Oliver Optic

Down the Rhine: Young America in Germany

A story of travel and adventure

Oliver Optic

Down the Rhine: Young America in Germany
A story of travel and adventure

ISBN/EAN: 9783337210731

Printed in Europe, USA, Canada, Australia, Japan

Cover: Foto ©Andreas Hilbeck / pixelio.de

More available books at **www.hansebooks.com**

DOWN THE RHINE;

OR,

YOUNG AMERICA IN GERMANY.

A Story of Travel and Adventure.

BY

OLIVER OPTIC.

BOSTON:
LEE AND SHEPARD, PUBLISHERS.
NEW YORK:
LEE, SHEPARD AND DILLINGHAM.
1873.

TO MY YOUNG FRIEND

RALPH OAKLEY,

𝔗𝔥𝔦𝔰 𝔙𝔬𝔩𝔲𝔪𝔢

IS AFFECTIONATELY DEDICATED.

YOUNG AMERICA ABROAD.

BY OLIVER OPTIC.

A Library of Travel and Adventure in Foreign Lands. First and Second Series; six volumes in each Series. 16mo. Illustrated.

First Series.

I. *OUTWARD BOUND;* or, YOUNG AMERICA AFLOAT.

II. *SHAMROCK AND THISTLE;* or, YOUNG AMERICA IN IRELAND AND SCOTLAND.

III. *RED CROSS;* or, YOUNG AMERICA IN ENGLAND AND WALES.

IV. *DIKES AND DITCHES;* or, YOUNG AMERICA IN HOLLAND AND BELGIUM.

V. *PALACE AND COTTAGE;* or, YOUNG AMERICA IN FRANCE AND SWITZERLAND.

VI. *DOWN THE RHINE;* or, YOUNG AMERICA IN GERMANY.

Second Series.

I. *UP THE BALTIC;* or, YOUNG AMERICA IN DENMARK AND SWEDEN.

II. *NORTHERN LANDS;* or, YOUNG AMERICA IN PRUSSIA AND RUSSIA.

III. *VINE AND OLIVE;* or, YOUNG AMERICA IN SPAIN AND PORTUGAL.

IV. *SUNNY SHORES;* or, YOUNG AMERICA IN ITALY AND AUSTRIA.

V. *CROSS AND CRESCENT;* or, YOUNG AMERICA IN GREECE AND TURKEY.

VI. *ISLES OF THE SEA;* or, YOUNG AMERICA HOMEWARD BOUND.

PREFACE.

DOWN THE RHINE, the sixth and last volume of the first series of "YOUNG AMERICA ABROAD," is the conclusion of the history of the Academy Squadron on its first voyage to Europe, with the excursion of the students and their friends into Germany, and down its most beautiful river. As in the preceding volumes of the series, brief geographical descriptions of the country visited are given, with a sketch of its history, and of whatever may be peculiar or interesting in its manners and customs. The travellers enter Germany by the way of Strasburg, and visit Freiburg, Schaffhausen, Constance, Friedrichshafen, Ulm, Stuttgart, Carlsruhe, Darmstadt, Baden-Baden, Heidelberg, Frankfurt, Mayence, Bingen, Bonn, Coblenz, Cologne, Dusseldorf, and Aix-la-Chapelle; but only the most interesting features of these places are noticed.

The story part of the volume relates mostly to a trip of the squadron from Havre to Brest, and the cruise of the Josephine up the Mediterranean, in which the writer has endeavored to show that even injustice is not to be redressed by resorting to evil deeds; and he is quite sure that the sympathies of his readers will always be with the members of the "Order of the Faithful."

As the author has before had occasion gratefully to acknowledge, the success of this series has far exceeded his anticipations; and in bringing the first series to a close, he again returns his thanks to his friends, young and old, who have so often and so earnestly encouraged him in his agreeable labors, — all the more agreeable because they are so generously appreciated. He intends, during the coming year, to make another trip to Europe, for the purpose of visiting all the countries mentioned in the titles of the second series; for he is not inclined to write about any country until he has seen it. If no unforeseen event intervenes to defeat his plans, the remaining volumes of YOUNG AMERICA ABROAD will soon follow.

HARRISON SQUARE, MASS.,
   October 28, 1869.

CONTENTS.

CHAPTER		PAGE
I.	CONFUSION IN THE SHIP.	11
II.	CLOSE QUARTERS.	27
III.	A GATHERING STORM.	42
IV.	THE YOUNG AMERICA MUTINY.	57
V.	THE ORDER OF THE FAITHFUL.	73
VI.	IN THE STEERAGE.	89
VII.	THE VISIT TO THE HOLD.	106
VIII.	SHORT OF WATER.	123
IX.	THE LAST OF THE MUTINEERS.	140
X.	WHAT THE RUNAWAYS WERE GOING TO DO.	158
XI.	A SHORT LECTURE ON GERMANY.	174
XII.	A MYSTERIOUS MOVEMENT.	191
XIII.	FROM STRASBURG TO CONSTANCE.	207
XIV.	THE STORM ON LAKE CONSTANCE.	224
XV.	LADY FEODORA AND SIR WILLIAM.	241

CONTENTS.

CHAPTER		PAGE
XVI.	UP THE MEDITERRANEAN.	260
XVII.	HEIDELBERG AND HOMBURG.	279
XVIII.	CASTLES, VINEYARDS, AND MOUNTAINS.	296
XIX.	COBLENZ AND COLOGNE.	309
XX.	HOMEWARD BOUND.	332

DOWN THE RHINE.

DOWN THE RHINE;

OR,

YOUNG AMERICA IN GERMANY.

CHAPTER I.

CONFUSION IN THE SHIP.

"ALL hands pipe to muster, ahoy!" screamed the new boatswain of the Young America, as he walked towards the forecastle of the ship, occasionally sounding a shrill blast upon his whistle.

At the same time the corresponding officer in the Josephine performed a similar service; and in a moment every officer and seaman in both vessels had taken his station. The squadron lay at anchor off the harbor of Havre. The students had returned the day before from a delightful tour through France and Switzerland — all except the thirty-one who had preferred to take a cruise on their own account in the Josephine; and these had been performing ship's duty, and making up back lessons, while the vessel lay at anchor in the port of Brest. Perhaps it was not strictly true that these malcontents were sick of the game of running away, but it is strictly true that they were disgusted with the penalty which had been imposed upon them by the authorities of the Academy. It is to be regretted that they were not moved to penitence by their punishment, and that they were ripe for any new rebellion which promised to be even a partial success. They had been deprived of seeing Paris, — which is France, — and the beautiful scenery of Switzerland, by their folly; and they had taste enough to realize that they had sacrificed the best part of a tour in Europe.

Those who had participated in the excursion were enthusiastic in their belief that they had had a good time; and the frequent discussion of the pleasures of the trip did not tend to diminish the discontent of the runaways. It was absolutely intolerable to think they had been compensating for past deficiencies in their studies, while their shipmates were gazing upon the magnificent palaces of Paris, the picturesque cottages, and the sublime mountain scenery of Switzerland. Perhaps their temper was not improved by the reflection that others had been permitted to enjoy what they were not allowed to see, for envy is one of the ugliest and most uncomfortable of human passions. Boys, like men and women, fret because they cannot have what others possess, either as the gift of partial Fortune, or as the reward of their own superior skill and perseverance.

If the runaways had not learned wisdom from their failure, they had acquired discretion. The leaders in the mad scheme could now see just why and wherefore they had failed; and they believed — if they were to have the opportunity to do the deed over again —

they could make a success of it. The machinery of the secret organization was now disgusting to them, though it had enabled them to make the capture of the vessel. They were disposed to cast it all aside, and resort to new methods for future occasions. As a general rule, they were wise enough to keep still, and only among themselves did they express their chagrin and disappointment, or suggest that they were not entirely cured of their tendency to run away. The strict discipline of the squadron could not be evaded, and they were compelled to perform all their duties.

It was the beginning of a new term in the school. New officers had succeeded the old ones, or the position of the latter had been materially changed. The members of the order of the Knights of the Golden Fleece found themselves scattered by the new arrangement. Not less than a dozen of them had been transferred to the consort, while Tom Perth, the leading spirit of the runaways, had attained to the dignity of second master of the ship, more by his natural abilities than by any efforts he had made to win a high place. As yet he had found no opportunity to arrange a plan for further operations with his confederates, for Mr. Fluxion, the vice-principal, was in the charge of the schooner, and his eyes and ears were always open. The return of the tourists from their excursion restored the routine on board of the vessels.

Everything was changed, and at first hardly an officer knew where he belonged, or what his duty was. Confusion reigned on board the ship and her consort, while the students were finding and preparing their new berths. Happily, the changes were all made before dinner time, and everything settled down into its wonted order and regularity. After the midday meal was served, all hands were piped to muster, in order that the officers and seamen might be exercised in their new situations. The details of sea duty were well understood by all. Those alone who had been promoted from the steerage to the after cabin were in the dark in regard to their duty, though in these instances the parties had a general idea of what was required of them. But it was necessary to have the crew ready to work together, for the seaman who had hauled on the weather-brace in tacking was now an officer, and the stations of many were new and strange to them.

Shuffles in the ship, and Terrill in the consort, proceeded to execute all the manœuvres required in handling the vessel, from getting under way to coming to anchor again. Nearly all the officers and crew were zealous to perform their several parts correctly; but there were enough of the discontented ones, who shirked as much as possible, to create considerable confusion. The captain of the Young America was not satisfied with the manner in which the various evolutions were performed; so he began at the beginning, and went over all the ground again, to the great disgust of the runaways in his crew, who had been doing this sort of thing for four weeks, while the others were enjoying the beauties of the mountain scenery.

"What's the matter, Captain Shuffles?" asked Commodore Kendall, when the commander finished the routine a second time, and was still dissatisfied with the result.

"It doesn't work well," replied Shuffles, biting his lip.

"A new broom sweeps clean, they say," laughed the flag officer. "Perhaps you are more particular than your predecessors were."

"I think not. The ship would have miss-stayed under such handling as we have to-day, to say nothing of the clumsy look of it," continued the new captain. "I shouldn't wish to be out in a gale with a crew as slack as ours is just now."

"What's the trouble?" asked the commodore, rather anxiously. "I saw that things did not work well."

"There is trouble somewhere, and I think I can see where it is."

"What is it?"

"Certain parties in this ship don't like me very well, just now."

"You mean the runaways," suggested Paul.

"Of course."

"They are making a mistake if they are slack in their duty," added the commodore, rather indignantly. "They wish to go with us on our next excursion: but I don't think they can win the privilege in this manner."

"Wilton and Howe are doing all they can to make things go wrong," said Captain Shuffles, who was more in sorrow than in anger at the conduct of these worthies. "If they are doing it to spite me, they are only spiting themselves. I am going through these manœuvres until they are a little more ship-shape, at least."

The new captain ordered all hands to take their stations for getting under way, and Commodore Kendall went aft, though he still carefully observed the conduct of the seamen. The clumsiness, and the intentional blunders of certain of the crew seemed to indicate that there was a conspiracy to defeat the purposes of the commander. First, Howe tumbled down while the hands were walking round the capstan; Spencer stumbled over him, and a dozen boys were thrown in a pile upon them. Then Richmond and Merrick dropped their handspikes overboard, through an open port, when the order was given to restore these articles to their proper places.

Little snarled himself up in the gasket on the fore-topsail yard, and dropped off, as though he had fallen, though he clung to the rope, and was brought up with a jerk ten or twelve feet below the spar. Some of his gang, believing he had really fallen, screamed, and the attention of the whole crew was drawn off from their duty. When the fore-topmast staysail and jib were to be set, somebody had fouled the downhauls, so that they could not be hoisted. There was a kink in the halyards of the main-top gallant-sail, so that it would not run through the block. Clewlines, clew-garnets, leachlines, and buntlines were in a snarl. The zeal of those who were striving to do their duty faithfully seemed to make the matter worse, and the officers found it difficult to determine who really made the mischief; for the malcontents pretended to be as enthusiastic as their shipmates. Strong expressions and hard words were freely used by the vexed seamen, and certainly such a scene of confusion had never before been observed on board of the ship, even when a large proportion of the crew were green hands.

Captain Shuffles was deeply grieved by the misconduct of the crew ; for, standing on the quarter-deck, he could not distinguish between the intentional and the unintentional blunders of the crew, and therefore believed that the disaffection was much more extensive than was really the case. The zealous efforts of one portion of the crew to rectify the mistakes of another portion only increased the confusion, and some of those who were actually doing their best appeared to be the real authors of the difficulty. The captain was drilling his crew in simultaneous movements, and it was difficult, if not impossible, to ascertain exactly the source of the unwonted confusion.

While the routine of evolutions was thus bunglingly performed, the principal and the professors, who had been discussing an interesting question of discipline in the main cabin, came on deck. Perhaps the fact that Mr. Lowington was not on deck had encouraged the conspirators in creating the confusion which pervaded the decks and rigging. As he was the last to ascend the companion-way, he paused on the steps, with his head on a level with the deck, to note the precision of the drill. He was not noticed by the conspirators, and, unfortunately for them, they continued in their career of insubordination. The quick eye of the principal readily detected the nature of the mischief, though it was as impossible for him as for the officers immediately to indicate the authors of the confusion which prevailed throughout the ship.

"This does not look much like going down the Rhine this week," said Mr. Lowington to Commodore. Kendall, as he stepped upon the quarter-deck.

"I don't think it does, sir," replied Paul, grieved and indignant at the miserable exhibition of seamanship which the crew then presented.

"This is a strange sight on board of this ship," added the principal, biting his lips with vexation, for, as usual, when the young tars displayed their seamanship, there were plenty of spectators on shore, and on board of other vessels in the roadstead.

"I certainly never saw anything like it since we first began to learn ship's duty in Brockway harbor."

"The crew appear to be hazing the new officers," continued Mr. Lowington, who could not fail to perceive that a large portion of the apparent blundering was intentional.

"Of course there isn't a seaman on board who does not know his duty."

"They are not familiar yet with their new stations, and a little confusion is unavoidable," said Mr. Lowington, willing to make all reasonable allowances.

"But they have already been through the routine two or three times," suggested Paul.

"Are the crew dissatisfied with the election?" asked the principal.

"I have not heard any dissatisfation expressed; but I suppose some of them don't like Shuffles, especially those who went off in the Josephine."

"There are not twenty of them left in the ship; and it seems as though the whole crew were engaged in this frolic."

At this moment a gang of the waist men, who were walking away with the main-topsail sheets, were suddenly piled up in a pyramid on deck. The second fellow in the line had fallen down; the next had tripped over him, and those that followed tumbled into the heap. It is more than probable that some, whose estimate of the value of good order was not very high, though they were tolerably good boys in the main, were tempted by their love of fun to take part in what appeared to them only a frolic. A scene of violent confusion ensued in this particular part of the deck. Some, who were near the bottom of the pile, were hurt by those who fell upon them, and the tempers of others were not improved by the mishap. Hard words followed, those at the bottom blaming those at the top, and those at the top growling at those at the bottom. Some were rubbing their elbows, others their shins, and all appeared to be anxious to ascertain who had produced the mischief.

"Pipe to muster, Captain Shuffles," said the principal, stepping up to the bewildered commander. "We have had about enough of this."

Shuffles gave the order to the first lieutenant, and it was duly transmitted to the boatswain, whose shrill pipe soon assembled the whole ship's company in the waist.

"We shall catch it now," said Spencer, one of the runaways, to Howe, as they met near the rail, a little outside of the crowd.

"No matter; he is only going to preach to us," replied Howe through the corner of his mouth, while he tried to look as innocent as one of the chaplain's lambs.

"We shall not have a chance to go down the Rhine if we do things in this way."

"I don't want to go down the Rhine; at least, not till I have been through Paris and Switzerland."

"But we want to go ashore with the other fellows, or we shall have no chance to go anywhere."

"Shut up! Don't talk about that here. If we don't go, no one will go. This is bully! We shall get things mixed so that the officers won't know a lamb from a goat."

"Bob Shuffles hasn't made much yet as captain," laughed Spencer.

"We'll get even with him yet," added Howe, still talking through the corner of his mouth, and looking all the time at the principal, who had taken his place on the hatch.

Mr. Lowington, as the rogue had suggested, only intended to "preach." He had observed the insubordination of the crew, and he regretted it exceedingly, for he was as careful of the reputation of the ship as of his own. There was an evident intention on the part of a large portion of the ship's company to haze the new officers. Such a purpose was unworthy the character of young gentlemen, and he hoped that such conduct as he had just witnessed would be discontinued. In a day or two he purposed to start for Germany, but he could not leave the ship unless he was satisfied that every one on board knew his duty; for on their return they might be compelled, by some unforeseen event, to go to sea at once, and the crew did not appear to know how to set and furl a sail. The officers, from the captain to the lowest rank, appeared to have performed their duty faithfully; and all the trouble was in the execution of their orders. In conclusion, he announced that the drill would be resumed in half an hour, and directed the commander to pipe down.

"That didn't hurt anybody," said Howe, as he walked forward with Spencer. "Let us keep it up."

"We may get caught at it."

"No need of that. Accidents will happen."

"Yes; but they don't happen all over the ship at the same time."

"Well, they may, you know," laughed Howe. "In fact, I don't see how accidents are to be avoided while we have such a fellow as Shuffles for captain. If there is any one in the ship that I despise, it is Shuffles."

"So say we all of us!"

"The snivelling, canting, whining puppy! Have you any idea that his merit-marks made him captain of the ship?" continued Howe.

"I suppose they did."

"Tell that to the marines! Wasn't he acknowledged to be the worst fellow in the ship when we crossed the Atlantic? Wasn't he the ringleader in all mischief and scrapes?"

"But he has reformed."

"Reformed!" sneered Howe. "He has turned hypocrite, if that is what you mean by reformed. I don't believe in that sort of bosh."

"He's the pet of the principal and the instructors."

"Yes; and they have given him marks enough to make him captain, just to show good fellows, like you and me, what a saint can do. It is all humbug! Why, he got more marks than Kendall, Gordon, Haven, and the rest of those cabin nobs, who are fit to enter the senior class in a college. I am satisfied that his merit-roll was doctored so as to make it come out as it did."

"I don't believe Lowington would do any such thing as that," suggested Spencer, shaking his head.

"Don't you? Well, I do. What's the use of talking! Didn't Shuffles jump from the steerage into the captain's state-room?"

"Any other fellow may do the same thing. Look at Tom Perth, who lost a heap of marks for running off in the Josephine, as the rest of us did. He is second master. If it hadn't been for our scrape, very likely he would have been captain."

"Don't you believe it."

"If Lowington had not been fair, and let every fellow go just where his marks carried him, Perth would not have had a place in the cabin."

"O, the principal only wanted to break us up by taking our best fellow away from us. He couldn't drive Tom Perth, and now he's going to lead him — bait him with sugar and offices."

"Some of the fellows say Shuffles can't handle the ship without the help of the principal," said Spencer.

"Of course he can't!" exclaimed Howe. "Hasn't he proved that already? If Paul Kendall had been captain, he would have spotted every fellow that made any trouble. Let us keep it up, Spencer, and we shall soon prove that Shuffles can't handle the ship. That will be enough to satisfy me."

The approach of an officer interrupted the conversation; but Howe passed from one to another of the malcontents, and instructed them what to do in the next drill. They were to create all the confusion they could in the discharge of their duty. They were to misunderstand the orders, and to blunder in the execution of them, in such a manner as to conceal their own agency in the mischief, and divide the responsibility of it among their companions. The runaway crew of the Josephine, mortified at their failure, were still fretting because they had not visited Paris and Switzerland. They were ready to listen to evil counsels, and regarding Howe as their leader since the promotion of Perth, they promised to follow his instructions to the letter.

"What are we going to make by it?" demanded Sheffield, who doubted the policy of the proceeding.

"We are going to prove, in the first place, that Shuffles can't handle the ship," replied Howe.

"Perhaps you may prove it, even if you don't believe what you prove."

"But I do believe he can't handle the ship."

"I don't. I hate Shuffles as bad as any fellow, but I believe he is as good a sailor as any person on board, man or boy."

"That's all in your eye!" retorted Howe, contemptuously. "He may be able to get along while we are lying in port, but I should like to see him work the ship in a gale of wind."

"He can do it," answered Sheffield, confidently. "But he is a flunky, and spoiled all our fun in the Josephine. I am willing to throw him over for being a hypocrite, and selling us out as he did. What else are we to gain?"

"We shall help along our chances of going down

the Rhine, and," whispered Howe, " of seeing Paris and Switzerland."

" I don't see it."

" Well, I do. If we cave in and pretend to be lambs when we are lions, we shall have to do duty while the rest of the fellows are having a good time on shore. If we show that we are still wide awake, Lowington will take us with him, because he will not dare to leave us on board."

" He will leave Fluxion with us."

" Not much! I heard some of the fellows say that Fluxion was going to Italy to see his mother, or his sister, or somebody that is sick there."

" I heard that."

" If it is true, Lowington will not leave us behind, especially if he finds we are not as gentle as lambs."

" Perhaps not; but as the matter stands, we are already condemned to stay on board during the rest of the season."

" I know that; but Lowington will let us off."

" He will be more likely to do so if we behave well."

" Not he! Don't you believe it."

" They say Shuffles is teasing him to remit the rest of the penalty."

" Shuffles! "

" That's so; and Lowington promised to consider the matter. Tom Perth told me this; and he heard Shuffles talking to the principal about it."

" Humph! I don't want to go on those terms," replied Howe, in disgust. " That's some more of Shuffles's cant! One of his sensations! He thinks he whipped us out on board of the Josephine, and now he wants to be magnanimous with his victims. If we go with the crowd, it will be because Lowington is afraid to leave us behind. We are not a set of babies, Sheffield, to be whipped and sent to bed when we are naughty. Neither are we sailors before the mast, to be kicked here and there, at the pleasure of our masters. What do you suppose the fellows came to Europe for, if it was not to see the country? Are we to be left on board just because we went on a little lark? Not much!"

"That's all very good, but it won't go down," laughed Sheffield.

"I'm not going to eat humble pie for any one. Do you mean to tell me I am not as good a fellow as Bob Shuffles?"

"I didn't say you were not."

"Am I not his equal?" demanded Howe.

"I suppose you are, if you behave as well."

"Behave as well!" sneered the orator. "I behave well enough, and I'm not going to be put down, nor beg my rights of Bob Shuffles. If I am left on board, for one, when the fellows go down the Rhine, I intend to break things."

"Don't break your own head."

"Let me alone for that. If our fellows have any spirit at all, they will not be left behind. In the next drill, things will be mixed, and no one can tell who makes the mischief. Our fellows are not the only ones that don't like Shuffles, and you will find that about half the crew will help snarl things up. Now, keep your weather eye open, Sheffield. Take my advice, and don't whimper. Our fellows have a little business in Paris and Switzerland, and we shall attend to it in a week or two. There goes the pipe. Mind your eye, Sheffield."

The boatswain's call sounded through the ship, and officers and crew hastened to their stations.

CHAPTER II.

CLOSE QUARTERS.

THE malcontents in the ship were, apparently, the most zealous seamen on board. Certainly no one would have suspected them of organizing any mischief, they looked so innocent and so determined to do their duty promptly. Howe, Wilton, Little, and others had done their work thoroughly and secretly. They had arranged at least a dozen different tricks for making confusion among the crew. To each one of the discontented a part had been assigned, which he was to perform in such a way as to conceal his own agency.

Captain Shuffles was planking the quarter-deck with the commodore. Everybody could see that he was not entirely at his ease. His position was a novel one to him, and he was oppressed by its responsibilities, especially since the crew had behaved so badly at the first drill. He could not help knowing that a portion of the crew were opposed to him, and would do anything they could to annoy him. The situation was a difficult one; for, at the commencement of his term of office, he did not wish to have any of the seamen punished for neglect or disobedience, even if he could discover the guilty ones.

Mr. Lowington was not on deck. He had purposely gone below, for he wished the new captain to act on his own responsibility, and overcome the difficulty alone. This was in accordance with his previous course, when, even in a gale of wind, he permitted the young officers to handle the ship without any dictation. Though the action adopted by the boys was not always in accordance with his own judgment, he never interfered unless an obvious and dangerous blunder was made. His policy had worked well thus far, and he was disposed to continue it. In the present instance, he was no better informed than the captain in regard to the real cause of the difficulty. He believed it was merely the effect of a fun-loving spirit on the part of the crew; a mere disposition to haze the new officers a little, and perhaps prove what they were made of. He hoped the new officers would satisfy them, and, if necessary, send a dozen or twenty of the mischief-makers to the mainmast for punishment.

"All hands, up anchor, ahoy!" piped the boatswain, after he had received the order from the captain, through the proper officers.

Those whose stations were at the cable and capstan sprang to their places with unwonted alacrity.

"Bring to, forward!" added the first lieutenant, giving the order to attach the messenger. "Ship and swifter the capstan bars!"

As it was not intended to get the ship actually under way, only a portion of the work indicated by the orders was really executed. The form of hooking on the messenger was gone through with, as also were the various preparations for catting and fishing the anchor. The capstan bars were inserted in the pigeon-holes.

"Heave round!" shouted the first lieutenant; and the order was repeated by the second lieutenant, whose station is on the forecastle.

Everything appeared to be progressing with proper order and regularity, and Captain Shuffles hoped the warning words of the principal had produced an impression upon the minds of the mischief-makers. But appearances are very deceptive. While the hands were walking around the capstan, four of the bars suddenly came out of the pigeon-holes at the same instant, and a dozen of the seamen were thrown, apparently with great violence, upon the deck. The bars, confined at one end by the swifter, swung round and cracked the shins of others, and a scene of confusion ensued, which set at nought all ideas of discipline.

No one was badly hurt, but every one was excited. Those who were not concerned in the plot caught the spirit of mischief from the others, and, with but few exceptions, the crew joined in the sport. The seaman who originated the trouble had simply neglected to insert the pins which confine the capstan bars within the pigeon-holes, or had left the bars with the heads against the pins. As nearly all joined in the frolic, there were none to inform against others, and it was simply impossible for Leavitt, the second lieutenant, or Ellis, the first master, — under whose eye this breach of discipline had occurred, — to determine who the ringleaders were.

Shuffles and the commodore were intensely annoyed

at this scene, and immediately went forward. By this time, those who had been thrown upon the deck, which included nearly all at the capstan, had picked themselves up. The Knights looked even more innocent than those whom they had dragged into the scrape, and the high officers from the quarter-deck were no wiser than the lieutenant and master. In the midst of the confusion, Howe and Wilton had removed the pins from the bars, which still remained in the drumhead of the capstan.

"Mr. Leavitt, how did this happen?" demanded Captain Shuffles.

"Half the bars dropped out of the capstan all at once, and the hands were thrown down," replied the lieutenant, who was hardly less annoyed than the captain.

"Were the bars pinned in?"

"I supposed they were, sir."

Captain Shuffles walked up to the capstan. Not a single pin was inserted.

"Let your midshipman see that the bars are properly pinned and swiftered next time," said the commander, as he walked aft to resume his place on the quarter-deck.

"Unship the bars!" said Leavitt; and they were restored to the rack, leaving everything as it was before the drill began.

The crew were piped to muster, and the order to weigh anchor repeated. The capstan bars were shipped, and this time, the midshipman whose station was on the forecastle satisfied himself that they were securely pinned, and so reported to the second lieutenant. As the rogues had made no provision for this state of things, they were thrown upon their own resources for the means of defeating the operation a second time. Commodore Kendall had placed himself in position to watch the movement, and the officers in charge had pinned their eyes wide open, fully resolved that the authors of the trouble should not escape a second time.

Directly abaft the capstan was the fore-hatch, over which lay the path of those who walked around at the bars. Ordinarily the hatch was closed when the capstan was used; but, on the present occasion, a plank had been placed across the aperture, to avoid the necessity of putting on the hatch, and thus excluding the air from the kitchen, where the cooks were baking their daily batch of bread.

"Heave round!" said the first lieutenant.

"Heave round!" repeated the second lieutenant; and the hands at the capstan began their circular march.

By some means not observed by the vigilant officers, the plank over the fore-hatch slowly travelled along until one end of it barely caught on the combing of the hatch. Half a dozen seamen had given it a kick with their heels as they passed over it, and it was soon in condition to drop into the steerage below. Little stepped upon it, and down it went. Releasing his hold of the bar, he dropped upon the steps below, and disappeared. Sheffield followed him, and then Ibbotson. The hands at the other side of the capstan took care that the party should keep moving. A few well-disposed boys, when they came to the hatch, — which was not more than four feet wide, — leaped across it, as any of them might have done, if they had not been infected with the spirit of mischief.

"Avast heaving!" shouted the second lieutenant.

At this instant one of the lambs was on the combing of the hatch, and he must either go over or hang by the bar; so he pushed along, and his movement brought another into a similar position. Seeing how the case was, the rogues kept the capstan going, in spite of the commands of the officers, until two thirds of the gang had dropped into the steerage. It was finally suspended by the efforts of the excited officers, who took hold of the bars with their own hands, and counteracted the efforts of the rogues.

The young rascals in the steerage pretended to be hurt more seriously than they were, though some of them had struck the steps or the floor below with force enough to make them feel a little sore. They began to limp, and to rub their shins and shoulders, their heads and arms, very vigorously, as though they believed that friction was a sovereign remedy for aching bones.

"Why didn't you stop, Hunter, when I ordered you to do so?" demanded Leavitt, indignantly.

"I couldn't, sir," replied the lamb, speaking only the simple truth.

"Yes, you could! I will report you for disobedience."

"I was right over the hatch, and I had either to go down or jump over: I couldn't stop there."

"And you did the same thing, Hyde," added the officer.

"I couldn't help it, sir," replied he. "When Hunter got over, he dragged me so far that I couldn't stop."

"Why didn't you let go, then?" demanded Leavitt, angrily.

"I was afraid the next bar would hit me in the head."

Both of these boys were ordinarily models of propriety, and they had not, for an instant, intended to do anything out of order. The real culprits were all at the foot of the stairs, rubbing their limbs and making the most terrible contortions, as though their legs, arms, and heads were actually broken. The officers had all seen Hunter and Hyde pushing along the bars after the order had been given to stop. They seemed to be guilty, and they were required to report at the mainmast to the first lieutenant, for discipline. The second lieutenant then went down the fore-hatch, where the appalling spectacle of a crowd of sufferers was presented to his view.

"Are you hurt, Little?" he asked, turning to the most prominent victim of the catastrophe.

"Yes, sir," groaned Little, twisting his back-bone almost into a hard knot, and trying to reach the seat of his injury with both hands at the same time.

"How happened you to fall through?" inquired Leavitt, more gently than he had spoken on deck, for the sight of all this misery evidently affected him.

"I don't know, sir," answered Little, with one of his most violent contortions. "I was looking up at the fore-yard arm, and — ugh! — the first thing I knew, I was — O, dear! — I was down here, with that — ugh! — with that plank on top of me."

"Are you much hurt?"

"I don't know. It aches first rate," cried Little, with a deep, explosive sigh.

"Well, go aft, and report to the surgeon."

"I don't want to go to the surgeon. He mauls me about to death. I shall be better soon."

"On deck, all who are able to do so!" added Leavitt. "Bennington, you will ask Dr. Winstock to attend to those who are hurt, and report to the first lieutenant."

But it did not appear that any one was so much injured as to require the services of the surgeon, for the whole party went on deck at the order. Little still writhed and twisted. Howe rubbed his knee, and Spencer nursed his elbow. Commodore Kendall, who had witnessed the whole affair, did not see how it was possible for them to tumble down the hatchway without injuring themselves, and he was willing to believe that the appearance was not deceitful. He had kept his eyes fixed upon the crew as they walked round the capstan, but he was unable to determine whether the mishap was the result of accident or intention.

Again the captain came forward; but after consulting with Paul, he returned to the quarter-deck without making any comments. The two lambs had reported to the first lieutenant, and the matter had gone to Captain Shuffles, who directed the culprits to be sent to the principal. They went into the steerage, and knocking at the door of the main cabin, Mr. Lowington came out, and heard their statement. They were ordered to their mess-rooms to await an investigation.

The hatchway was closed, and the order to man the

capstan was given a third time. The injured seamen had in a measure recovered the use of their limbs, and though they still limped and squirmed, they took their places in the line. Either their will or their ingenuity to do mischief failed them, the third time, for the form of heaving up the anchor to a short stay was regularly accomplished. The commodore and all the officers in the forward part of the ship watched the operation with the keenest scrutiny, and when it was successfully finished, they hoped the end of all the mishaps had come.

"Pawl the capstan! Unship the bars! Stations for loosing sail!" continued the first lieutenant. "Lay aloft, sail-loosers!"

The nimble young tars, whose places were aloft, sprang up the rigging.

"Man the boom-tricing lines!"

But the boom-tricing lines appeared to be in a snarl, and it was some time before they were ready for use, being manipulated by some of the mischief-makers.

"Trice up!" shouted Goodwin, the executive officer. Up went the inner ends of the studding-sail booms.

"Lay out!" added Goodwin.

"Lay out!" repeated the midshipmen in the tops; and the seamen ran out on the foot-ropes to their several stations for loosing sail.

At the same time, the forecastle hands were loosing the fore-topmast staysail, jib, and flying jib, and the after-guard, or quarter-deck hands, were clearing away the spanker.

"Loose!" said the executive officer; and the hands removed the gaskets, stoppers, and other ropes, used to confine the sails when furled.

"Stand by — let fall!" was the next order.

At this command all the square sails should have dropped from the yards at the same instant, but as a matter of fact, not half of them did drop. Sheets, buntlines, bowlines, lifts, reef-pendants, and halyards were fearfully snarled up. Some of the seamen on the yards were pulling one way, and some another; some declared the snarl was in one place, others in another place. The rogues had realized an undoubted success in the work they had undertaken. Vainly the midshipmen in the tops tried to bring order out of confusion. Those who were actually laboring to untangle the ropes only increased the snarl.

The condition of affairs was duly reported to the captain, who had become very impatient at the long delay. The masters were then sent aloft to help the midshipmen unravel the snarl, but they succeeded no better. It was evident enough to all the officers that this confusion could not have been created without an intention to do it. An accident might have happened on the main or the mizzen-mast, but not on every yard on all three of the masts.

"What are you about?" asked Perth, who had been sent into the main-top, as he met Howe.

"We have come to the conclusion that Bob Shuffles can't handle this ship," whispered the ringleader of the mischief, with a significant wink.

"You are getting us into a scrape."

"Well, we all are in the same boat."

"Don't carry it too far," suggested Master Perth.

"Carry what too far?" demanded Robinson, the midshipman in the top, who had heard a word or two of the confidential talk — enough to give him an idea of what was in the wind.

"Dry up, old fellow," said Perth, with some confusion, as Howe, who had come down from the yard to cast off a line, sprang back to his place.

"What did you mean by that remark of yours?" inquired the midshipman.

"I told Howe not to carry the end of the buntline too far. It was wound three times around the topsail sheet."

"Was that what you meant?" asked Robinson, suspiciously.

"Don't you see that buntline?" replied Perth. "It is fouled in the sheet, and he was pulling it through farther, so as to snarl it up still worse."

"All right," replied the inferior, who, however, was far from being satisfied with the explanation.

"All right!" retorted Perth, smartly. "Is that the way you address your superior officer. One would think I was responsible to you for my words and actions."

"I didn't mean that," added Robinson.

"What did you mean?"

"I only said all right to your explanation."

"You did — did you?" said Perth, severely. "Then you called me to an account, and now you acquit me!"

"I beg your pardon. Whatever I said, I did not mean anything disrespectful," pleaded Robinson.

"Is this the 'kind of discipline among the officers? If it is, I don't wonder that the crew get snarled up. I don't like to blow on a fellow, but I'm tempted to send you to the mainmast."

"I didn't mean anything."

Master Perth turned from his abashed inferior, ascended the main rigging, and with a few sharp orders, compelled the topmen to unsnarl the ropes. He was afraid the midshipman would report what he had said to the captain, and he had attempted to intimidate him into silence by threatening him with a similar fate.

"On deck!" hailed Perth from the top. "All ready in the main-top, sir," he added, when the third lieutenant answered his hail from the waist.

After a delay of half an hour, a like report came down from the fore and mizzen-tops. The masters returned to their stations on deck, and everything was in readiness to continue the manœuvre. Captain Shuffles was in earnest conversation with Commodore Kendall. A more unsatisfactory state of things could not exist than that which prevailed on board of the Young America. The conduct of the crew amounted almost to mutiny. Those who had maliciously made the mischief, and those who had been engaged in it from a love of fun, had succeeded in confounding those who meant to do their duty. It was impossible to tell who were guilty and who were innocent; for three quarters, at least, of the crew seemed to be concerned in the confusion.

"It is clear enough that they are hazing me," said Captain Shuffles, sadly. "I don't know that I have done anything to set the fellows against me."

"Certainly not," replied Paul, warmly. "You have only done your duty. I have no doubt those fellows who ran away in the Josephine are at the bottom of it. If I am not very much mistaken, I saw Howe, on the main-topsail yard, tangling up the buntlines and sheets."

"I have heard that these fellows intended to get even with me," added Shuffles, with a smile, as though he had not much fear of them.

"I should keep the crew at work until they did their duty. I would keep them at it night and day, till they can get the ship under way without any confusion," added Paul, earnestly.

"I intend to do that, but I do not like to be hard upon them."

"There is no danger of your being too hard."

"Whether I am hard or not, I'm going to have the work done in ship-shape style, if we drill till morning. All hands, furl sails," said he to the first lieutenant.

The boatswain's call sounded through the ship. The necessary orders were given in detail, and after considerable confusion, the sails were all furled, and the ship restored to its original condition.

"Pipe to muster," continued the captain.

Under this order all the officers assembled on the quarter-deck. Captain Shuffles addressed them in the mild tones in which he usually spoke, as though he was not seriously disturbed by the ill conduct of the crew. Assigning a lieutenant, a master, and a midshipman to each mast, he directed them to set each sail separately, without regard to others. They were to set the topsails first, then the other sails up to the royals. Other officers were directed to drill the seamen stationed at the head sails and the spanker.

During this conference Howe and his associates were congratulating themselves upon the success of their vicious schemes, and encouraging each other to persevere if another drill was ordered. They were curious to know what the captain was doing with the officers on the quarter-deck; but they concluded that it was only a meeting to "howl" over the miserable discipline of the ship. But their wonderings were soon set at rest by the boatswain's call of "All hands, make sail, ahoy!"

They sprang to their stations as zealously as though they had no thought but for the honor of the ship. They soon discovered that a new order of proceeding had been introduced. The masters and midshipmen perched themselves in the rigging, where they could see the movements of every seaman. The adult forward officers — Peaks, the boatswain, Bitts, the carpenter, and Leech, the sailmaker — also went aloft, and stationed themselves on the topmast-stays, so that, besides the lieutenants on deck, the commodore, and the past officers, there were three pairs of sharp eyes aloft to inspect the operations on each sail.

Howe and his associates were not a little disconcerted at this array of inspectors, and still more so when the order was given to loose only the topsails. Peaks, on the main topmast-stay, caught Howe in the very act of passing the gasket through the bight of the buntline. The veteran tar came down upon him with such a torrent of sea slang, that he did not attempt to repeat the act. The topsails were then set as smartly and as regularly as ever before. After the inspectors had seen all the sails set and furled in detail, the topsails, top-gallant sails, and courses, with the jib and spanker, were set as usual, when the vessel got under way.

By the time the routine in detail had been practised two or three times, the officers began to know where to look for the mischief-makers. Peaks had exposed the ringleader, and the conspirators were finally beaten at their own game. But Captain Shuffles was not satisfied; and when the crew were dismissed from muster, he hastened to the main cabin to consult with the principal.

The conspirators, at close quarters, had lost the day, and discipline was triumphant.

CHAPTER III.

A GATHERING STORM.

"MR. LOWINGTON, I should like to go to sea for a day or two," said Captain Shuffles, when he had obtained the ear of the principal.

"Go to sea!" exclaimed Mr. Lowington. "Why, I thought you were all in a hurry to go down the Rhine."

"I am not at all satisfied with the discipline of the ship," answered the new captain. "It requires about as many officers as seamen to execute any manœuvre, and I think we need more practice in ship's duty before we make any more tours on shore."

"How did you succeed in your second drill?"

"We went through with it after a while; but it was only with two officers in each top, and the adult forward officers on the stays, that we could set a single sail."

"Have you ascertained who is at the root of the mischief?"

"Howe, for one."

"The runaways, probably," added Mr. Lowington, thoughtfully.

"I have no doubt all of them were concerned in it; but at least half the crew took part in the mischief. We finally went through all the forms with tolerable precision. Two or three days' service at sea will enable us to put everything in good working order. The officers also ought to have a little practice in their new stations."

"When do you wish to go to sea?"

"Immediately, sir," replied Shuffles.

"To-night?"

"Yes, sir. I think any delay would be injurious to discipline. The crew have been hazing the officers now for two hours, and have had the best of it most of the time. If we went to sea without any delay, I think it would be understood."

"You are right, Captain Shuffles. Where is Commodore Kendall?"

"In the after cabin, sir."

"Send for him, if you please."

The commander sent one of the waiters to call Paul, who presently appeared.

"Captain Shuffles wishes to go to sea to-night," said Mr. Lowington, with a smile, as the young commodore entered the cabin; "and I think he takes a correct view of the situation."

"To-night!" exclaimed Paul, whose thought immediately flashed from the ship to the Hotel de l'Europe, in Havre, where Mr. and Mrs. Arbuckle and Grace were domiciled, having come down from Paris by the morning train, to be in readiness to start with the ship's company for the Rhine.

"I know what you are thinking about, Paul," laughed the principal. "You may go on shore, and invite the Arbuckles to join us; or, as we can work the ship very well without a commodore, you may stay on shore with them until our return."

"Invite them to go with us," suggested Shuffles. "I think the presence of our friends will have a good effect upon the crew."

"I should be very glad to have them go with us," replied Paul.

"It is a little doubtful whether we return to Havre again, for Brest would be a better place for the vessels to lie during our absence in Germany," said Mr. Lowington.

"We cannot sail at once — can we?" asked Paul.

"We can get off this evening," replied Mr. Lowington. "Let the stewards of the ship and the consort go on shore, and get a supply of fresh provisions. The commodore, in the mean time, can wait on the Arbuckles. I see no difficulty in getting off by sunset."

"It will be rather short notice for the Arbuckles," suggested Paul.

"They are ready to go to Germany at an hour's notice, and it will require no more preparation for this voyage. You can go on shore at once, Commodore Kendall. Captain Shuffles, you will hoist the signal for sailing; send a boat to the Josephine, and I will give you a letter for Mr. Fluxion."

The arrangement agreed upon, Captain Shuffles went on deck, and directed the first lieutenant to pipe away the commodore's barge. The third lieutenant was detailed to serve in this boat. As its crew went over the side, Captain Shuffles saw that Howe, Spencer, and four others of the runaways were of its number, under the new station bill. This fact induced him to send Peaks with the lieutenant in charge, so as to guard against any mischief. The third cutter was sent to the Josephine, with the principal's letter. In this boat, Little was the only runaway. The first cutter soon after left the ship with the steward, to bring off a load of fresh provisions.

As the third cutter was obliged to wait for Mr. Fluxion to write an answer to Mr. Lowington's letter, the crew were allowed to go on board of the Josephine. The sight of the signal for sailing, which had been hoisted on board of the Young America, caused no little excitement in the consort, as, in fact, it did on board of the ship. It looked like a very sudden movement, for all were anticipating their departure for Germany by the next or the following day. The principal had told them they would leave in a few days, and not a word had been said about going to sea in the interim.

"What's up?" asked Greenway, one of the runaways, who had been transferred to the Josephine, as Little came on deck.

"I don't know — only that we are going to sea," replied Little. "We have had high times on board of the ship."

"What have you been doing?"

"Hazing Shuffles," said Little, in a whisper.

"And I'll bet that is the reason why we are going to sea, instead of going to Germany," answered Greenway, with something like disgust in his looks and in the tones of his voice.

"No matter; we have proved that Shuffles can't handle the ship. He had to call on old Peaks to help him before he could get the main-topsail set."

"But if you play these games we shall be left on board while the rest of the fellows go down the Rhine."

"Not much! Fluxion is going to Marseilles to see his grandmother, or somebody else, and if we only make mischief enough, Lowington won't dare to leave us on board."

Little explained the views of Howe, which he had adopted as his own, to the effect that the more mischief they made, the better would be their chances of joining the excursion to Germany. Greenway was foolish enough to take the same view of the question. If the vice-principal was obliged to go away, Mr. Lowington would not dare to leave the runaways with any other person.

"But we don't want to go to Germany," added Little.

"Why not?"

"Simply because we have not been to Paris and Switzerland," replied the little villain, as he led his companion to the forecastle, where no one could overhear them. "We are going to have the time we bargained for when we sailed in the Josephine. If we go with the rest of the fellows, we intend to take French leave of them as soon as we find an opportunity to do so. On the whole, I had just as lief stay if Fluxion is not to have the care of us, for we can slip through the hands of any other man in the squadron."

"There is some money in Paris waiting for me," said Greenway.

"There is some waiting for a lot of our fellows," replied Little. "I intend to claim mine as soon as the party begin to go down the Rhine."

"What's the plan? How are the fellows to get off?" asked Greenway.

"Every one must manage that to suit himself. We had better go in little parties of three or four."

"O, no; it's better to keep together," protested Greenway.

"I don't think so. If we attempt to do anything together again, we shall be watched. We must look out for our chances."

"But our fellows are separated now, and we can't do anything alone."

"Yes, you can. When you see a good opportunity to start for Paris, start. That's all you have to do."

"I don't like this way."

"It's the best way. Don't you see that when we are missed we can all be caught in a bunch again. If we go in a dozen different squads, they will have to chase us in as many different directions. If we start with the fellows for Germany, we shall step out as we have the chance to do so. I don't believe in more than two or three going together."

"But some of us may not have any money," suggested Greenway.

"Then they must borrow some of those who have it."

"Lowington got hold of two or three drafts, or bills, sent to the fellows."

"Only two or three," replied Little, lightly. "Those fellows can either borrow, or go with the lambs."

The Knights of the Red Cross, afterwards of the Golden Fleece, had written to their fathers, asking them for remittances to be sent to Paris, where, after sailing around to Marseilles in the Josephine, and going the rest of the way by railroad, they were to get their letters. Most of their parents had complied with the request, but two or three of them had taken the precaution to inform the principal of the fact, and the bills had been cashed, the proceeds being placed to the credit of the students in whose favor they had been drawn. As long as the boys wrote home, the fathers and mothers seldom communicated with the principal. Most of the rogues had been informed in their letters from home that the money wanted had been remitted, and awaited their order in Paris. The runaways, therefore, would be in funds sufficient for their stolen excursion as soon as they could reach their destination. The only thing that disturbed them was the difficulty of obtaining enough in the beginning to pay their railroad fare to Paris.

While Little was instructing Greenway in the programme for the future, the crew of the third cutter were called away, and the conference was abruptly closed. The purport of the letter which the officer in charge of the boat bore to the principal, was, that Mr. Fluxion did not desire to leave the consort for his visit to Marseilles until the close of the week. Howe was perhaps nearer the truth than he really believed when he declared that Mr. Lowington would not dare to leave the runaways on board of either vessel in charge of any other person than the vice-principal. He had been strongly inclined to grant the petition of Shuffles in their favor; but when it was almost proved that the party were the cause of all the confusion which had occurred on board of the ship during the afternoon, that they were in a mutinous frame of mind, he was not willing to encourage their insubordination. He was much disturbed by the difficult problem thus thrust upon him. Dr. Carboy, the professor of natural philosophy and chemistry, who had spent several years in Germany, had volunteered to take charge of the runaways, and he seemed to be the only person who was available for this duty. He was no sailor, and only a fair disciplinarian, and Mr. Lowington had not entire confidence in his ability to manage thirty of the wildest boys in the squadron — discontented under the punishment to which they were subjected.

Though everything was orderly on board of the ship, there was a great deal of suppressed excitement, not to say indignation, for the crew did not like the idea of keeping watch and reefing topsails, instead of voyaging down the beautiful Rhine. The movement looked like a punishment, and many of the crew felt themselves to be entirely innocent of the blunders and failures made in handling the ship. They had done their best, and thought it was not fair to punish the innocent with the guilty. Doubtless it was not fair; but it was a question which related to the discipline of the crew, as a whole, and not a dozen of those who had made the mischief could be identified, even by the seamen who had worked in the rigging with them, much less by the officers.

The mischief-makers themselves did all they could to foment this spirit of discontent among those who were ordinarily well disposed. They assumed the responsibility of declaring that the trip into Germany had been indefinitely postponed. Probably, with the self-conceit incident to human nature, they really believed they were no worse than the best of the crew, and they desired to involve all their shipmates in the odium of the insubordination which had taken place.

"No Rhine, except pork rind," said Little, as he met Raymond in the waist, after the latter had expressed his dissatisfaction at the new order of things.

"Do you think so?" asked Raymond, who had read enough of the splendid scenery of the Rhine to make him very anxious to see it.

"A fellow that isn't blind can see — can't he? — if he opens his eyes," demanded Little. "What did the new captain do this afternoon, the very minute the crew were dismissed from their stations?"

"I don't know. What did he do?" inquired Raymond, curiously.

"Didn't he rush down into the main cabin? Didn't he have a long talk with Lowington? Then, wasn't the signal for sailing hoisted at once? I tell you this is all Shuffles's doings."

"Why should Shuffles want to go to sea any more than the rest of us?" asked Raymond.

"Why should he? Isn't he the captain of the ship now? Doesn't he want to try on his new authority, and see how it fits? Don't he want to punish the crew because they didn't drill well this afternoon? I believe you are a little deaf in one eye, Raymond, or else you can't hear in the other. It's all as plain as the figure-head on a French frigate," continued Little, with enthusiasm enough to convince any dissatisfied seaman.

"Perhaps it is as you say."

"I know it is."

"The drill was very bad. Every fellow knows that."

"What if it was? Whose fault was it?"

"I don't know whose fault it was; but everything went wrong, and I suppose the new captain is not satisfied with the state of discipline on board. I should not be, if I were he."

"Two of your little lambs are cooped up in their state-rooms now for disobedience of orders."

"Who are they?"

"Hunter and Hyde."

"Two of the best fellows in the ship — never got a black mark in their lives," said Raymond.

"O, well! The new captain will put you pious fellows through a course of sprouts that will open your eyes. Shuffles is a liar and a hypocrite. He has his reward, while an honest fellow, like me, will stick to his bunk in the steerage till the end of the cruise."

"I don't believe Shuffles is a liar, or a hypocrite. You don't like him because he broke up your cruise in the Josephine."

"That's not the reason. I am willing to obey the orders of all the officers, but I don't like to see the crowd punished for nothing," replied Little, leading the auditor back to the original topic.

Raymond was not yet a good subject for the mischief-maker to work upon, though, like a majority of the crew, he was dissatisfied with the change in the programme. Going to sea meant strict dicipline; and after making up their minds to have a good time on shore, it was not pleasant to think of hard work and hard study for the next week or two.

"There comes the commodore's barge," continued Little, as he pointed to the boat, which was rapidly approaching the ship. "The Arbuckles are on board, with all their trunks. What do you think of that, Raymond?"

The mischief-maker looked triumphant. The pile of baggage in the boat seemed to furnish sufficient testimony to clinch the argument he had used.

"That looks like a long cruise, certainly. I suppose they are going with us," replied Raymond, with a sorrowful and disappointed look.

"To be sure they are. In my opinion we are going to sail for Belfast, to convey the Arbuckles home. You won't see any Rhine, except a pork rind, on this cruise. If the fellows have any spunk at all, they won't stand this thing."

"Stand it! What can they do?" asked Raymond, who really believed the crew to be unfairly treated.

"Don't you know what they can do? Who works the ship?"

"We do, of course."

"Who would work her if we did not?"

"Well, I suppose she would not be worked at all," replied Raymond, smiling.

"Then, if all the fellows respectfully refuse to man the capstan, or to unloose a sail, till they have their rights, who will get the ship under way?"

"We are not going to do anything of that sort," answered Raymond, rather indignantly. "It would be mutiny."

"You needn't call it by that name, if you don't wish to. Lowington promised the fellows a trip

THE ARRIVAL OF THE ARBUCKLES.—Page 52.

down the Rhine. Now, because the new captain could not handle the ship, we are to be sent off to sea. If the fellows had any grit at all in their bones, they would show Lowington that they are not slaves to him, or any other man."

"I think we won't talk any more about that," said Raymond, as he moved off, for the bold speech of the mischief-maker alarmed him, and caused him to realize that he was listening to one of the ringleaders of the runaways.

The commodore's barge came up to the gangway. The ladies were assisted up the steps, and the trunks hoisted on board and stowed away in the after cabin. The two state-rooms, which had been built for the use of the commodore and the past officers, were appropriated to their use.

If Raymond, and such as he, were not willing to listen to the mutinous counsels of the runaways, he was not the less dissatisfied and discontented. The arrival of the Arbuckles, with their baggage, indicated that the trip to the Rhine had been abandoned. Perhaps the well-disposed students could have submitted to this disappointment, if it had not been inflicted upon them as a punishment. It seemed to them that they were to suffer for a whim of Shuffles. The runaways had taken pains to disseminate this idea among the crew, as they had also succeeded in involving the whole of them in the mischief which induced the principal to go to sea that night.

All over the deck and throughout the steerage, the boys were grumbling and growling like regular old salts, whose prerogative it is to find fault. When

Howe and Spencer returned in the barge, they readily perceived the state of feeling on board. Little told them what he had said and done, and convinced them that the whole crew were ripe for a strike. The entire ship's company were discussing their grievances, and even a large portion of the officers were dissatisfied. Very likely the sudden elevation of Shuffles had created a feeling of jealousy in the minds of a portion of them.

The mischief-makers were prompt in taking advantage of this state of feeling in the crew. They fanned the flame of discontent, and it was not difficult to convince their shipmates that they were very hardly used; that the new captain was imposing a heavy burden upon them. Some of the best disposed of them were in favor of waiting upon the principal, and representing their view of the case to him; but the more impetuous ones laughed at this plan. Shuffles was the principal's pet, and he would support his *protégé* against everybody else on board. The students talked as boys talk, and acted as boys act. At that moment Shuffles was the most unpopular fellow on board, for it was understood that he had proposed and advocated the obnoxious measure. The ship's company were willing to believe that Mr. Lowington had yielded his assent to please the new captain, rather than because he deemed it necessary to go to sea himself.

By the time the first cutter returned, a large majority of the students had decided that something should be done. They could not agree upon the precise step to be taken. Some advocated a protest, others a respectful refusal to do duty; and a few went in for a square mutiny. The provisions were transferred from the cutter to the ship, and the boat was hoisted up before the perplexing question could be settled.

"After supper, let every fellow go to his mess-room. Don't answer the boatswain's call to weigh anchor;" said Raymond, who had made considerable progress in rebellion since his conversation with Little.

"Ay, ay! That's the talk!" responded half a dozen of the group, who had been anxiously discussing the question.

"No, no!" added half a dozen others.

"Why not?" demanded Raymond of the opponents of the plan.

"Because the Arbuckles are on board, for one reason, and because it will be mutiny, for the second," said Tremere, who volunteered to be spokesman for the opposition. "Mr. Arbuckle has taken us through Switzerland, and paid all the bills, and has invited us to another excursion on the same terms. Now, when he comes on board with his family, to take a little sail with us, we refuse to do duty. It looks like contempt and ingratitude to him."

"It has nothing to do with him," replied Raymond, warmly. "Here is the whole matter in a nutshell. Mr. Arbuckle invited us to take a trip into Germany, and Mr. Lowington promised that we should go. Then, because we don't drill quite as well as the new captain wishes, he insists upon going to sea. The cruise down the Rhine is given up, and we are to carry the Arbuckles to Belfast."

"Who says we are going to Belfast?" demanded Tremere.

"All the fellows say so."

"That doesn't prove that we are going there. I go for obeying orders, wherever we go."

"No, no!" replied a dozen of the group.

"We don't intend to do anything wicked," said Raymond. "When the boatswain calls, we don't answer — that's all. Then the officers will want to know what the matter is, and we shall have a chance to explain our position. When we get fair play, we shall be all right, and return to duty."

The group separated, and while the ship's company were waiting for the supper call, those in favor of the strike used all their influence to carry their measure, while those who were opposed to it remained passive.

CHAPTER IV.

THE YOUNG AMERICA MUTINY.

IT was impossible for the advocates of the mutiny to determine what success had attended their efforts, when the crew were piped to supper. Howe and Little were delighted to find the work in which they were interested progressing so finely. Nearly the whole crew were arrayed against the new captain, and in half an hour the grand explosion would take place. Not more than twenty of the students were expected to respond to the boatswain's call to get under way, and it would be impossible to go to sea. The seamen went below at the supper call, but most of them were too much excited to eat their usual allowance.

The officers, who were to take their supper at a later hour, were all on deck. Paul Kendall was seated by the side of Grace Arbuckle, enjoying a pleasant chat, while her father and mother were in conversation with the principal. Captain Shuffles was planking the deck, apparently engaged in deep thought. Possibly the events of the afternoon disturbed him, for he had already received a hint that the ship's company were much dissatisfied at the idea of going to sea. He could not see why they should be. If the crew did their duty, and everything worked well, the squadron would proceed immediately to Brest, and the cruise need not last more than two days. He knew the programme himself, but he forgot that it was the policy of the principal to keep the destination of the ship a secret, as a general rule, until she was out of sight of land. The Arbuckles had brought their baggage with them, because the party was to proceed to Brest, and would not return to Havre.

Popularity is certainly a very insecure possession; for, three weeks before, Shuffles had been the favorite of the whole ship's company. Now, he was the most unpopular person on board; partly, it is true, because he was misunderstood. Both officers and seamen regarded him as the cause of the present movement. Most of them believed, or at least feared, that the trip to the Rhine had been abandoned, and that the new captain was responsible for this change in the programme. They concluded that he preferred to exercise his new authority, to roaming on shore, where he was, practically, no more than any other student. It was true that Shuffles had suggested to the principal the idea of going to sea, as a measure for perfecting the discipline of the crew. Mr. Lowington had permitted the captain to fight his own battle with the crew, and he fully believed that a little sea service was necessary, after the disorder and insubordination which had prevailed in the ship during the drill. Some of those who complained the loudest had permitted their love of fun to get the better of their discretion, and had joined in the disorder which prevailed during the drill. Many well-disposed boys had assisted the conspirators against the peace of the ship by joining in what appeared to them to be but a mere frolic, while it was, in fact, an organized attempt to make mischief. They had encouraged the spirit of insubordination, without supposing they were engaged in anything more than a mere lark, involuntary on their part, and suggested only by the circumstances of the moment.

From the captain's stand-point, the confusion had a very grave aspect; while from that of the seamen, it was a matter of trivial consequence. The commander was mortified to find the discipline so weak; and he could have no confidence in himself or his crew until his orders were promptly obeyed. He was thinking only of the welfare of the ship and her crew. He had no intention of punishing the students, when he suggested the plan of going to sea, — only of perfecting the discipline. It seemed to him just as though three weeks on shore had demoralized the ship's company. Though he was now aware that the runaways had done what they could to make trouble, the confusion seemed to be too extensive to be accounted for by their agency. Two of the best boys on board had been sent to the mainmast for disobedience; and it was clear that the runaways had not produced all the trouble.

The commodore fully sustained him, and believed that it was best for the ship to go to sea. If the students had forgotten the ropes, or were so much embarrassed in their new stations, that they could not set a sail or get up the anchor without making a mess of it, the ship ought to go to sea. On the return of the excursionists from Germany, it might be necessary to put to sea without an hour's delay, as the principal had suggested. Shipwreck and disaster might follow if the crew were not in working order. It was a plain case to the captain.

Paul Kendall had explained the situation to the Arbuckles as mildly as he could. He had told them that the seamen were a little disorderly, and that it was necessary to have them in perfect discipline before they went to Germany. Without intending to do so, he had produced the impression on their minds, that the trip would be given up unless the boys performed their duty to the entire satisfaction of the principal. In talking with the officers, they had expressed their fear that the proposed excursion would not take place. Perhaps the guests were not far from right; for certainly the students would not be allowed to step on shore if the discipline of the ship was not satisfactory. Miss Grace was sadly disturbed at the thought of depriving the students of the pleasure of seeing the Rhine, its wonders and its beauties.

"Why, I thought your crew were in perfect discipline, Captain — no, I mean Commodore — Kendall," said she, as they sat upon the quarter-deck, discussing the great question of the hour.

"They are, generally," replied Paul. "But you know we are a little world by ourselves, and we have our troubles just like other people. It will be all right, I hope, in a day or two. The students get a little wild sometimes."

"Captain Shuffles is such a noble fellow, I should

think they would all wish to do their best. I'm sure I should, if I were a sailor in your ship."

"Shuffles is a capital fellow," added Paul, who was certainly more pleased to praise the commander himself, than to have his fair companion do so.

"I shall never forget his noble conduct on that terrible night when the steamer was burned," said Grace, warmly.

"Probably none of us will ever forget it. But I am sorry to say that there is a great deal of dissatisfaction with the new captain, just now, even among the officers," added Paul.

"I'm very sorry."

"But it is not his fault; really it is not," continued Paul, fearing that he had said too much.

"I'm sure it is not," protested Grace. "I wonder if I have any influence with the officers."

"I think you have: indeed, I know you have with one of them," replied Paul; but he began to choke before he had uttered the last clause of the sentence.

"With one of them?"

"Yes, with all of them; but perhaps more with one than with others," stammered Paul, studying the seams in the quarter-decks.

"Who is he, pray?" asked Grace, rather timidly.

"With the commodore," answered he, desperately.

"Thank you, Commodore Kendall. Then we will both use our influence to have the captain set right with the officers and the crew."

"Well, it is not exactly the right thing for so dignified a personage as the commodore to persuade his inferiors that his views are correct. He issues orders, and others obey them," laughed Paul. "But really I cannot, in courtesy, meddle with the discipline of the ship."

"I'm going to meddle with it, if I can do anything to set Captain Shuffles right," said Grace, who was very confident that it was quite impossible for her noble preserver to do, or even think, anything wrong.

"The officers will do their duty, whatever they think," added Paul. "In due time they will be satisfied that the captain is right. I fully agree with him, and think that the ship ought to go to sea."

"Of course, I expect to find you on the right side, Commodore Kendall," said Grace.

"Certainly I'm always on your side," he replied, becoming astonishingly bold for him.

"Then we are both on Captain Shuffles's side. Who is the officer standing near us?"

It happened to be Master Perth; and Miss Arbuckle called him, intent upon finding some one who was not on the captain's side. Paul, however, did not think it was in accordance with the dignity of the commodore of the squadron to listen to any criticism of the captain's action, and he reluctantly left the pleasant seat he occupied by the side of the young lady. If there was any one on board who hated Shuffles, Perth was he.

"I wanted to get acquainted with you, Mr. Perth; for it seems to me I have not met you before," she began.

"Probably not, Miss Arbuckle, for I was not one of the party who went to Paris and Switzerland with you," replied the second master.

"Indeed!" exclaimed she, understanding, without further explanation, why he was not one of the party, and that he was one of the runaways, though she could not exactly comprehend how he happened to be an officer if he had been a rebel.

"I had the honor to command the Josephine during a portion of the time the ship's company were absent," laughed he, with anything but penitence for his past offences.

"I am very sorry you were not with the others."

"So am I, for one reason — it deprived me of the pleasure of seeing your pretty face for three or four weeks," said Perth, lightly.

"Perhaps I shall change my mind if I find your absence saved me from such annoyance as I feel at the present moment," replied Grace, blushing, and looking much displeased.

"I beg your pardon! I meant no offence," stammered Perth.

Grace smiled again; for she did not believe he would again venture to indulge in an impudent compliment.

"I am very sorry to learn from what you say that you were one of the runaways," she continued.

"I was one of them — I may say that I was the chief of them," replied Perth, without a blush.

"Of course you are very sorry for it, and very glad that Captain Shuffles brought you back."

"That's an open question," laughed Perth. "I don't think Shuffles made much by what he did. I don't believe any fellow makes anything by being a hypocrite, and selling out his friends."

"I don't think so, either. But you certainly cannot mean to say that Captain Shuffles is a hypocrite, or that he ever betrayed his friends?"

"I suppose I ought not to say anything to you about it, knowing that he is a strong friend of yours."

"Whatever you say, Mr. Perth, shall not be repeated. I have been told that some of the officers are opposed to the new captain; and I do not see how it can be true, when he is so noble and good."

"Noble and good!" ejaculated Perth.

"Certainly. You know what he did for me on the night the steamer was burned."

"There isn't a fellow on board that would not have given all he had for a chance to do the same thing for you," protested Perth.

"But all the students like him."

"I don't believe he has twenty friends in the ship."

"Then they do not know him as I do," replied Grace, indignantly.

"They know him better than you do. He's smart, and a good officer; but when you have said that, you have said all that can be said," continued Perth, bluntly.

"I am sorry to hear you say so," added Grace, really grieved, even while she was incredulous. "I am afraid you are prejudiced against him because he broke up your plan to run away with the Josephine."

"He didn't break it up. Our fellows disagreed among themselves; that's the reason why we had to come back," explained Perth, whose pride did not permit him to acknowledge that he had been beaten by the superior skill and energy of Shuffles. "Now, all the fellows are on the very verge of mutiny, because he insists upon taking the ship to sea, instead of going down the Rhine."

"I'm sure he is doing no more than his duty," persisted Grace, stoutly. "It appears that Mr. Lowington thinks he is right, or he would not send the ship to sea. I am really sorry to hear you speak so unkindly of your captain, for I must say that I cannot believe a word you say about him."

"Thank you," replied Perth, dryly.

"I think you are sincere in your belief," added she. "Paul Kendall says that the captain is right."

"Well, he is commodore, you know, and must believe everything the principal says," laughed Perth. "It is not quite proper for any of us to have opinions of our own, but you see some of us have them."

Perth was certainly good-natured, whatever else he was, and as Grace said no more, he touched his cap, and passed on. The devoted admirer of Shuffles's nobleness and goodness was greatly disconcerted by the blunt statements of the second master, who had declared that the ship's company were almost in a state of mutiny against the captain. She continued her inquiries among other officers; but, though some of them thought it was quite unnecessary to go to sea, they all spoke very handsomely of Shuffles. It was plain enough that Perth had injured himself more than the object of his calumny, by what he had said.

"Are you ready to go to sea, Miss Arbuckle?" asked the captain, as he came on deck, and touched his cap to her.

"I am quite ready; indeed, I am afraid I am more ready than many others on board of this ship," she replied. "I am sorry to hear that some of the officers and seamen are very much displeased at the idea of going to sea."

"So far as the seamen are concerned, it is their own fault, for they have not done their duty," added the captain.

"Not the fault of all of them, I hope."

"Not all, certainly; but if they don't know their stations, they must learn them. If you are all ready to go, I think we will be off," said Shuffles, as he glanced at his watch. "You will get the ship under way, if you please, Mr. Goodwin," he added, addressing the first lieutenant, who was standing near him.

"I really hope there will be no trouble, Captain Shuffles," continued Grace.

"There can be no trouble. All sailors grumble, you know, Miss Arbuckle, and our boys imitate their elders in this respect. They will growl for a while, but just as soon as they work the ship with skill and promptness, we shall put into Brest, and make our trip down the Rhine. I think we shall not be at sea beyond a couple of days."

"I hope not, for the sake of the crew."

"All hands, weigh anchor, ahoy!" shouted the boatswain, as his sharp pipe rang through the ship.

Less than thirty of the seamen answered to the call, and it was apparent that a very large majority of them had chosen to follow the evil counsels of the runaways, or the foolish counsels of other discontented spirits. It was the first time since the ship went into commission that any considerable number of the crew had failed to respond to the call. Shuffles was confounded, and the first lieutenant actually turned pale. It looked like such a mutiny as the Chain League had planned.

"Pipe again," said Shuffles, as quietly as he could.

Again the boatswain sounded the call, and repeated the order, but with no better success than before. Not another seaman appeared upon deck.

"What does this mean?" said the commodore to the captain.

"As near as I can interpret it, the greater part of the crew do not intend to obey orders," replied Shuffles.

"It certainly looks so."

"Mr. Goodwin, will you inquire of those who obeyed the order, whether their shipmates heard the call?" continued the captain, laboring very hard to appear cool and collected, as a commander ought to be in every emergency.

Paul Kendall's curiosity prompted him to follow the executive officer to the waist, where the seamen who had obeyed the call were waiting for orders. He was unwilling to believe the evidence of his senses, though he knew that there was considerable disaffection on board.

"Did the rest of the crew hear the boatswain's pipe?" asked Goodwin of the faithful few.

"Yes, sir," replied Tremere.

"Where are they now?"

"In the mess-rooms."

"Why don't they obey?"

"They say they don't want to go to sea: they say they haven't done anything to deserve punishment, and they object to being punished," replied the spokesman.

"What do they mean by being punished?" asked the commodore.

"Sent to sea. Mr. Lowington promised us a trip down the Rhine; and now that excursion is given up. The fellows say the ship is bound to Belfast, to convey the Arbuckles home. They say they are willing to do their duty, if they can have fair play."

"What do the seamen intend to do?" asked Paul.

"Nothing, sir. They say they will give their reasons when called upon."

"Probably they will, when called upon," said Paul, who had very high ideas of discipline.

The executive officer returned, and explained the situation to the captain. It was impossible to get the ship under way with less than thirty seamen, and he felt that his powers were exhausted. Fortunately, Mr. Lowington, who had heard the boatswain's pipe, came on deck at this critical moment.

"Didn't I hear the boatswain's pipe?" asked the principal, surprised to find only a few hands in the waist.

"Yes, sir; we have called all hands twice, and only about thirty answer the call."

"It was a mistake to call more than once," replied Mr. Lowington, who did not seem to be taken aback by the astounding intelligence. "What's the matter?"

The captain explained, reporting the statements made by the faithful ones in the waist.

"A mutiny, then — is it?" added the principal, with a smile. "Well, I am glad it is no worse."

"The mutineers are willing to explain, when called upon for an explanation," added Paul, who was indignant at the conduct of the malcontents.

"We don't usually call for explanations in such

cases on board ship," said the principal. "It is plain enough that this is only a second edition of the confusion of this afternoon. The young gentlemen have been listening to evil advice."

"What shall be done, sir?" inquired the captain, rather nervously, in spite of his laborious efforts to keep cool.

"Mutiny is mutiny," replied the principal; "but in this case, I think we need not treat it with the severity which prevails in the navy. The students below say, and probably believe, that the excursion to the Rhine has been abandoned, and that the ship is bound to Belfast. Though they are mistaken, we can only tell them so when they return to their duty. We will go to sea, as we intended."

"How can we go to sea with a crew of less than thirty?" asked Shuffles.

"Keep perfectly calm, Captain Shuffles. I am willing to grant that, in a man-of-war, with men in a state of mutiny, the case would be a very serious one. I do not so regard it in the present instance, but we will profit by the lesson it may teach. For an officer to permit a sailor to see that he is disconcerted is yielding too much. Therefore, young gentlemen, I wish you all to be perfectly composed, whatever happens. This affair is rather ludicrous than otherwise, since the mutineers declare that they are ready to explain when called upon to do so, which is very kind and condescending on their part," the principal proceeded, addressing the officers who had gathered around him for the solution of what seemed to them a very difficult and trying problem.

But they were not permitted to hear the solution, for the principal invited the commodore and the captain into the main cabin, to discuss the matter, desiring, even in the present embarrassing situation, to have everything done in accordance with his ideas of discipline. He meant that the captain should be the apparent, if he could not be the real, manager of the difficult affair.

"How many hands responded to the boatswain's call?" asked the principal, when the party were seated.

"Less than thirty," answered Shuffles.

"Twenty-eight. I had the curiosity to count them," interposed Paul.

"Twenty-eight," repeated the principal. "Very well; we can —"

"I hope you will excuse me, sir," said Shuffles, interrupting him. "If this state of thing is caused by any dislike to me, sir, I am willing to resign."

"So far as I know, you have done your duty, Shuffles; and to permit you to resign would be to abandon the plan of the Academy Ship, and acknowledge that discipline is an impracticable thing. You cannot resign."

"Many of the fellows dislike me," added the captain.

"That is not your fault, as I understand the matter. That the runaways, who, I suspect, are at the root of this mischief, should be prejudiced against you, was to be expected. If others are also, it is because they are misinformed. You can afford to wait till time justifies your good intentions."

"I am willing to own that I have no desire to resign. I like the place, but I am willing to sacrifice my own wishes for the peace of the ship."

"Peace is not to be bought on any such terms. Say nothing more about resigning. Twenty-eight hands, you say, are ready to obey orders."

"Yes, sir."

"On an emergency, the captain and four lieutenants can officer the ship. Masters, midshipmen, and pursers must do duty as seamen. They will gladly consent to do so. Let it be voluntary on their part. How many will that make?"

"Thirty-eight."

"Peaks, Bitts, and Leach will make forty-one. The Josephine is fully manned, and can spare us nine more. That will make fifty. If we lay aside the school work, we can sail the ship round the world with that number."

Shuffles displayed a smile of satisfaction at this solution.

"But we will procure the services of a tug-boat to tow us to sea, so that there will no hard work in getting clear of the harbor," added the principal. "Send Leavitt in the second cutter to the Josephine for the extra hands, and let Foster go in the third for one of the steam-tugs up by the jetties. Above all things, Captain Shuffles, do not mention your plans to any person."

"I will not, sir," replied Shuffles, as he hastened on deck to put in force the solution of the problem.

"What is to be the result of this, Mr. Lowington?" asked Paul.

"I don't know — nothing serious, however. The young gentlemen are waiting very impatiently in their mess-rooms to be called and asked for the explanation, which I doubt not is a very plausible one. Let them wait," continued the principal, leading the way to the deck, where he sat down with the Arbuckles, and was soon busy in conversation with them, as though nothing had happened.

CHAPTER V.

THE ORDER OF THE FAITHFUL.

THE appearance of Captain Shuffles on deck produced a decided sensation among the officers, some of whom believed that the mutineers would be dragged from the mess-rooms by the adult forward officers, and tied up to the rigging. The decided character of the principal certainly pointed to the most decided measures. Something terrible was to be expected, and the young gentlemen were astonished when Mr. Lowington came on deck, immediately after the captain, seated himself with the Arbuckles, and began to converse with them as pleasantly as though no mutiny had ever been dreamed of.

The captain called the officers around him, and all of them eagerly obeyed the summons.

"We are going to sea immediately," said he, with none of the anxiety which was visible in his face before. "As we are short-handed, I have a favor to ask. Those below the rank of lieutenant, who are willing to serve as seamen until the discipline of the ship can be restored, will signify it by walking over to the starboard side."

All below the grade indicated, with a single exception, promptly marched over to the other side of the ship. The four lieutenants stepped out of the way, so that the single dissenter might stand alone. It is hardly necessary to say that Perth was the person who was so largely in the minority among the officers.

"You decline to serve with the other masters?" said Shuffles.

"I prefer to be excused. I have had considerable experience as a seaman, and would like a little more as an officer," replied Perth, politely.

"We shall dispense with the services of all the officers except the lieutenants," added the captain. "There will be nothing for you to do, but you shall not be compelled to serve as a seaman."

"Permit me to take his place," interposed Gordon, the senior past officer.

"Thank you, Gordon," replied Shuffles.

"Please enroll me also as a seaman," added Haven, good-naturedly.

"And me also," laughed Paul.

"I suggest that the past officers take the places of the second, third, and fourth lieutenants, who shall do duty as seamen," said Leavitt, the second officer.

"By all means," added Foster, the third.

"With all my heart," followed Prescott, the fourth.

The captain adopted this suggestion, and Gordon, as second lieutenant, was sent off to the Josephine in the second cutter, which was pulled by three masters and the three midshipmen. When it was ready to leave, Mr. Lowington stepped into the boat, for he desired to satisfy himself that the crew of the consort were not also demoralized. Haven in the third cutter, with a volunteer crew, left the ship to procure a tug-steamer. Peaks, Bitts, Leach, and the head steward had been privately requested to be on deck, in case any unexpected demonstration was made by the mutineers.

In the steerage everything was very quiet. The sensation below was decidedly superior to that on deck. The rebels were patiently waiting to be called upon for an explanation of their remarkable conduct. Probably none of them even noticed that the grating had been put upon the main hatch by the cautious Peaks, to prevent them from leaving the steerage. The boatswain's call had sounded twice, and they supposed the faculty of the Academy were consulting upon the proper measures to be taken. Most of them believed that they would be invited on deck, where the principal would "preach" to them, as usual, and thus afford them an opportunity to state their grievances. Perhaps, with the exception of the runaways, they were willing to return to their duty after they had recorded their protest. The principal still purposed to let them wait.

The third cutter, all of whose volunteer crew wore shoulder-straps, came up to the gangway of the Josephine, which, like the ship, was all ready to weigh anchor.

"You come with a very nobby crew," said Mr. Fluxion, as the principal stepped upon the deck of the consort.

"The ship is in a state of mutiny," replied Mr. Lowington, with a smile upon his face, which softened the astounding declaration.

Mutiny!" exclaimed Mr. Fluxion.

"Precisely so. We called all hands to weigh anchor, and less than thirty answered to the summons. We learned from them that the rest of the crew refused to do duty till their grievances were heard. Do you know of anything of this kind on board of your vessel?"

"We haven't called all hands yet, for we don't begin to get under way till the ship mans the capstan. It is possible that we shall have the same difficulty."

"Let your captain get under way at once, for the ship will be towed out. If your crew is all right, I should like to transfer a few seamen to the ship, for we are rather short-handed," added the principal.

Mr. Fluxion called Captain Terrill, and the order was given to pipe all hands. As the boatswain's whistle sounded, the principal and the vice-principal descended to the cabin. Mr. Lowington had begun to explain his method of dealing with the difficulty, when a messenger from the captain reported that twelve seamen refused to answer the summons.

"Ascertain who they are, and get under way without disturbing them," said the principal, after the messenger had retired.

"That's a novel way to deal with a mutiny," added Mr. Fluxion, who was always in favor of decisive measures.

Mr. Lowington stated his views fully, and explained his plan. Though the vice-principal did not agree with him in regard to his corrective measures, he consented to adopt them. When they went on deck, the captain handed Mr. Fluxion a list of the names of the Josephine's mutineers. They were the twelve runaways who had been transferred to the consort. Little had succeeded in inducing them to engage in the plot, but the rest of the crew would not follow their vicious example, even with the assurance that the mutiny was general on board of the ship. Under these circumstances, none of the crew of the Josephine could be spared for service in the Young America, and the boat returned without them. The principal decided that the ship could be handled with the available force, which might include a portion of the cooks and stewards, some of whom were sailors.

The tug-boat had come alongside when the cutter reached the ship. In order to give any rebel, who had repented, an opportunity to return to his duty, the grating was removed from the main hatch, and the boatswain again called all hands to weigh anchor. Only two of them, however, answered the call. The capstan was manned by the faithful thirty, reënforced by the officers and the men on board. A long hawser had been passed from the bow to the steamer, and as soon as the anchor was up to the hawse-hole, the signal was given to go ahead. The Josephine followed as promptly as though every seaman on board performed his duty, though the sails were not set with the usual precision. The little squadron went off to the north-west, carrying its double mutiny with it.

As soon as the ship began to move, after the anchor was secured, the officers devoted themselves to the duty of stationing the crew. They were divided into two watches, and their places for making and taking in sail, reefing and tacking, were assigned to them. As the officers who had volunteered to serve before the mast were thorough seamen, the task was speedily accomplished. There were no "green hands" to be favored, for every one was competent to hand, reef, and steer. By the time the squadron was well in the offing, the ship's company was in condition to make sail. About ten miles outside of the harbor, the steamer was discharged.

"All hands, make sail, ahoy!" shouted the boatswain, and every officer and seaman sprang to his station.

Lieutenants, masters, midshipmen, and pursers mingled with the seamen, and the work was done with promptness and precision. Topsails, top-gallant-sails, and courses were set, and with the wind abeam, the ship went off to the north-west as comfortably as though no mutiny had distracted her routine. When everything was made snug for a night at sea, the roll was called, and the names of the mutineers checked on the list.

"Young gentleman," said Mr. Lowington, while the faithful were still assembled in the waist, "I regret that so many of your companions have resorted to a silly and stupid expedient to redress real or imaginary grievances. Mutiny is never respectable, under any circumstances; and I wish to draw a sharp line between those who do their duty and those who do not. I desire that none of you hold any communication whatever with the mutineers. Be dignified and gentlemanly, but avoid them. Give them no information in regard to what transpires on deck. I *request* you to do this. I do not give you any order to that effect.

"None of the mutineers will be allowed to come on deck, and I shall have some means of distinguishing the faithful from the unfaithful."

"Will you allow me to furnish a badge for each of the faithful?" asked Grace Arbuckle, who stood near the principal, and was deeply interested in the proceedings.

"Certainly, Miss Arbuckle; and I am sure the young gentlemen will set an additional value upon the decoration if it is bestowed by you," replied Mr. Lowington, as gallantly as though he had been a much younger man.

"Thank you, sir," answered Grace, blushing at the compliment.

"Miss Arbuckle will give a badge to each of you," continued the principal to the faithful few.

The crew on deck applauded lustily.

"It will be a white ribbon on the left breast," said Grace.

"A white ribbon on the left breast," repeated Mr. Lowington, as Grace hastened to the cabin to procure the materials for the decoration. "I learn that those who refused to answer the boatswain's call, expected to be asked for an explanation of their conduct. I cannot make terms with mutineers. I should have proceeded in a different manner if I had not believed there was a misunderstanding. I am willing to explain for your benefit, but not for those below. Do you understand?"

"Ay, ay, sir!" shouted the students.

"With a promise on your part to keep your own counsels, I will explain. Those of you who will agree not to communicate anything I may say to the mutineers will signify it by going abaft the mizzen-mast on the quarter-deck. Those who decline to agree to these terms will remain in the waist."

Every officer, including Perth, and every seaman, promptly marched to the quarter-deck.

"At the wheel, do you agree to the terms?" said the principal, addressing the quarter-master and seaman who were steering.

"Yes, sir," replied both.

"Mr Peaks, you will see that no one is at the ladder of the main hatch," continued the principal, turning to the adult boatswain.

"Ay, ay, sir," replied Peaks, who soon reported that all the mutineers were still in the mess-rooms.

"Now, young gentlemen, I am told it is generally believed in the steerage that the trip down the Rhine has been abandoned; that the ship is bound to Belfast to convey our good friends to their home. This is a mistake, and probably the one which made the mischief in part. I have no idea of going to Belfast, and no idea of abandoning the excursion into Germany."

The boys applauded with a zeal which indicated how satisfactory the intelligence was to them.

"Certainly the discipline of the ship needs improving, but I was satisfied that two or three days' service at sea would restore it to its former standard. If the squadron remains at Havre during our absence, both vessels must go into the docks, which involves considerable expense. I therefore purposed to make a harbor at Brest, and go from there to the Rhine. For this reason the baggage of our friends was brought on board. That is really all that need be said. Are you satisfied?"

"Ay, ay, sir!" shouted the crowd.

"But remember that this explanation is made for your benefit, and not for that of the students in the steerage. They have chosen their own remedy, and they must abide the issue. You are now dismissed."

"Not yet, if you please, Mr. Lowington," interposed Grace, who had stationed herself, with her mother on the port side of the mizzen-mast. "If the young gentlemen will pass this way, they shall be decorated with the white ribbon of the Order of the Faithful."

"The Order of the Faithful!" exclaimed Mr. Lowington, laughing, while all the students applauded. "You will pass forward on the port side of the mizzen-mast, and be initiated into the Order of the Faithful."

"I shall join that order," said Commodore Kendall, as he placed himself in the single line formed by the boys.

"Let the flag-officer go first," added some of the students, dragging Paul to the head of the column.

"Commodore Kendall, you are received into the Order of the Faithful," said Grace, as she pinned upon the left breast of his coat the white ribbon, which was doubled, so that the two ends hung down.

"Thank you, Miss Arbuckle. I will endeavor to be faithful," replied the flag-officer, as he touched his cap to the fair initiator.

Captain Shuffles followed him, and in half an hour the entire party were duly initiated and decorated.

As fast as Mrs. Arbuckle could cut off and double the ribbons, Grace adjusted them. She explained that she had purchased a large quantity of narrow white and blue ribbon in Paris to make trimmings for a dress; and when the principal had spoken of a distinguishing mark for those who did their duty, it had suggested to her the white ribbon of the Order of the Faithful. She was delighted to have her idea so well received.

"We have had some secret societies on board this ship," laughed Paul Kendall, after he had received his decoration. "I move you we form another — the Order of the Faithful."

"We have already taken the obligation," added Shuffles.

"And we have been initiated by Miss Arbuckle," said Gordon.

The suggestion was received with favor, though rather as a pleasantry than as a serious matter; and, after the faithful had all marched by the mizzen-mast, the subject was again taken up in the waist.

"I move you that Commodore Kendall be chosen Grand Commander of the Order of the Faithful," said Shuffles.

"I beg you will excuse me. I couldn't walk if I had to carry around with me such a magnificent title as that," replied Paul, shrugging his shoulders like a Frenchman. "I suggest that Miss Grace Arbuckle be the chief of the order, and that no one be admitted unless initiated by her. As she is the founder of the order, it is fair that she should be its head."

"Good!" shouted several of the officers and seamen.

"What shall her title be?" added Shuffles.

"Queen," replied Gordon.

"No; that's too commonplace," answered Haven.

"What shall it be, then?"

"Something outlandish, just for the fun of the thing," said Haven, who was not a very warm advocate of secret societies.

"The Amazon," suggested one of the seamen.

"O, no! don't call her an Amazon," protested Paul. "It would be a libel upon her."

"The Queen of the Fairies."

"We are not fairies," objected Haven.

"She is one, at any rate."

"Call her the Empress."

"Simply the President."

"No; the Directress."

The question seemed to be a trying one; and one after another suggested titles which were satisfactory to no one but the proposers.

"How will the Protectress do?" inquired Shuffles.

"Rather formidable and commonplace," replied Haven. "Make it the Grand Protectress, and I am with you."

"I like Protectress," added Paul Kendall.

"So do I," said half a dozen others.

"Grand Protectress is better," persisted Haven, who could not help making a burlesque of the affair.

"Grand Protectress!" shouted a dozen others, who believed in high-sounding titles.

"Put it to vote," suggested Shuffles.

"Ay, ay! put it to vote."

"Those in favor of Grand Protectress say, ay," continued Haven.

"Ay!" responded a large number.

"Opposed."

"No."

"The ayes have it. Grand Protectress it is."

"I move you that Commodore Kendall and Captain Shuffles be a committee to wait upon Miss Arbuckle, and inform her that she has been unanimously chosen Grand Protectress of the Order of the Faithful. Those in favor say, ay; those opposed, no. It is a vote."

The committee went to the quarter-deck, where Grace and her mother were conversing with Mr. Lowington. Paul, who was by seniority the spokesman, touched his cap, and looked as dignified as though he had been the minister plenipotentiary of one of the great powers.

"Miss Arbuckle, I have the honor — and I should do injustice to my own feelings if I did not add, the pleasure — to inform you, that you have been unanimously chosen Grand Protectress of the Order of the Faithful."

"The what?" asked Grace.

The principal, usually very solemn and dignified, laughed heartily.

"Grand Protectress," replied Paul, gravely. "The order has been duly established; and, as you have initiated all the members, it is eminently proper that you should preside over its destinies."

"Please to assure the members of the order, that I accept the high position, and that I am very grateful to them for the honor they have done me," answered Grace, when she could restrain her laughter so as to speak.

"I am happy to be the bearer of such a pleasant message," said Paul, as he bowed and retired.

"Grand Protectress!" laughed Grace, repeating in measured tones her magnificent title.

Paul reported the acceptance of the Grand Protectress; and the society was further organized by the choice of a secretary, whose only duty was to keep a record of the names of the members.

"Now, we want a motto," said Gordon; "something that will express, in few words, the objects of the society."

"I don't happen to know what the objects of the society are," replied Haven; "but I suggest, '*Honi soit qui mal y pense.*'"

"The Queen of England has a mortgage on that motto," said Paul. "*Semper paratus* will be better."

"What does it mean?" asked a student.

"Some praties," replied a wag.

"Let us have a motto in plain English, and one that has not been used by all the engine companies in the United States," added Haven.

"*Semper paratus* is good, I think," persisted Paul. "*Always ready* to answer the boatswain's call, and *always ready* to do our duty."

"But it is worn out," protested Haven. "I move you we invite the Grand Protectress to give us a motto."

The motion was carried, and the same committee appointed to make the request. Paul led the way to Grace again, who was still highly amused at the grand honor which had been conferred upon her.

"The Order of the Faithful instructs me humbly to petition the Grand Protectress for a motto suitable to the needs, and expressive of the objects, of the association," said Paul.

"O, dear me!" exclaimed Grace. "If you ask such things as that of me, I shall not wish to be Grand Protectress. I think, as your great philosopher said, it will be paying too dear for the whistle. Must it be in English, French, Latin, or German?"

"That must be left to the discretion of your Grand Protectresship," answered Paul, gravely.

"Please to help me, father," said she, appealing to Mr. Arbuckle.

"Whatever the Grand Protectress vouchsafes to give us shall be cherished by the order," added Paul.

Mr. Arbuckle wrote a sentence on a slip of paper, and handed it to Grace.

"Ah, here is your motto!" exclaimed she, laughing heartily.

"Please to repeat it," said Captain Shuffles.

"*Vous ne pouvez pas faire un sifflet de la queue d'un cochon,*" added Grace, reading from the paper, which she handed to Paul, choking with mirth.

"Thanks, most excellent Grand Protectress," replied the commodore, who found it very difficult to maintain his gravity.

"It is a literal translation of the English proverb, and perhaps the idea is not expressed in similar phrase in French," said Mr. Arbuckle; "but I think it will answer very well for a motto."

Paul smoothed down his face as well as he could, and conveyed the motto to the assembled order in the waist.

"I have the honor to inform you that the Grand Protectress has provided a motto," said he.

"What is it?" demanded a dozen.

"It is in French."

"The motto!" called the impatient Faithfuls.

"*Vous ne pouvez pas faire un sifflet de la queue d'un cochon.*"

Only two or three laughed, for only a few were as good French scholars as Paul and Shuffles.

"What's the English of it?" asked several at the same time.

"You must excuse me, for I do not think it is quite proper to translate the motto," replied Paul.

Those who understood it enjoyed the joke too much to afford the others any light on the subject. Haven was delighted with the motto, and moved that it be accepted. As it had been furnished by the Grand Protectress, it was unanimously adopted. The weak scholars were very curious to know the meaning of the mystic words. Most of them could make out a part of the sentence, but not enough to translate it. The business of the meeting was completed, and the members separated, all of them feeling that the mutiny of the Young America was more like a merry-making than anything else. To be decorated with the white ribbon of the order by a beautiful young lady was a privilege which they appreciated, and all of them were thankful that they had not been led astray by the evil counsels which had prevailed in the steerage.

"If you do not like the motto, I can give you another now," said Grace, when Paul joined the little party on the quarter-deck.

"The one you gave was unanimously adopted by the order," replied Paul.

"Was it, really?" asked Grace, laughing more heartily than before.

"Certainly it was."

"Did they understand its meaning?"

"Some of them did."

"If you like this one better, it is at your service: 'High aims produce noble deeds.'"

"While I hope we all believe in the English one, I think the members of the order prefer the French one."

"If they are suited, I am," replied Grace, cheerfully.

The ship was still going along under easy sail, though the weather promised to be unfavorable before morning. At eight o'clock, the starboard watch, with the first and third lieutenants in charge, took the deck, and the port watch went below. They were to be ready for duty at twelve. Everything on deck was as pleasant as a merry-making. None of the passengers were seasick.

Everything was not so lovely in the steerage, and it is necessary to go back a few hours in order to ascertain what passed among the mutineers.

CHAPTER VI.

IN THE STEERAGE.

AFTER the students finished their supper, those who had decided to rebel against the authorities of the ship retired to the mess-rooms, agreeably to the instructions of the leaders. There were forty-four of them, including the eighteen runaways who still remained in the ship as seamen, and who were the real mischief-makers, forming a class by themselves, hardening their hearts in sheer ugliness against the discipline of the ship. In their exploit with the Josephine, they had "bucked" against authority, and had suffered the consequences, which unfortunately had not produced a favorable impression upon them. They were disposed to do the same thing again.

The rest of the mutineers belonged to a different class. They were generally well-disposed boys, fond of fun and excitement, not exactly the "lambs" of the flock, but certainly not the black sheep. If some of them had assisted in creating the confusion during the drill, they had not done so with any malicious purpose, as the runaways had, but from a thoughtless love of sport and excitement. They would never have thought of such an expedient as rebellion if they had not been cunningly worked upon by the real mischief-makers. They were not strong-minded young men, who dare to do right under all circumstances. With good impulses in the main, their principle was not hardened into that solid element which constitutes a reliable conscience. They were easily led away, and believing they had a real grievance, they resorted to doubtful means for its redress.

Of this class Raymond had been the leading spirit. He would have resented the appellation of mutineer as an insult. All he expected and desired to obtain was an explanation; and he was confident that when two-thirds of the crew mildly, and even respectfully, declined to do duty, the principal, either in person or by deputy, would come below to ascertain the nature of the difficulty. He had cautioned his party to be perfectly respectful to the officers, and especially to the principal and professors. If it was to be a mutiny in any sense of the word, it was to be a very gentlemanly one. Having reduced the intended rebellion to this mild form, he had no fear that the rough hand of Peaks would be laid upon them, or that the party would be driven by force from the messrooms.

"How do you suppose it will come out?" asked Hyde, one of Raymond's messmates, in a low tone, as a group of the rebels gathered in their room.

"It will come out all right," replied the leader of the mild mutineers, confidently.

"I'm not so sure of that," added Hyde, shaking his head. "Mr. Lowington is a great stickler for discipline; and he is not exactly the man to come below, and coax us to attend to our duty."

"I don't expect he will coax us to do it. But there are so many of us in the scrape that he can hardly do anything else."

"How many do you suppose there are?" inquired Hyde.

"I can't tell exactly, but I am satisfied that more than two thirds of the whole crew will stand out."

"I don't know about that."

"I know that every fellow in the ship is mad because the trip to the Rhine is given up; and I think that at least two thirds of them are mad enough to do something about it. I should not be surprised if not a single fellow answered the boatswain's call."

"I should; for I know half a dozen who have said they should; but they mean to let the principal know that all the fellows are dissatisfied with the idea of being cheated out of the run into Germany. I'm not sure that this wouldn't be the better way."

"O, it wouldn't amount to a row of pins! What does the principal care whether the fellows are satisfied or not? We must do something to prove that we are somebody," persisted Raymond.

"That's so," added Lindsley, earnestly. "I don't believe in all Howe's nonsense, but there is a good deal of truth in what he says. We are not common sailors, but the sons of wealthy men. We were sent to this ship because we could have a chance to see the world while we were getting an education; and it isn't just the thing to deprive us of the privileges we pay for. Of course we don't mean to make any row. If the principal don't choose to set us right, why, we must go to our duty, and make the best of it; but for one, I shall write to my father, and tell him just how the matter stands."

"That's the idea," responded Raymond. "I shall do the same thing, and I know my father will send for me immediately. My mother would be glad enough to have me go home."

"I'll tell you what it is, fellows," added Lindsley, warmly; "if about fifty of us will only hang together, we can have our own way. If we write home that we are dissatisfied, that the principal is rough on us, and won't let us see the country, we can blow up the Academy Ship higher than a kite."

"I think we have seen the country pretty well," suggested Wilde.

"Yes; but we are not to go into Germany," replied Raymond. "We are to go to sea, just because the new captain demands it."

"For my own part, I like the ship first rate, and should hate to have my father send for me," continued Wilde. "I don't believe there are a dozen fellows on board who wouldn't think it a hard case if they had to leave."

"Not if we are to be treated in this manner. If we are allowed to see the country, and have a good time, every fellow will be satisfied," replied Raymond. "But I think it will all come round right if we keep a stiff upper lip, and stand up for our rights. I like Lindsley's idea first rate. We can talk that up, and it will help us out, if nothing else will. We can easily get forty or fifty of the fellows to say they will ask their fathers to take them away from the ship if they don't have fair play. Then we can mildly suggest the idea to Mr. Lowington; and, I tell you, he can see that the loss of fifty of us would make an end of his big idea."

"I'm not ready to say I will ask my father to take me out of the ship," protested Wilde.

"I am," said Raymond.

"So am I," added Lindsley.

"And I," chimed in others.

"While we are waiting, suppose we circulate the idea."

At this moment Tremere and Willis, who were the other occupants of the mess-room, came in, and the proposition was stated to them.

"No!" exclaimed Tremere, very decidedly. "When the boatswain pipes, I shall go on deck, and do my duty as long as I have two legs to stand on, and two hands to work with."

"So shall I," added Willis. "I don't believe half the stories that have been told through the ship. In my opinion, if any of the fellows don't go down the Rhine this year, it will be because they are rebels or runaways. I shall take my station when the boatswain pipes, if I am the only fellow on board that does so."

"If you haven't spunk enough to stand up for your rights, you deserve to lose them," replied Raymond, disgusted with the answers of those high-toned students.

"My rights! Humph! I value them too highly to throw them away by any such stupid conduct as you suggest," answered Willis.

Lindsley, thinking that Tremere and Willis did not

understand their plan, volunteered to explain that they did not intend to use any violent measures; that they meant to be entirely respectful to the officers and to the faculty.

"Disobedience is disobedience, whether you are respectful or disrespectful; whether you say 'no' squarely, or 'excuse me;' only the former is less cowardly than the latter," said Tremere, in reply. "As I understand the matter, you are getting up a row, asking fellows to write to their fathers to take them away from the ship."

"All hands, up anchor, ahoy!" shouted the boatswain, at the main hatch.

Raymond returned to the mess-room, while the two incorruptible fellows hastened to their stations on deck.

"Now we are in for it!" said Lindsley.

"Let us stick to our text," added Raymond, fearful that some of the party would back out as the decisive moment had come.

"Ay, ay! Stick to the text!" added Hyde.

"Hold on, and I will see how many fellows answer the call," continued Raymond, nervously, as he stationed himself at the door of the room, where he could see the seamen who went up the ladder.

"Count them," said Lindsley.

It was an exciting moment to the rebels, for however real they believed their grievances to be, probably not many of them were satisfied with the expediency or the justice of the measure they had adopted to redress them.

"Only twelve!" exclaimed Raymond, when the last of the faithful had ascended the ladder.

"That's bully!" said Hyde, rubbing his hands with satisfaction at the assumed success of the scheme.

"Are you sure that you counted right?" inquired Lindsley.

"I counted ten, and added Tremere and Willis to the number, for they had gone up before I began. I didn't expect even as many as that would go."

But the enthusiastic rebel had made a blunder. A portion of those who intended to obey orders, having no motive for remaining below, had gone on deck as soon as they finished their suppers. Sixteen of these, added to the twelve who went up from the steerage, made the twenty-eight who first answered the call.

"Only twelve!" repeated Hyde.

"If we have nearly the whole crowd, we can do something more than explain our position," said Lindsley.

"I'm not in favor of doing anything more than that," added Raymond, shaking his head.

"All hands, up anchor, ahoy!" shouted the boatswain, the second time, at the main hatch.

"It's all right," said Howe, appearing at the door; "not a fellow answers it."

"Only a dozen have gone on deck in all," added Raymond.

"Is that all?" asked the runaway.

"That's all; I counted them."

"Good! We shall make a big thing of it," answered Howe, as he left the room to look into others, in all of which it is safe to say that the strong-minded rebels were engaged in stiffening the backs of the weaker ones, for a large portion of them were in a very novel position.

"Some one will be down very soon to know what the matter is," said Hyde, fidgeting about his berth, where he had stretched himself to await the time.

"Who shall speak for us?" asked Raymond.

"You shall," replied Lindsley.

"Very well; I will do the best I can," answered Raymond, modestly. "I am to say, very respectfully, that the fellows are dissatisfied with the idea of going to sea, and giving up the trip to the Rhine."

"Yes; and we respectfully request that the principal will make good his promise to take us into Germany," added Hyde.

"Don't you mean to say anything about the letters to our fathers, asking them to take us away from the ship?" inquired Lindsley.

"That looks a little like a threat," objected Raymond. "Besides, we don't know how many fellows will agree to send such letters."

"Let us go round and see," suggested Lindsley.

"We will, if there is time."

As the record of the preceding chapter testifies, there was an abundance of time to carry out this or any other preliminary measure. Raymond and Lindsley proceeded to canvass the rebels in regard to the letters. The eighteen runaways were ready to assent to anything, but only about half of the others were willing to give in their allegiance to what they regarded as a mean scheme. Some even declared they would back out if anything of this sort was to be attempted. Raymond was politic enough not to press the measure very hard, and he returned to his room with the names of only thirty, instead of fifty, which he had expected to obtain.

"That's enough to make a show with," said Lindsley. "But I don't intend to say anything about the letters to the principal, if he is willing to do the fair thing by us."

"What are they about on deck? It is half an hour since the boatswain piped all hands," said Hyde, jumping out of his berth.

"I'm sure I don't know," replied Lindsley, uneasily. "I should think they had found out by this time that something was the matter."

"I know one thing," said Wilde, with a significant shake of the head, as though he had made an important discovery.

"What's that?" demanded the others, in the same breath.

"They have put the grating on the main hatch, so that we can't go on deck if we wish to do so," replied Wilde, who had begun to be regarded as one with a weak back.

"No matter for that," answered Raymond, with an effort to laugh, though he was far from being satisfied with the situation as indicated by the closed hatch. "As we don't want to go on deck, it makes no difference to us."

"That's so," added Lindsley. "They have put on the grating to make a show. They can't do anything while sixty of the crew are below."

"Are you sure there are sixty?" asked Hyde, doubtfully.

"Take twelve from the whole crew, and it leaves sixty. But count them for yourself, if you are not satisfied with my figures."

"I will;" and he left the mess-room for this purpose.

He had the curiosity to look up the hatch, and made another discovery — that the stout boatswain was there, apparently keeping watch. The faithful had just marched to the quarter-deck, to indicate that they were willing to "keep their own counsel," as requested by the principal. Hyde returned to the room to report the fact. It looked like decided measures to him.

"I think we are caged," said he.

"No matter if we are," replied Raymond, with a sneer. "One thing is plain enough; they can't go to sea without us."

"No; twelve fellows can't get the anchor up, even with the help of Peaks," added Lindsley.

"O, we've got them," persisted Raymond. "We are a majority of all hands, even if you count the officers on the other side; and I happen to know they are as much dissatisfied as we are."

Hyde left the room again, and succeeded in making a count of all the seamen in the steerage.

"Humph!" snuffed he, on his return. "You counted the fellows with your elbows, Raymond. There are only forty-four in the steerage."

"Forty-four!" sneered Raymond. "Does twelve from seventy-two leave forty-four?"

"No; but twenty-eight from seventy-two leaves forty-four," retorted Hyde. "I'm sure I'm right."

Raymond was not satisfied, and counted for himself, but with no different result; and Lindsley suggested that some of the twenty-eight were on deck when the boatswain's call sounded.

"Well, what's the odds?" demanded the mortified leader of the moderate party. "They can't get the ship under way with twenty-eight much better than with twelve. It takes thirty-two to man the capstan. What are they doing on deck?"

"I don't know," replied Hyde. "I was going up the ladder to ascertain, but Peaks drove me away. I heard them lowering boats, but I could not make out what they intend to do."

"O, it's all right. You needn't fret about it," added the leader.

Probably no one was more disturbed than he. The lowering of the boats was discussed in full, but nothing could be made of it, though Raymond insisted that the ship could not go to sea while the boats were away. Half an hour later they heard the faithful on deck hoisting up the boats. Hyde stood at the door of the mess-room watching the hatchway, for any chance revelation of the principal's intentions. The same doubt and uncertainty, as well as curiosity in regard to the movements on deck, prevailed in all the other mess-rooms. It had been agreed that all hands should remain in their rooms; but this agreement was now violated, and most of the mutineers were gathered at the doors, anxious to obtain intelligence from the deck.

Suddenly the grating was removed from the hatch.

"All hands, up anchor, ahoy!" shouted the boatswain, for the third, and, as it proved, the last time.

But no one came below to remonstrate, or ask for the explanation which a majority of the rebels were now exceedingly anxious to give. The moment the call sounded, Wilde walked towards the ladder.

"Where are you going?" demanded Raymond, angrily.

"I have had enough of this thing," he replied, and, without waiting for any further parley, went on deck, though the rebels hissed him.

Another seaman from one of the other mess-rooms followed his example, though Howe seized him by the collar, and attempted to detain him by force. Fortunately he was a stout fellow, and shook off his assailant. A storm of hisses and abuse followed him as he went up the ladder. Doubtless this treatment of the weak-backed, as they were considered, deterred others from imitating their example, for the faithful had only these two added to their number.

"I'm glad we are rid of them," said Raymond. "Fellows with weak backs don't do us any good."

"They add to our number, at any rate," replied Hyde, who, if he could have escaped the odium of the movement, would have gone on deck himself.

"No matter for that; we have forty-two left, and the ship can't go to sea without our help," added Raymond.

"I'm not quite sure of that," answered Hyde.

"No matter if she does go to sea," said Lindsley.

"But she can't go," persisted Raymond. "All we want is a chance to state our grievances; and the principal is not going to let us stay down here a great many days without knowing what the matter is."

"Hark!" said Hyde, as the boatswain's whistle sounded on deck.

"Man the capstan!" shouted Goodwin, the first lieutenant.

"Doesn't that look as though the ship was going to sea?" added the sceptical Hyde. "I tell you what it is, fellows, we are sold!"

"Sold? Not a bit of it! We are in the winning boat."

"Not exactly."

The rebels listened to the merry pipe of those who walked around the capstan, and heard the grating of the chain cables as they passed through the tiers into the lockers in the hold. It was plain enough that thirty-two hands had been found to man the capstan, for the anchor was certainly coming up from its miry bed. These sounds produced something like consternation among the mutineers, for they indicated at least a partial failure of the scheme in which they had trusted for redress.

"Go ahead!" shouted the executive officer through his trumpet.

"Go ahead?" repeated Raymond, as he went to the sky-light. "Not a sail has been set."

"But she is moving," said Hyde. "I see how it is. They have taken a tug-steamer."

"They are not going to tow the ship to Belfast," answered Raymond, as he went to one of the port gangways from which the mess-rooms opened. "There goes the Josephine, under sail. In my opinion, they are only dropping down to another anchorage. The principal will not think of such a thing as going to sea with only thirty seamen. It isn't safe to do so."

"When it isn't safe, Peaks will be down here, and you will have to turn out and do duty," said Hyde.

At that instant, as if to verify the prophecy of the croaker, the stalwart boatswain, with the assistance of the carpenter, lifted the grating off the main hatch. Most of the rebels retreated to their rooms; but it was a false alarm, for the two adult seamen, instead of coming below themselves, only lifted up the ladder, and drew it on deck, restoring the grating when it was done.

"That looks like something," said Lindsley.

"I tell you we are sold," added Hyde. "The principal isn't coming down here to ask us for an explanation. It isn't his style."

"Don't croak any more, Hyde," protested Raymond, in disgust.

"I only say we are sold, and you can't deny it."

"Wait and see."

They did wait, and after a while they heard the order to shake out the topsails. Looking up through the main skylight, they saw lieutenants, masters, and midshipmen, on the yards. They listened to the voices of Paul Kendall, Gordon, and Haven, issuing orders which were usually given by the lieutenants. From what they saw and what they heard, they were enabled to arrive at a tolerably correct solution of the means by which the ship was at present handled. They understood that the larger portion of the officers were doing duty as seamen, while the past officers were serving as volunteers under the captain.

"We might as well cave in, and go on deck," said Hyde, after the movements on deck had been thoroughly discussed.

"Humph! You can't get on deck, to begin with," replied Raymond. "But I haven't any idea of giving it up so."

"The plan has failed — that's plain enough," added Hyde.

"Not yet."

"I think it has. We are whipped out, and the sooner we make our peace with Mr. Lowington, the better it will be for us."

"If you mean to back out, say so, Hyde."

"I don't want to back out while the rest of the fellows stick."

"How will it do to send a messenger to the principal, state our grievances, and have the thing over?" suggested Johnson.

This idea met with considerable favor, but the principal objection to the measure was, that the messenger could not get on deck, as the ladder was removed from the main hatch, and the forward one was closed. The ship careened, the waves dashed against the bow, and it was evident that she was going to sea in good earnest. A large portion of the rebels were now studying up a plan to get out of the scrape, rather than to establish their rights. The boatswain's whistle sounded on deck, and all hands were piped to muster. Vainly the mutineers tried to ascertain what was going on, while Mr. Lowington was making his explanation to the faithful; but the parties were on the quarter-deck beyond their sight and hearing. Only the applause which followed Grace's proposition to decorate the members of the Order of the Faithful reached their ears. The ceremony itself, which took place in the waist, indicated that those on deck were having an exceedingly jolly time, though the nature of the performance was not understood. Then, when the Grand Protectress was elected, the hilarious mirth of the Faithful was positively sickening to the rebels. Those on deck appeared to be making fun of those below, for what else could they be laughing at, since the refusal of the rebels to do duty must be the all-absorbing topic on board? The situation was very unsatisfactory to the mild mutineers, and not very hopeful to the runaways.

"Let them laugh," said Raymond, whistling up his courage, so that he could maintain the dignity and firmness of a leader. "If we hold out, we shall carry our point. I have looked at the tell-tale, and the ship is headed to the north-west. If the course means anything, it means Belfast."

"What's the use of talking?" exclaimed Johnson. "The plan I proposed is the only one now. I move you we send a messenger to the principal."

"You can't get on deck," retorted Raymond.

"We can hail some one on deck, or knock at the door of the main cabin."

"It looks like backing out," added Lindsley.

"That is what we shall have to do in the end, and we may as well do it first as last," said Hyde.

"Hold on! Here comes Howe," continued Lindsley. "Let us hear what he has to say."

"I don't care what he says," muttered Hyde, who, like many other of the mild rebels, was not willing to join hands with the virulent and intense ones.

"I say, fellows, we are not making much on this

tack," Howe began, as he joined the group at the door of the mess-room. "We are going to have a meeting abaft the foremast, to decide what shall be done next. All hands are invited."

Howe moved on to extend the invitation to others.

CHAPTER VII.

THE VISIT TO THE HOLD.

"I DON'T attend any meeting with those fellows," said the prudent Hyde, as the rebels began to gather at the place indicated.

"There is no harm in hearing what they have to say," replied Lindsley.

"I don't care what they have to say. I won't have anything to do with them. In my opinion they are trying to get us all into a scrape."

"You are in one now, and you may as well be hung for an old sheep as a lamb."

"I would rather be hung for a lamb," answered Hyde, turning on his heel, and walking as far from the foremast as the limits of the steerage would permit.

About a dozen others followed his example, for the meeting was understood to be called by the runaways, who represented the most virulent type of rebellion. They had already lost all their privileges for the season, which could be restored only by the grace of the principal, and they had nothing to sacrifice. It was not prudent to enter into their counsels, and the mildest rebels, like Hyde and Johnson, avoided them.

"We are not making much on this tack," said

Howe, when the rebels, who chose to take part in the meeting, had assembled.

"That's so!" exclaimed Lindsley.

"Well, what's to be done? That's the next question."

"Nothing," added Raymond, who dreaded any extreme measures, and did not mean that Howe's party should obtain control of the movement. "As I understand the matter, all is going on right. We have only to hold out, and everything will end well for us."

"But we are shut up in the steerage. We are prisoners. The tables are turned upon us," replied Howe.

"Not at all. We have carried our point so far. We refused to do duty, and we haven't done any. I am in favor of fighting it out in this manner to the end."

"It is a milk-and-water affair as it is now, and won't amount to anything."

"What's the reason it won't?" demanded the champion of the mild party.

"Suppose the main hatch were opened, and the boatswain should call all hands — how many of us do you suppose would be left? There are a dozen of your chickens that would back down so quick it would make your eyes smart," added the champion of the intense party, pointing to the group which had collected around Hyde, who appeared to be forming a party of his own. "And the next time the call was made, a lot more would slump. Before long we should be so reduced in numbers that the brig would hold us all, and a few of us would have to stand the punishment for the sins of the crowd. You led us into the scrape; now you must help us out of it."

"Who led you into it?" asked Raymond, indignantly.

"You and your fellows, of course," retorted the heavy champion.

"I don't see it."

"Don't you? Then you are as green as a tame pigeon," continued Howe, smartly. "Our fellows — of course you know I mean those who ran away in the Josephine — are under the ban already. Did you suppose we were going into an affair like this alone? Not much! We went in because you did; to back up your movement. Now we are in it, you want to back out, and let your fellows show the white feather."

"I don't mean to back out," protested Raymond.

"But those fellows out there do," added the wily rogue.

"Well, there are thirty of us here, who will stick to the end. What do you say, fellows?"

"Of course we will," replied several, very mildly.

"Will you agree, upon your word and honor, to stick as long as any one does?"

"That depends upon circumstances," interposed Lindsley.

"I suppose it does," sneered Howe. "It isn't fair to leave us to bear the brunt of the whole."

"All we ever proposed to do was simply to refuse to do duty till we had explained our position to the principal," added Raymond.

"And kiss the rod, whether you get fair play or not," replied Howe.

"We can't do anything more than that. When the principal understands that over forty of us are dissatisfied, we have gained our point."

"Have you indeed!" flouted Howe. "Then I fancy you have already gained it, for he has found out that you are dissatisfied by this time."

"Well, what do you want to do?" demanded Raymond.

"It's no use to mince the matter. We have made a failure of it so far. The lambs on deck are having a good time, laughing, cheering, and carrying on — making game of us, no doubt, while we are shut up here as prisoners," replied Howe, rolling up his sleeves, as though he intended to do something savage. "We ought to make ourselves felt, which we haven't done yet, for the rest of the ship's company seem to regard our movement as a good joke, and to think we are having the worst of it. Well, I think we are; and we must make ourselves felt."

"Do you call it making yourselves felt when you are pounded on the head with belaying pins, as you were in the Josephine?" inquired Lindsley, dryly.

"We raised a breeze there, and we are bound to do it here."

"A breeze that first knocks you down yourself. I would rather have the wind blow another way," added Raymond.

"I don't mean to get up a fight, or anything of that sort."

"Well, what do you mean?" asked Raymond, impatiently.

"We have plans of our own; but we are not going to disclose them till we have some assurance that the other fellows will stand by us," answered the cautious leader of the intense party. "We are going to make ourselves felt."

"We are not going to agree to anything without knowing what it is," said Lindsley.

"And we are not going to let on to fellows that may go to the principal, and blow the whole thing. I will say this: If your fellows will pledge themselves, word and honor, to stand by us to the end, I will agree that the ship shall return to Havre, or some other port in France, within twenty-four hours, and that the tables shall be turned in our favor."

"How are you going to do it?" asked Lindsley.

"Leave that to me. I have a plan which cannot fail. Do the fair thing by us, and we will get you out of the scrape."

"I will agree to this, and nothing more: I will stand out till we have a chance to be heard," replied Raymond, who began to have some hope of the mysterious movements of Howe. "I will do nothing but stand out."

"We don't ask you to do anything else. We will do the rest, if you back us up."

"We don't back you up, for we don't even know what you are going to do."

"We will tell you what we are going to do."

"Hold on! Perhaps we had better not know anything about it," interposed Raymond.

"No, you don't!" exclaimed Howe. "We will tell those who will take the oath."

"The oath!" ejaculated Lindsley. "Are we joining the Knights of the Golden Fleece?"

"No, no! I mean the promise," answered Howe, impatiently. "Word and honor — that's all I want."

The runaway portion of the rebels were doubtless already familiar with the extraordinary means which was to turn the ship back to the ports of France. The others, who attended the meeting, were largely influenced by curiosity. They were intensely mortified at the defeat, which they were unwilling to acknowledge. It would afford them immense satisfaction to have the tables turned in their favor; but they were utterly unable to imagine what powerful machinery Howe and his associates could bring to bear upon the obdurate principal; how they were to compel him to put the ship about, and return to France.

The mild party retired to consider whether it would be prudent for them to enter into a compact of this description with such dangerous characters as the runaways. They were prejudiced against the measure, but victory in the undertaking, in which they had engaged, was so earnestly coveted, that they were tempted to join hands even with Howe, Little, Wilton, and other desperate fellows. When a person has once gone astray, the inducements to go farther increase. But Raymond and his friends were not quite willing to pledge themselves in advance to measures which they were not allowed to understand; and they finally agreed to bind themselves to secrecy, in regard to the nature of the scheme, if Howe would explain it on these terms, and then engage in it if it were not too wicked. The party returned to the foremast, and Raymond stated their position.

"That won't go down," promptly replied Howe, with his bullying, self-sufficient air. "We are to tell you what our plan is, and let you adopt it or not, as you please! No, sir!"

"We pledge ourselves beforehand to keep your secret, whether we join with you or not."

"We won't trust you."

"Very well," added Raymond, decidedly. "Nothing more need be said. Come, fellows."

The leader of the mild party turned on his heel, and moved aft, followed by his adherents.

"What do you suppose they mean to do?" asked Lindsley, as they halted under the skylight, near the middle of the steerage.

"I don't know; but it must be something desperate to compel the principal to put back," replied Raymond. "It may be to make a few auger-holes in the bottom of the ship."

"I wouldn't do anything of that sort," added Lindsley, shaking his head.

"No matter what it is; we offered to do the fair thing."

"Suppose you had agreed to keep still, and they had proposed to bore holes in the bottom of the ship; would you have kept your promise, and said nothing about it?" asked Lindsley.

"I would not have let them do it; and then there would have been nothing to conceal," answered Raymond.

"Precisely so! That's a good idea. Why not agree to their proposition, and then, if they mean to do anything which endangers the ship, we can easily prevent them from doing it," said Lindsley, who was exceedingly curious to know what the runaways wished to do.

Others were affected with the same desire, and their curiosity was rapidly overcoming their prudence. While they were discussing the question, Hyde and his party, seeing that Raymond and his associates had withdrawn from the runaways, came to the spot, and disturbed the conference with irrelevant questions. If all the mild mutineers could be induced to cling together, they could easily overrule Howe and his party. Just then, there was not that unity which alone insures success. There were actually three parties in the steerage, and it was necessary to reconcile them, or the rebellion would end in an ignominious failure. But this was found to be quite impossible, so far as Hyde and his party were concerned; for if the boatswain's call had sounded at that moment, they would have returned to their duty, if permitted to do so. Raymond would not consent to make terms with Howe, without the concurrence of all the others, including Hyde.

Howe was quite as much disgusted with the situation as any of the milder rebels. He had hoped and expected to drag them into any desperate scheme which might be adopted, and after Raymond and his party retired, he looked rather blankly at his friends.

"They are nothing but babies — little spoonies!" said he, contemptuously. "It isn't safe to do anything with them."

"Nor without them," suggested Spencer.

"I don't believe that," added Little. "They are in for it already. They will be held responsible for anything done below, as well as we. Let's go on with the job, just as we intended."

After considerable discussion, the suggestion of the little villain was adopted, with a modification, however, proposed by himself, by which the whole party were to be implicated in the mischief. No time was to be lost, for a portion of the faithful, who appeared still to be having a good time on deck, would soon come below to turn in. Howe and Little went to the main scuttle, which opened into the hold, and raised it.

"What are you going to do?" asked Raymond.

"We are going to hide in the hold, just for the fun of the thing," replied Little. "Won't you come down with us?"

"That's not a bad idea," suggested Lindsley. "When they come down to look for us, they won't find us. That will make a sensation, at least, and then we shall not be entirely ignored."

"Are you going to stay there all night?" inquired Raymond.

"Yes — why not?" answered Lindsley. "It is not quite so comfortable a place to sleep as the mess-rooms; but we can stand it for one night."

Even the mild rebels, Hyde and Johnson, were pleased with the plan, for it looked like an adventure. The persuasions of Lindsley induced them to yield whatever scruples they had. It would be a rich thing to have the principal or the officers come down into the steerage, and find it empty. There was still a chance to make the principal do something, even if it were only to call them up for punishment; for anything seemed better than being entirely ignored.

Little and Howe, each with a lantern in his hand, which he had taken from the lamp-room forward, led the way into the hold. All the members of the three parties followed; the mild rebels regarding the movement rather as a piece of fun than as anything which added to the guilt they had already incurred. When the last one had descended the ladder, Howe put on the scuttle, and the steerage was "like some banquet hall deserted," for the stewards were either on deck or in the kitchen, where they spent their leisure hours.

As soon as the rebels were all in the hold, they separated into three parties again, as they had been in the steerage. Little, with his lantern, went forward, where he was soon joined by the rest of the runaways; Hyde and his companions went aft; and Raymond's party remained near the main scuttle. The hold was divided into store-rooms, forward and aft, while the space amidships was devoted to the stowage of boxes, barrels, water casks, and other articles. The water tanks were near the heel of the foremast, where Howe and his party had located themselves. They contained the entire supply of the ship, while she was going from port to port, or lying in harbor. They had been fitted up under the direction of Mr. Lowington. The water was drawn from them by means of a pump in the kitchen, the pipe of which could be adjusted to either of them with screw connections.

"We must do the job quick, and get out of this place, or we may be fastened down here, as we were in the steerage," said Little, in a low tone, though he need not have troubled himself to use this precaution, for the dashing of the sea against the side of the vessel made so much noise, that those who were twenty feet distance could not have heard him.

"Are you sure we are not burning our own fingers?" asked Ibbotson. "My experience in the Josephine, when we were short of water, taught me what it was to be without it, especially when you have to feed on salt horse and hard bread."

"That's so," added Spencer.

"Can't we save some for ourselves?" inquired Wilton.

"What's the use? We shall return to Havre as soon as the officers find that the water tanks are empty," added Little.

"But why not save some?" persisted Wilton. "There are lots of bottles on the ballast, and a tunnel on the vinegar barrel. Hurry up, and fill a bottle for each fellow."

A dozen of the rebels rushed aft, and procured the bottles, while Little started the faucets which were used in drawing off the water, when it was necessary to clean out the tanks, or for use when the pump above was out of order. This was the precious scheme by which the intense rebels intended to compel the principal to return to port immediately. There could be no doubt that it would be an effectual one, for with no fresh water the ship could not remain a single day at sea without causing great discomfort, if not actual suffering, to those on board. This happy expedient had been devised by Little, and it was diabolical enough to be the invention of his fertile genius.

The bottles were brought up, and with the aid of

the tunnel, a dozen and a half of them were filled — just enough for the Howe party, for they did not intend to look out for the comfort of those who would not fully join them in their plans. The water rushed from the tanks, and flowed away into the ballast underneath. The faucets were large, and in a short time the tanks were empty. As the ship rolled each way, almost the last drop in them was poured out.

"Now let us get out of here before we are fastened in," said Little, after he had adjusted the faucets.

"There will be a sweet row when they find out the tanks are empty," added Howe, fully believing that the party had now done something to make themselves felt.

"It will please me to hear them howl," continued Wilton.

"Keep your bottles out of sight," said Howe. "Don't let those fellows see them, or they will smell a mice."

. "Don't you suppose they know what we have been doing?" inquired Monroe.

"How should they? The swashing of the sea made so much noise they couldn't hear the water running out," answered Little.

"Don't let on."

The party concealed their bottles under their clothing, and moved towards the ladder by which they had descended.

"What were you doing with all those bottles?" asked Raymond.

"What bottles?" demanded Little.

"We saw you take a lot of bottles from the ballast there," replied Raymond, whose party had been discussing the probable use to which they were to be applied, though they reached no satisfactory conclusion.

"Well, I'll tell you what they were for," answered Little. "We were going to have some fun, pelting them with stones, just as we used to play duck on shore, you know; but we concluded not to do so, lest the stewards in the kitchen should hear the noise, and make a row about it — that's all."

"Where are you going now?" inquired Lindsley, who was not quite satisfied with this lucid explanation — as though fellows engaged in a mutiny would care to amuse themselves pelting bottles!

"We have just made up our minds that it is not quite safe to stay down here any longer."

"Why not?"

"Suppose they should fasten us in?"

"Suppose they should? I thought you intended to stay down here," said Raymond, who concluded that the runaways were very fickle in their purposes.

"We did intend to do so; but we hadn't looked over all the ground. It has just occurred to us that the thirty lambs, who kiss the rod that smites them, would not come into the steerage to-night. It will take about the whole of them to stand watch, and if any of them go below, they will sleep on the floor of the main and after cabins, where they cannot be corrupted by such wicked fellows as you and I, Raymond. So, you see, if we can't get up any sensation by sleeping on the ballast, what's the use of making yourself uncomfortable for nothing. That's the idea. Let us go into the steerage, and turn in for the night."

"I don't believe in backing out," said Raymond, not very well pleased to hear Little class him with himself.

"Don't back out, then, my dear fellow. Stay here all night, and have a good time," added the little villain, as he ascended the ladder, and opened the scuttle.

"I'm not going to stay here if the rest don't," interposed Lindsley; and all the Howe party followed the runaways.

Hyde's party, seeing that all the others were retreating, came to the ladder, and asked for an explanation. Howe replied that the runaways were sick of the game, and had returned to the steerage; and the third squad followed the example of the other two. The hold was left as empty of human beings as the tanks were of water.

By this time the watch on deck had been stationed, and the rest of the crew were permitted to retire. As there was no danger that the mutineers would escape from the ship, the grating was removed from the main hatch; but a portion of the watch, including Peaks and the head steward, were posted near it, to prevent any seaman not wearing the white ribbon of the Order of the Faithful from coming on deck. Fifteen of the thirty who had done their duty came below to turn in. Their appearance created a sensation among the disaffected. Now they would ascertain what had been said on deck about their refusal to answer the call. Now they could hear, second-handed, the sermon which the principal had preached, and which they had heard the faithful applaud. Now, they could learn what terrible fate had been marked out for the rebels.

When the faithful came into the steerage, the first thing the rebels noticed was the white ribbons which adorned their breasts. Of course they wanted to know what it meant; but they felt a little embarrassed under the circumstances, and did not like to ask direct questions at first. They wished and expected the faithful to open the subject by telling them what a mistake they had made in not being "good." But the lambs did not say a word to them; did not appear to notice them, or to indicate by their actions that any unusual event was in progress on board. There was a great deal of silent skirmishing in the steerage. Raymond, who had always been pretty intimate with Tremere, as they both berthed in the same mess-room, continually threw himself in the way of the latter, in order to tempt him to speak of the evening's occurrences. Tremere was as silent as a marble statue, though he looked as composed and good-natured as ever; indeed, rather more so than usual.

"How's the weather on deck, Tremere?" finally asked Raymond, when no hint would induce the faithful one to speak first.

"It looks like a change. I shouldn't wonder if all hands were called to furl top-gallant sails and reef topsails before eight bells," answered Tremere.

"How did you get along working ship?"

"For further particulars, inquire of the principal," replied he.

"What do you mean by that?"

"Speech is silver, silence is golden."

"Humph!" sneered Raymond, puzzled by the singular replies of his friend.

"Yours truly," laughed Tremere.

"Why don't you speak?"

"I haven't learned my piece."

"You have learned a piece of impudence."

> "'He that hath but impudence
> To all things has a fair pretence.'"

"Are you mad, Tremere?"

"'Though this be madness, yet there's method in it.'"

"Quit your quotations! What's that on your coat?"

"A coat-ation."

"If you are mad with me, Tremere, say so."

"'I am not mad! no, no, I am not mad!'" shouted the member of the Order of the Faithful, with appropriate gestures and expression.

"Come, quit fooling! Can't you talk sense?"

"I can and will; for

> 'Want of decency is want of sense.'
>
> 'In college halls, in ancient times, there dwelt
> A sage called Discipline.'"

But you didn't go to school to the old fellow, Raymond."

"I believe you have lost your wits! Now, be reasonable, and talk like a sensible fellow. What is this?" asked Raymond, putting his finger on the white ribbon.

"A ribbon."

"What is it for?"

"For me."

"Who gave it to you?"

"The person who had it next before I did."

"Humph! How silly you are! Where did you get it?"

"On deck."

"But who gave it to you."

"The donor thereof."

"Who is the donor thereof."

"The one who gave it to me."

"If you won't answer me, say so. Don't try to make a fool of me."

"I usurp not nature's kindly office."

"Do you mean to insult me?"

"No; I mean to turn in, for I may be called before I have had my snooze out;" and Tremere, yawning as if he were bored and very indifferent, walked into the mess-room which contained his berth.

Those who had listened to the conversation were very much amused by it, and the rest of the Faithful took their cue from Tremere. Not one of them would answer a question or give a particle of information in regard to what had transpired on deck. All of them appeared to be astonishingly good-natured, and no one seemed to be disconcerted by the rebellion, except the rebels.

CHAPTER VIII.

SHORT OF WATER.

"THEY may play bluff as much as they like; but you had better believe there will be a sensation in the morning, if not before," said Howe, — after the fifteen members of the Order of the Faithful had retired to their rooms, — addressing Raymond, who manifested no little vexation at the cavalier manner in which he had been treated by his friend and messmate.

"What will that be?" asked the milder rebel.

"Wait, and you will see," replied Howe, mysteriously. "We didn't go down into the hold for nothing."

"What did you go down for?"

"You will find out soon."

"Well, I want you to understand that I didn't have anything to do with your plots and schemes," added Raymond, cautiously.

"You didn't! Who said you didn't? I say, Raymond, you are a good fellow to kiss the hand that smites you; and I hope you will keep on kissing it. What did you try to pump Tremere for, after you saw what he was up to?"

"I wanted to know what he was up to."

"Don't you know? It is a game of bluff. Those fellows pretend to be indifferent to what we are doing."

"They certainly seem to be very indifferent. Have you any idea what that white ribbon means?"

"Have I? Certainly I have. Can't you see through the side of the ship, when there's a port in it? That ribbon is to distinguish the lambs from the black sheep, like you and me."

"Pooh! What's the use of that?"

"So that the officers can tell them in the dark as well as at noonday. But Little has given those fellows a name already. He calls them the White Feathers. We must laugh at them, make game of them, whip them with their own weapons. Hark!" said Howe, suddenly turning his head towards the kitchen, near the door of which they stood.

"What's the matter?"

"They are trying the pump," replied Howe, as both of them plainly heard the sucking, "squilching" noise made by the copper pump, from which the cook was trying to draw water from the tanks below.

"What of it?" demanded Raymond, who did not see anything remarkable in the circumstance.

"Never mind; you will find out soon enough," answered the chief runaway, as he left his companion thoroughly mystified, and not a little alarmed; for it was evident that some terrible mischief had been perpetrated.

The pump sucked and groaned under the efforts of the cook, who had been directed to make a pot of coffee for the use of the watch, and was now trying to obtain water for that purpose. None would come, and it was plain to him that the pump was out of order. Taking a bucket and a lantern, he passed into the steerage, and opened the scuttle. The runaways observed him with intense interest; for the time had come when they were to "make themselves felt." The cook went down into the hold, and was absent about a quarter of an hour. He returned with an empty bucket in his hand, and hastened on deck with the alarming intelligence that the water tanks were all empty, which he communicated to the head steward.

As the tanks had been filled just before the ship left the dock at Havre, the head steward was not willing to believe the startling report. He went into the hold himself with the cook. By this time the runaways thought it prudent to keep out of sight, and all of them retired to their rooms, and most of them to their berths. The head steward tried the tanks, and was satisfied with the truth of the report. When the ship rolled, the faucets on the lee side poured out a few drops of water. Sounded with a mallet, the tanks gave forth only a hollow, empty sound. The steward was astonished and mortified at the discovery, for he was responsible for keeping the ship supplied with water, as well as with all other necessaries in the culinary department. He inquired very particularly in regard to the state of the faucets when the cook had first come below to draw water, and was assured that they were firmly closed. He lifted up some of the ballast, and saw that it was wet. He went to the well, where all the leakage of the ship is collected to be thrown up by the pumps.

The ship was regularly pumped out twice a day, and this duty had been performed just before the crew were piped to supper. There should have been but little water in the well; but there was enough to satisfy the head steward that the contents of the water tanks had flowed into it. Dipping one of his fingers into the water, he tasted it, and its freshness was another convincing proof of the fact.

"Has any one but the cooks and stewards been in the hold?" he inquired.

"Not that I know of," replied the cook. "I haven't been out of the kitchen since supper."

"Over forty of the students have been in the steerage since the ship sailed."

"The stewards told me that the boys were standing out."

"In my opinion, some of them have been in the hold, and started those faucets."

"You don't think they'd do that — do you?" exclaimed the cook.

"Some of them would sink the ship, if they dared. I think the principal did not manage this affair just right. He ought to have seized the young rascals up to the rigging, and kept them there till they were ready to do duty without grumbling. Now let us see if there is water in any of the casks."

"No, sir; the boatswain broke 'em out, and cleaned the casks, while we were in the dock."

The head steward took the mallet, and sounded upon the head of each cask. They were all empty; and it was clear enough that there was not a drop of fresh water in the hold, except that which was already mingled with the foul bilge-water under the ballast. The ship was going to sea, and both clouds and barometer indicated heavy weather. The steward was troubled, and immediately hastened to the principal with the alarming intelligence. He found Mr. Lowington in the main cabin, and announced the discovery he had made.

"It is a scheme to drive the ship back to port," added the principal, after he had satisfied himself, by questioning the steward, that the tanks had really been filled while the ship was in the dock."

"Well, sir, it seems to me that the plan must be successful," added the steward, with a grim smile.

"Doubtless it will be; but we will not return to Havre. We shall be off Cherbourg in the morning, and we will make a harbor there. But there must be some water on board."

"Only what is in the water-jars, sir. Possibly there are ten or fifteen gallons in all of them."

There was a large water jar in the steerage, and one in each of the two cabins, which had been filled just before the ship sailed. The steward was directed to draw them off, and save the water, to be dealt out as sparingly as the emergency might require. There were several tons of ice in the store-room, which had been filled at Havre; and there was no danger of any suffering for the want of the needed element. The principal went on deck with the steward, and observed that the wind was freshening, with a decidedly nasty look to windward. It might not be possible to go into Cherbourg the next morning with safety; and Mr. Lowington did not like the idea of being driven into port before the mutiny had been suppressed. The Josephine was half a mile to windward, under easy sail; and, in the present state of the sea, it was an easy matter to communicate with her, as it might not be a few hours later. He therefore explained the situation to Captain Shuffles, — who was still on deck with Grace and Paul, too nervous and too anxious to retire, — and directed him to call all hands.

The boatswain piped the call. Peaks and the head steward at the main hatch, in accordance with their instructions, would permit none who did not wear the white ribbon of the Order of the Faithful to come on deck. Hyde and his party proposed to return to their duty. They had had mutiny enough, and their leader, speaking for the whole, asked permission to be reported to the principal. The steward bore the message to him, while the twelve penitents waited at the ladder. The runaways remained in their rooms; but Raymond made an ineffectual effort to induce them to be firm.

"Come up!" said Peaks, when the principal appeared at the hatch, and gave the order.

"We wish to return to our duty, sir," Hyde began; "we are very sorry for our disobedience, and are willing to take the consequences."

"How many of you are there?" asked Mr. Lowington.

"Twelve in our party, sir."

"Will you conform, in every respect, to the requirements of the present occasion?"

"We will, sir."

"But they must join the order," interposed Grace,

who had accompanied Paul to the waist. "They are not entitled to the white ribbon, for they have come in at the eleventh hour."

Mr. Lowington smiled, and directed the penitents to repair to the quarter-deck.

"I am so glad they have yielded!" said Grace.

"So am I. You can let them take the second degree to-night," laughed Paul.

"Yes; and that shall be a blue ribbon. The next ones that come shall have the yellow ribbon, and be the first degree. That's all the different colors I have," added Grace, as she hastened to her state-room to procure the material for the decoration of the penitents, who were standing before the principal, abaft the mizzen-mast.

"Are you really sorry for what you have done, or do you back out because your plan does not work well?" asked the principal of the delinquents.

"I am really sorry for it, sir," answered Hyde; and there is not a doubt that he spoke the simple truth.

"Have you been into the hold this evening?"

"Yes, sir," replied Hyde, promptly.

"For what purpose?"

"We only went because the others did; but we did not stay there long."

"Have you meddled with the water tanks?"

"No, sir."

"Has any one?"

"I do not know, sir. Down in the steerage, we were divided into three parties, because we did not agree very well;" and Hyde explained the views of each party, and the localities which they had occupied during their visit to the hold.

Mr. Lowington readily comprehended the object of the runaways, when they induced the other two parties to visit the hold. In fact, he saw the whole truth just as it was; that the Howe party had made the mischief from the beginning, and that the others were the victims of their cunning schemes. He believed that his plan was working well, since it was eliminating the comparatively innocent from the guilty.

"You may return to your duty, on this condition — that you have no communication with either the Howe or the Raymond party," added Mr. Lowington. "You will not inform them in regard to anything which has transpired, or may transpire, on deck. Do you accept the conditions?"

"I do, certainly, sir," replied Hyde.

Others gave the required pledge, astonished to be restored to their duty on such mild terms. They took their stations with the crew. But Grace Arbuckle soon appeared with the blue ribbons, and Hyde was conducted to her by the commodore.

"I confer upon you the second degree of the Order of the Faithful, and decorate you with the blue ribbon. When you have proved yourself faithful to your duty, and worthy of promotion, you will be advanced to the third degree, the emblem of which is the white ribbon," said Grace, as she pinned the decoration upon his breast.

"Thank you," replied Hyde, rather bewildered by the ceremony.

The rest of the penitents were brought up, and, in

like manner, initiated into the Order of the Faithful. Of course they wanted to know more about it, and the new organization was explained to them.

"I'm glad you backed out, Hyde," said Tremere. "When are the rest coming?"

"I don't know that they are coming at all. I got enough of it."

"What do those fellows want to do?"

"Get their rights."

"Well, they'll get them when they return to their duty, and not before, unless it is the right to be punished for their disobedience," added Tremere.

"I still think it was not fair to give up the trip to the Rhine, after the promise that we should go, though it was a great mistake of mine to refuse to do duty," added Hyde.

"Who says the trip is given up?"

"All the fellows;" and Hyde rehearsed the arguments which had been used to sustain the proposition.

"As you are now a member of the Order of the Faithful, you may know its secrets," laughed Tremere. "Mr. Lowington made an explanation to those who did not take the law into their own hands;" and he proceeded to give the substance of this statement.

Hyde was all the more disgusted with the course he and his friends had adopted, and was fully resolved to do his duty in future, whatever his personal opinions might be. The mildest of the mutineers were thus disposed of, and a dozen pair of hands added to the force of the ship.

While this conversation was in progress, the Young

America had been headed towards the Josephine. Peaks had fired one of the guns on the forecastle, which was the signal, in the night, for the consort to heave to. Hyde's party had been restored to their several stations, while the volunteer officers still filled the places of those who did not answer the boatswain's call. The Josephine promptly obeyed the signal, and the ship ran up to her, as near as it was prudent to go, backed her main-topsail, lying to on her quarter. The first cutter was manned and lowered, vacancies in her crew being filled with the stoutest hands available. A dozen breakers, or kegs, used for boat service, were put on board, and with Peaks to assist in the stowage, the cutter shoved off, and pulled for the schooner.

The officer in charge of the boat explained to Mr. Fluxion what had occurred on board of the ship, and the twelve breakers, with six more belonging to the consort, were filled and stowed in the boat, which returned without delay to the Young America. The cutter was hoisted up, and again the squadron stood on its course. The new supply of water was immediately secured under lock and key, in one of the store-rooms. The quantity was still very meagre, being hardly enough for two days' consumption on full allowance. The watch below was again dismissed. It included one half of the penitents, who were beset by Raymond's party with questions and abuse; but they were true to their pledge, and the rebels were none the wiser.

The noise of the gun and of the lowering of the cutter had been heard by the runaways, and the appearance of the eighteen breakers, as they were passed down into the hold, was the assurance of another failure to them.

"We are dished," said Monroe, as the forward officer passed down the kegs.

"Perhaps we are, and perhaps we are not," replied Howe. · "The end hasn't come yet."

"I suppose there is room enough in the run for the contents of all those breakers," added Little.

"Hyde and the rest of those babies have returned to their duty," continued Monroe, who was always the first to despond.

"No matter for that; we will keep on this tack till something happens," persisted Howe. "By this time we are pretty sure of being left behind when the fellows go to Germany; and for my part, as Fluxion is going away, I think that is the best thing that can happen to us. We shall find a chance to strike out on our own hook."

But the arrival of the water breakers carried consternation to the runaways, whatever they said and did. They were tired of the battle, though, if any of them had a thought of repentance, they subdued it. Raymond's party were angry at the defection of Hyde and his associates, and the future looked dark and hopeless, so far as remedial agencies were concerned, but their pride still prompted them to hold out. Wearied with anxiety and hope deferred, they turned in as the night advanced.

At eight bells, all hands were called again. The wind was blowing half a gale, and the starboard watch had taken in the light sails. It was deemed advisable still further to shorten sail, and a reef was put in the topsails. The starboard watch then turned in, the port having the deck till four in the morning. The wind came in heavy gusts from the south-west, and shortly after midnight it began to veer to the west, which brought up a dense fog. At four bells in the mid watch, the wind came square from the west in heavy squalls. The ship went about, and stood to the southward, the principal intending to go into Cherbourg if the weather would permit.

At eight bells, when the morning watch was called, another reef was put in the topsails. At daylight the fog was too dense to think of making a port, and the ship tacked again. There was a heavy sea running, but everything went along very well. Captain Shuffles remained on deck all night, but no emergency occurred which required the exercise of more than ordinary skill and energy. The wind was blowing a gale, though not a very severe one. All the students on board had been in worse weather, and it produced no excitement whatever.

At seven bells in the morning, the port watch was called to breakfast, according to the regular routine of the ship. The meal consisted of coffee, beefsteak, fried potatoes, and the rolls which had been baked the preceding afternoon. Peaks and the head steward were in the steerage, and when some of the runaways appeared, and attempted to seat themselves at the mess tables, they were forbidden to do so. Only those decorated with white or blue ribbons were allowed to breakfast. At eight bells the port watch went on deck, and the starboard, relieved from duty, came down to their morning meal, when the tables had been reset. A fresh supply of hot steaks and potatoes was brought from the kitchen, for the breakfast of each watch was cooked separately, and they fared precisely as the other watch had. The rebels were still excluded from the mess tables, and violent was the grumbling thereat.

When the regular breakfast was finished, the tables were again cleared, and the mutineers began to think they were to be starved into subjection; but they were mistaken, in part, at least, for the tables were again set. This time there were no hot beefsteaks, no fresh rolls, no fried potatoes, no coffee — nothing but cold corned beef and hard tack. None of the cooks or stewards said anything, no one made any remarks of any kind. There was the breakfast — salt junk and hard tack — regular sailor's fare. The head steward mildly indicated that breakfast was ready for those who had not already been served. The two parties of rebels seated themselves, and turned up their noses at the fare.

"Steward, bring me a mug of coffee," shouted Howe to the nearest waiter.

"It takes water to make coffee," replied the man, solemnly, and as he had doubtless been instructed to answer.

"What if it does? Bring me some coffee," repeated Howe, angrily.

"No coffee for this crowd," interposed the head steward, as solemnly.

"But I'm going to have my coffee," added Wilton, whose temper was not the sweetest in the world, as he rose from his stool, and rushed towards the kitchen door.

"Avast, my lad!" said Peaks, taking the rebel by the collar with no gentle force. "It takes water to make coffee."

Wilton was afraid of the boatswain, for there was a tradition on board that he had, on one occasion, laid hands upon a refractory boy, and he was evidently in the steerage for a purpose. He skulked back to his place at the table.

"Can't I have some coffee?" demanded Raymond, of the head steward, when that official came near his seat.

"You cannot."

"Why not?"

"Because it takes water to make coffee."

"What of that?"

"Owing to circumstances, the supply of water on board is rather short," answered the head steward, as solemnly as before.

"That's nothing to do with me. I didn't start the water tanks."

"I obey orders, and don't argue with any one; but there's an old saying that a man is known by the company he keeps, and I suppose a boy is, too."

The steward passed on, and refused to answer any more questions.

"If we can't have coffee, give us some water," said Lindsley.

"Water is water," replied the steward.

The rebels were hungry, and they ate, though very sparingly, of the unpalatable food which was set before them. Like most other boys belonging to "the first families," they did not relish corned beef at any time; and that before them, though of excellent quality, was very salt, having been a long time in the brine. They partook of the beef and the hard bread simply because there was nothing else with which to satisfy their hunger. Some of them wanted to "make a row" about the fare; but Peaks was a very formidable obstacle in the way of any such demonstration. They ate what they could, rather than what they wanted, and retreated to their mess-rooms.

"Well, what do you think now?" said Lindsley, as he threw himself into his berth.

Raymond only shook his head and grated his teeth.

"I think we are sold, and the sooner we back down, the better," added Lindsley.

"I won't back down!" snapped Raymond, savagely.

"How long do you think you can eat salt horse, without any water to wash it down?"

"I can stand it till I die!"

"I don't think it is worth while to stand it quite so long as that."

"I do! What right has the principal to deny us even a drop of water?"

"What right have we to stand out, and refuse to do our duty? Howe's fellows started the water tanks, and—"

"We didn't do it!" interrupted Raymond, savagely. "I won't stand it."

Rushing out into the steerage, he went to the water jar, in one corner. It was empty, though there was a breaker of water on deck for the use of the Faithful, who were thirsty. He was mad, and ready for desperate steps. He hastened to the mess-room of Howe, and entered just as that worthy was taking a draught from the bottle he had filled at the tanks the evening before.

"What's that?" demanded he.

"Water," replied Howe, good-naturedly.

"Give us a drink — will you? I'm almost choked," asked Raymond, glad to see that there was still an alternative.

"No, I thank you," answered Howe, putting the stopper back into the bottle. "We don't do the heavy jobs, and then provide for those who are too cowardly to help us."

"We are in the same boat with you; and it isn't fair to let our fellows suffer while you have water."

"You wouldn't go in with us. We have only a bottle apiece," pleaded Howe.

Raymond appealed to others in the room, but all of them were of one mind. The salt beef had created a tremendous thirst among those who had eaten it, and all who had water made large draughts upon the supply. The bottles had contained pickles, olives, ketchup, and other similar articles, so that the water was not very palatable. In the course of the forenoon, Raymond and his party stealthily attempted to obtain possession of these bottles, but the runaways were too vigilant for them; and before dinner the thirsty ones were exceedingly uncomfortable, to say the least. They tried to conceal their condition from the Faithful as much as possible, but they were all very nervous and disquieted.

At one o'clock, after the regular dinner of roast

beef and rice pudding had been served to the Faithful, the tables were again prepared for the rebels; but the bill of fare was corned beef and hard bread — not a drop of water. Peaks and the head steward paced the unsteady floor, as they had done at breakfast time. Raymond, whose tongue and lips were parched with thirst, became desperate again, and attempted to force his way into the kitchen. He was seized by the boatswain, and the more he struggled, the more he was shaken up. He refused to behave himself, and Peaks thrust him into the brig.

CHAPTER IX.

THE LAST OF THE MUTINEERS.

THE gale continued to blow ugly and gusty during the day, until eight bells in the afternoon. The fog hung heavy over the ocean, and the bell was rung every five minutes, in accordance with the English Admiralty instructions. The ship had been standing close-hauled to the north-north-west since noon, when she had tacked, at the warning of the fog signal, made at some light station on the coast of France, in the vicinity of Cape de La Hague. For four hours she had been on her present course, and was therefore approaching the coast of England again. At the beginning of the first dog-watch, there were some signs of a change of weather. The fog appeared to be lifting, and the wind came in less violent gusts.

In the steerage, among the rebels, the most unalloyed misery prevailed. The runaways had exhausted their supply of water under the pressure of thirst caused by the salt provision, though they had not yet begun to be very uncomfortable. Certainly they had, as yet, no thought of yielding, but were rather studying up the means of obtaining a new supply of water. Raymond's party were only waiting for the boatswain's call to ask permission to join their shipmates on deck;

but, most provokingly, no call came. Their leader had been discharged from the brig as soon as he ceased to be violent; for the principal did not wish to punish any one for the mutiny, preferring to let it work its own cure on the diet he had prescribed.

With the exception of the rebels, every one seemed to be particularly jolly. The principal had explained his policy to them, and they were entirely satisfied. All the evolutions of seamanship were performed with remarkable precision even in the gale, demonstrating that the crew had not lost their prestige, when the will was right. In the cabin, even, the rough sea did not dampen the spirits of the passengers, who had been, in a measure, accustomed to the rude action of the sea by their voyage in the steamer and in the Josephine. The Grand Protectress of the Order of the Faithful was full of life and spirits, and watched with the deepest interest the progress of the rebellion in the steerage.

In Raymond's party the suffering from thirst had become intolerable. Lindsley's back had been broken early in the forenoon, but Raymond declared that he would never yield — he would die first.

"What's the use?" demanded Lindsley. "We are whipped out, sold out, played out, and used up. My tongue is as dry as a piece of wash-leather."

"I don't like to give it up," replied Raymond. "It looks mean to back out."

"Just look at it a moment. We are suffering for the sins of Howe's fellows. They let off the water, saving a supply for themselves, and our fellows are really the only ones who suffer for their deed. We are sustaining them, even while they won't give us a drop of water to moisten our lips. For one, I never will get into such a scrape again. We have been fools, and whenever I see the runaways go one way, I'm going the other."

"All hands, on deck, ahoy!" shouted the boatswain at the main hatch.

"That means me," said Lindsley, rushing to the ladder. "Come along, Raymond. Howe and his fellows have been stingy and mean enough to be left alone."

Most of the crew were on deck when the call was piped. Lindsley led the way up the ladder, and Raymond followed him. The last argument of his friend had evidently converted the latter, for, however much he disliked to yield, it was not so bad as supporting the cause of such fellows as Howe, who would not even give him a drink of water. And the idea of enduring positive suffering for the evil deed of the runaways was not pleasant. They had let the water out of the tanks, but Raymond and his friends were the only ones who had thus far suffered in consequence of the act. It was these reflections which absolutely drove him upon deck, rather than any disposition to undo the wrong he had done.

A lift of the fog had revealed the Bill of Portland, a narrow neck of land projecting outside the channel from the English coast. The wind was hauling to the northward, and the prospect of fair weather was very good. The order was given to turn out one of the reefs in the topsails. The appearance of the Raymond party was noticed by Mr. Lowington, and even the passengers observed those who wore neither the white nor the blue ribbon. As soon as the rebels reached the deck, they discovered the water breaker in the waist. They charged upon it with a fury which required the interference of an officer; but half a pint was served out to each of them before they were sent aloft.

The reefs were turned out, and the ship came about on the other tack. Nothing had been seen of the Josephine since the fog settled down upon the squadron the night before; but the principal had no fears in regard to her safety. Fog-horns, guns, and bells warn the voyager of his approach to any of the perils of the shore; and the experienced navigator can interpret these signals so as to avoid all danger.

"South-west by west, half west," said Paul Kendall, who was the acting sailing-master on duty, giving out the course to the quarter-master in charge of the wheel.

"South-west by west, half west," repeated the latter.

"Where will that take us?" asked Grace Arbuckle, who watched everything that was said and done with deep interest.

"That course will take the ship to a point off Ushant, which is an island near the coast of France, not far from Brest," replied Paul, who took especial pleasure in explaining to her the working of the vessel.

"How far is it from here?"

"From the Bill of Portland, which is the land you see astern of us, the distance to Ushant is one hundred and fifty-seven miles."

"How long will it take us to go there?"

"That will depend entirely upon the wind," laughed Paul. "We are logging ten knots just now, which would bring us off Ushant about ten o'clock to-morrow forenoon. But the wind is going down, and we may not get there till to-morrow night."

"Well, I'm in no hurry; and I rather hope it will not blow very hard," added Grace.

"That's just my wish. If the water only holds out, I don't care."

"But there is something more for the Grand Protectress to do," said Grace.

"A dozen more who are to take the first degree; but I do not know whether they will be willing to be initiated."

"Why not?"

"Raymond, who is generally a good fellow, has been very ugly. Perhaps he feels better now he has quenched his thirst."

"May I speak to him?"

"Certainly, if you wish to do so."

Paul conducted the Grand Protectress to the waist, where the head steward was giving the Raymond party another half pint of water apiece. They were very thirsty, and, as boys understand the word, they had doubtless suffered a great deal for the want of water. As they had returned to their duty, and yielded the point, Mr. Lowington had directed that they should be frequently supplied, until they were satisfied. The general opinion was, that they had already been severely punished, not only by the thirst they had endured, augmented as it was by their diet of salt beef and hard bread, but in the mortification they had experienced at the failure of their scheme. The latter punishment was quite as severe as the former.

"Miss Arbuckle wishes to speak to you, Raymond," said Paul, addressing the discomfited leader of the mild party.

"What for?" demanded he.

"She will explain for herself."

"Does she want to preach to me?"

"I think not. Of course you are not compelled to see her, if you don't wish to do so," added Paul, who could not see why any one should not wish to converse with Grace.

"I will hear what she has to say," said Raymond, with a condescension which Paul did not like.

The commodore presented the delinquent to the young lady. Raymond touched his cap, and bowed politely.

"I am very glad to see you on deck, Mr. Raymond, for I have wished to make your acquaintance since last evening," Grace began.

"Thank you. I was not aware that I had any claims upon your consideration."

"I see you wear no ribbon. Shall I furnish you with one?"

"I don't know what it is for?" said Raymond, glancing at the white ribbon on the commodore's breast. "What does it mean?"

"I can't tell you anything about it just yet. I suppose you are very sorry for what you have done."

"I feel better since I have had a drink of water," replied Raymond, good-naturedly; and there was no doubt that he spoke the literal truth.

"I regret that it was necessary to deprive you of water."

"It was not my fault. I had nothing to do with emptying the water tanks," pleaded the culprit. "It was the runaways who did that."

"Then you were in bad company."

"I think so myself," answered Raymond, candidly, for he was still under the influence of the clinching argument which had induced him to come on deck.

At this point the conversation was interrupted by the call of the principal, who summoned the Raymond party into his presence on the quarter-deck.

"Are you satisfied?" asked Mr. Lowington, with a pleasant smile on his face, when the rebels had assembled before him.

"No, sir," replied Raymond, promptly, and before any other of the party could give a different answer.

"Why did you come on deck, then?"

"We couldn't stand it any longer without water."

"Is that the reason why you came on deck?"

"Yes, sir."

"Then you may return to your former diet till you are satisfied," added the principal, pleasantly.

"We don't wish to do that, sir."

"Didn't I understand you to say that you were not satisfied."

"I am not, sir," continued Raymond, stoutly. "I don't think it was fair to —"

"Stop!" interposed the principal, rather sharply. "I do not purpose to listen to your grievances. You have undertaken to redress them yourselves, and I see no reason why you should not persevere till you are satisfied."

"We can't live on salt junk and hard bread without any water, sir."

"Can't you, indeed? You should have thought of that before you joined hands with those who started the water out of the tanks."

"We did not even know that they meant to start the water, or, afterwards, that they had done it, till the cook said so. We are not responsible for what they did."

"Perhaps not; yet you were in the hold, in full fellowship with them. But I do not intend to argue the matter with you."

"We are ready to return to our duty, sir, whether we are satisfied or not," added Raymond.

"O, you are?"

"Yes, sir."

"Well, as long as you are willing to do your duty, I suppose it does not matter whether you are satisfied or not."

Raymond made no reply, and could not help wondering that he had been so simple as to believe the principal would ask an explanation of mutineers.

"Are you willing to obey all orders?" continued Mr. Lowington.

"Yes, sir."

"And the others?"

"Yes, sir," replied Raymond's followers.

"Will you refrain from all communication with those in the steerage who still refuse to do duty?"

"I will," answered Raymond, who had before made up his mind to do this.

"Especially you will not inform them of anything which takes place on deck, or give them the benefit of any explanation you may hear," said the principal. "Those who assent to these terms will walk over to windward."

The party, who could not help wondering at this singular treatment of what they regarded as a very difficult matter, walked squarely up to the weather-rail of the ship, and halted there. The remarks of the principal, and the pledge he exacted, seemed to explain the strange conduct of the white and the blue ribbon bands in the steerage. No one had been able to ascertain definitely what those badges meant.

"Very well. I am satisfied, if you are not," said Mr. Lowington, mildly. "You deserve punishment, but it shall depend upon your future conduct whether you receive it or not. You will go forward."

When the party reached the waist, they were confronted by Grace and Paul.

"You have promised to be faithful — have you not?" asked she.

"Yes; but I'm not satisfied," replied the leader.

"Then I confer upon you the first degree of the Order of the Faithful," added Grace. "Its emblem is a yellow ribbon;" and she pinned the decoration upon Raymond's breast.

"What does it mean?" he asked.

She explained its meaning, and then initiated his companions.

"How happens it that we have yellow ribbon while others have white or blue ones?" asked Lindsley.

"Because you have taken only the first degree, being the last ones to come. If you do well, and are faithful, you shall be raised to the second, and then to the third degree," replied Grace, with a vivacity which was not at all impaired by the laughter of the initiates, who, as others before them had, regarded the order as a pleasant joke.

"When you have proved yourselves worthy, you will be advanced to the second degree by the Grand Protectress," added Paul. "The motto of the concern is, '*Vous ne pouvez pas faire un sifflet de la queue d'un cochon;*' and I think you have fully proved the truth of the saying. The meaning of the sentence is one of the secrets of the order. Do you promise not to reveal it?"

"I do, for one," laughed Lindsley. "I haven't the least idea myself what it means."

"Nor I," added all the others.

"Then you will all be discreet. The motto contains a very valuable moral lesson, which bears on your case, and I hope you will take it to heart," said Paul.

"I should like to take it to head first," replied Lindsley.

"I hope you are satisfied now, Mr. Raymond," continued Grace.

"Not at all. I am willing to do my duty, rather than be starved on salt junk, and choked to death for the want of water; but I am not satisfied."

"Not satisfied!" exclaimed Grace. "Not after you have been initiated into the noble and magnanimous Circle of the Order of the Faithful!"

"Not much!"

"You should say, '*Nicht viel*,' when you want to use that expression," laughed Grace, who did not like

American slang, and had already partially cured Paul, who had a slight tendency in that direction.

"Well, *nicht viel*, then. It was not fair, when we had been promised a trip into Germany, to send us off to sea, just to please Shuffles."

"Captain Shuffles is a good young man. If you say anything against him, you shall be expelled from the Order of the Faithful!"

"Well, I won't say anything against him, then, Miss Arbuckle; but they say the ship is bound for Belfast."

"Do you see that land, Mr. Raymond?" she added, pointing to the light on the headland.

"I do."

"What land is it?"

"I don't know."

"It is the Bill of Portland. Now, which way is the ship headed?"

"About south-west," replied Raymond, after looking through the skylight at the tell-tale in the steerage.

"South-west by west, half west," she added.

"Bully for you!"

"Instead of that, you should say, '*Bulle für ihnen.*' In other words, you should utter all your slang in German: it sounds better."

"I only meant to say that you reeled off the course like a regular old salt," laughed Raymond.

"If the ship were bound to Belfast, its course would be nearer west. We are not going to Belfast. We are going to Brest. Mr. Lowington said the ship's company needed a little exercise to perfect the discipline, and to save the trouble and expense of going into the dock at Havre, the vessels will be left in the harbor of Brest. He never had a thought of giving up the trip down the Rhine."

"Is that so?" asked the leader of the mild rebels.

Paul repeated the explanation to the penitents which the principal had given the day before.

"We understood that we were going to sea just to please Shuffles," said Lindsley.

"The captain certainly wanted better discipline, and he did propose a day or two at sea for its improvement," added Paul.

"I don't care for two or three days at sea, if we are to go to the Rhine," continued Raymond. "I'm satisfied now."

The conversation was continued till the starboard watch was piped to supper. Raymond was fully satisfied now that he had made a fool of himself, and, what was even worse, that he and his companions had been the dupes of the runaways. Those who belonged in the starboard watch were permitted to go to the table, and they did ample justice to the cold roast beef, butter toast, and tea which covered the mess tables. Peaks and the head steward paced the steerage, as before, and no one without a ribbon was allowed to partake. At six o'clock, after the port watch had been relieved, the second supper was served, and the rest of the hungry and thirsty delinquents enjoyed the change in their bill of fare.

Then the runaways sat down to their supper of salt beef and hard bread, without tea or water. The food did not suit them, and they turned up their noses at it. The thirst created by their salt breakfast in the morning had required large draughts upon their water bottles, and before dinner they had exhausted the supply. They were very thirsty, though none of them were actually suffering. The fact that they could not get any water made them want it all the more. They ate none of the salt meat, which by this time was loathsome to them. Ship bread was dry feed, and they could eat very little of it. Doubtless it was a hard case for them, the sons of rich men; but they had only to obey the boatswain's pipe, and "eat, drink, and be filled."

"I can't stand this," said Monroe, when a group of them had gathered in their mess-room after the unpalatable supper.

"Can't you? What's the reason you can't?" growled Howe.

"I'm almost choked."

"So am I," added several others.

"Are you going to back out?" demanded the leader.

"Rather than perish with thirst, I am," answered Herman.

"What's the use? All the rest of the fellows have deserted us," added Ibbotson. "Even Raymond is sporting a yellow ribbon, and is as jolly as a lord now."

"We can't make anything by it," said Monroe. "I move you we back out, and get a drink of water. All hands will be called at eight bells, I think, to put on more sail."

"No, no! Don't back out," interposed Howe. "We haven't made ourselves felt yet."

"That's so," groaned Herman. "No one takes

any notice of us. Even those fellows that went up last won't speak to us, not even to answer a civil question. The principal evidently regards us with perfect contempt. I go in for doing something, or backing out. As it is, we are making a milk-and-water affair of it. We are starved and choked. That's all we have to show for what we have done."

"Why don't you preach, and say, 'The way of the transgressor is hard,' or something of that sort, which is original," snarled Howe.

"I should judge from your talk that you did not feel very good," added Herman.

"I don't; I'm as dry as any of you, but I have no idea of backing out."

"What are you going to do? What's to be the end of this?" demanded Ibbotson. "I've got enough of it."

"That seems to be the general opinion," continued Herman.

"Where's Little?" demanded Howe, who could not help realizing that the fortunes of the last of the mutineers were becoming desperate, and that it was not an easy thing to contend against such enemies as hunger and thirst. "I shall not give it up so. Let us do something. Let us make ourselves felt, even if we are hanged for it."

"What can we do?" inquired Herman, earnestly. "We are caged here like a lot of donkeys, and I have had enough of it."

"Will you hold on for a couple of hours longer, fellows?" persisted Howe.

"I will hold on till the boatswain calls all hands,

and not an instant longer," replied Herman. "My tongue feels as though it were cracking with thirst."

Howe rushed out of the room to find Little, who was the man of expedients for the runaways. He found him in an adjoining room, and stated the case to him. The little villain was as uncomfortable and unhappy as the rest of the mutineers, and, to the surprise of Howe, counselled yielding rather than suffering any longer.

"I didn't think that of you, Little," sneered Howe.

"Didn't you? Well, it's only a question as to who can stand it the longest on a diet of salt horse without water," replied Little. "I can hold out as long as any fellow; but we shall not make anything by it. If we could, I would stick."

"Let us do something, at least, to make a sensation before we give in. I don't like the idea of being conquered just in this way."

"What can we do?"

"Let us set the ship afire, or bore holes in the bottom," whispered Howe.

"Of course, you don't mean anything of that sort," added Little, with a grim smile.

"I would rather do it than be whipped out in this manner. I never felt so cheap and mean in my life," continued Howe, kicking the front of the berth, and pounding with his fist to indicate the intensity of his wrath.

"Nor I either; but what are you going to do about it."

"Well, you furnish gumption for the crowd, and I came to ask you what to do. Our fellows' backs are broken, and they will go on deck when the boatswain's pipe sounds again."

"I shall go with them," replied Little, quietly.

"Can't we get into the hold, and find some water?"

"No; Bitts put a lock on that scuttle this morning, and the forward officers are watching all the time. You can set the ship afire if you like. I don't think of anything else you can do to make yourself felt."

"I'll do it!" exclaimed Howe.

"No, you won't," added Little, mildly.

"What's the reason I won't?"

"You dare not."

"You see!" said the discomfited leader, bolting out of the room.

Some men, and some boys, are the most easily overwhelmed by letting them severely alone. If Howe could have made a sensation, he would have been better satisfied, even if he had been committed to the brig. He was vain and proud, and it hurt him more to be ignored than to be beaten. It was questionable whether he was desperate enough to put his savage threat into execution; but he collected a pile of books and papers in his mess-room, and declared his intention to Herman, Monroe, and others, who were his messmates. No student was allowed to have matches, and he lacked the torch to fire the incendiary pile.

"Don't be an idiot, Howe!" said Herman, disgusted with the conduct of his leader.

"I'm going to do something," persisted he.

"You are not going to do that."

"Yes, I am! As soon as the steward leaves the steerage, I shall borrow one of the lanterns, and there will be a blaze down here."

"No, there won't!"

"What's the reason there won't?"

"The fellows won't let you do any such thing. A fellow is a fool to burn his own ship at sea."

"Of course it won't burn up; but it will bring Lowington down here, and he will find out we are somebody."

"Nonsense!"

"But I mean it."

"No, you don't! It is all buncombe."

"You wait and see if it is. If I can only bring Lowington down here, and see him scared out of his wits, I shall be satisfied. I shall be willing to go into the brig, then, and stay there for the rest of the cruise."

"You are a fool, Howe."

"I'm desperate."

"You shall not kindle any fire here. If you say you mean to do it, I will call Peaks at once."

"I said it, and I'll do it," said Howe, leaving the room.

His messmates followed him. The steward had left the steerage, and Howe, in order to take down the lantern, leaped upon a stool. Herman kicked it from beneath him, and he fell upon the floor.

"What do you mean by that?" demanded Howe, with clinched fists.

"Don't you touch that lantern — that's all!"

"Yes, I will;" and he tried to mount the stool again.

Herman, Ibbotson, and Monroe seized him, and dragged him back into the room. The noise attracted the attention of the rest of the mutineers, and some others, who were below.

"Go, and call Peaks, Monroe," said Herman. "I will hold him till you come back."

"Don't do that," interposed the desperate leader, becoming suddenly calm, and apparently reasonable. "You are all cowards. Let me alone. I might as well yield, with such milk-and-water fellows around me. Don't say anything to Peaks."

"You are a bigger fool than I thought you were," added Herman, taking no pains to conceal his disgust at the conduct of his leader.

"All hands, on deck, ahoy!" piped the boatswain.

All hands, Howe included, answered the call. The mutiny was ended.

CHAPTER X.

WHAT THE RUNAWAYS WERE GOING TO DO.

IT was an astonishingly stupid mutiny, not relieved, even a shade, by the sensational conduct of Howe, the leader, in its last moments, that terminated twenty-four hours after its commencement, on board of the Young America. However, it was hardly more stupid than any other wilful evil-doing. Captain Shuffles, like the potentates of the old world, wishing to have his accession to power signalized by an act of clemency, had pleaded earnestly that the runaways might be forgiven, and permitted to visit Germany with the rest of the ship's company. Mr. Lowington had endeavored to reconcile the granting of the request with his views of discipline. It is not necessary to ask with what success he considered the matter, for the delinquents had now effectually put it out of his power to grant them any favor.

The fog had lifted, and from the north-west came up the clearing of the blue sky, as the sun went down. The wind had moderated, though the sea still rolled uneasily in the channel. The principal had directed the head steward to estimate the supply of water on board, and on his report had decided that the ship should proceed directly to Brest. She had been under easy sail, but as soon as the course was given to the captain, he called all hands. For the first time since the departure from Havre, all hands answered the call. Though it was quite dark, the presence of the runaways was promptly recognized. The volunteer officers, who were serving as seamen, were directed to take their regular stations in working ship.

The water breaker in the waist was in demand, as soon as the last of the mutineers came on deck; and without a word in regard to the past, the steward served them out a pint of water apiece. Their prompt attention to the water ration caused a smile among the Faithful, and the officers considerately deferred further orders until their pressing want was supplied.

"Shall we admit them to the Order of the Faithful?" said Grace to the commodore, when it was announced that the bottom had dropped out of the mutiny.

"I think not," replied Paul. "They have been the cause of all the trouble on board, and Mr. Lowington does not wish that anything should be said to them. They are the ones who emptied the water tanks."

"Really, I don't think they deserve to be admitted to the Order of the Faithful — at least, not till they have proved their fidelity to duty."

"Raymond, and those who came on deck before, are generally very good fellows; and we all believe now that they were led away by the runaways," added Paul. "We shall soon see whether all hands intend to do their duty."

When the thirsty ones had been supplied with water, the order to set the courses was given, and the runaways severally took their stations, and performed their duty without making any confusion. The top-gallant-sails and royals were then shaken out. The discipline now seemed to be perfect, and the principal's method of dealing with the mutiny was fully justified, though he took pains to explain to some of the professors that he did not consider this treatment practicable in all cases. The conduct of the rebels, and the facts developed, indicated that they wished to be noticed; that they believed the ship could not sail without their permission and assistance. This blunder was fatal to all their calculations, and they were unable to "make themselves felt."

But the runaways were no better satisfied than Raymond had been; and though they performed their duty in setting sail with entire precision, they were sour and morose. The sting of an overwhelming defeat thorned them. They were mortified, humiliated, and crest-fallen. They were enraged at the conduct of their rebellious companions of the milder stripe, who had deserted them, and they were reaping the general consequences of evil-doing. They did their work, but when it was done they avoided their shipmates, and even avoided each other. Howe had ruined himself as a leader by his silly conduct, and there was not likely to be any further concerted action among them.

Mr. Lowington had faithfully followed out his plan, and had directed Mr. Fluxion to adopt the same treatment for those who refused to do duty in the Josephine — to keep them in the steerage, and feed them on sailors' fare. The result of the treatment in the consort was yet to be learned, for she had not been seen since the supply of water had been procured from her.

At midnight the wind blew fresh from the northwest, and with all sails set, the ship logged twelve knots. The three lights on the Casquets, at the western extremity of the Channel Islands were in sight, and the prospect of seeing Ushant early in the forenoon was good. As all hands were now on duty, the system of quarter watches was restored, so that each part could have six hours of uninterrupted sleep. There was nothing for the watch on deck to do, except to steer, and keep a lookout; and there was a great deal of discussion about mutiny in general, and the Young America mutiny in particular. It was generally conceded even by the rebels, that it "did not pay."

After the runaways had in some measure recovered from the first blush of defeat, some of them wanted to know about the ribbons; but the members of the Order of the Faithful did not consider themselves authorized to impart the secrets of the organization, and declined to explain them. Doubtless they enjoyed the mystery, and desired to keep it up for their own amusement. Howe, when he found a tongue, reproached his companions in mischief for their cowardice, and boasted of what great things would have been accomplished if they had supported him to the end; but his most intimate associates were disgusted with him, and avoided him as much as possible.

At seven bells in the morning, a breakfast of coffee, mutton chops, potatoes, and hot biscuit put most of the runaways in the port watch in better humor than before, and another did a similar service for those in the starboard watch half an hour later. They ate and drank all they could, rather than all they needed, and probably shuddered when they thought of the consequences of evil-doing, as embodied in salt beef and hard bread, without a drop of water.

At one bell in the forenoon watch, the lookout in the foretop shouted, "Land, ho, on the lee bow." An hour after, the bold rugged shores of Ushant were plainly in sight, and Dr. Winstock informed Paul and Grace that they were in the very waters where the English fleet, under Admiral Sir Edward Hawkes, had won the great naval victory over the French in 1759.

"Sail, ho!" shouted the lookout.

"Where away?" called the officer forward.

"On the weather bow. It's a topsail schooner, and looks like the Josephine."

Glasses were in demand, and the officers soon satisfied themselves that the sail ahead was the consort. It was evident that, hugging the wind closely, she had gone farther from the coast than the Young America. She took a pilot off Ushant, and continued on her course, though Mr. Lowington was anxious to communicate with her, and learn the result of the mutiny which had also prevailed on board. Off the island, the ship was boarded by a pilot, and following the Josephine, passed through the Goulet de Brest, which is the only entrance to the harbor. This passage is not more than a mile wide, and is defended on each side by strong forts. The harbor is a land-locked bay, deep enough for vessels of the largest class, and with space enough to accommodate, at least, five hundred of them. Brest is the most important naval station of France, and its fortress and docks were full of interest to the young tourists. The city, which contains a population of eighty thousand, is built on the summit and slopes of a hill, some of the streets upon whose sides are so steep as to be impassable for vehicles.

The Josephine had already come to anchor, and the ship followed her example, taking position as near to her as it was safe to lie. As usual, when the vessels came into port, there was a great excitement on board, for new sights and sounds are peculiarly agreeable after the voyager comes from the monotony of the swelling ocean; and the students made the most of them. In coming into port, all hands had been on duty; and after the sails had all been furled, Captain Shuffles declared that he was perfectly satisfied with the discipline of his crew. The runaways, who were generally good seamen, whatever else they were, did not deem it prudent to "pipe to mischief" again, or to attempt to create any confusion. All eyes were fixed on them if anything went amiss, and if they were disposed to do wrong, they made a merit of necessity. But Brest was an old story to them, and brought up unpleasant memories. They knew the harbor, and were familiar with the sights, having served on board of the Josephine in this port for three weeks after the runaway cruise. Indeed, their knowledge of the harbor brought them into favor with others, who asked them many questions about the objects to be seen.

After everything was made snug on board of the ship, the yards squared, and every rope hauled taut in man-of-war style, the first cutter was lowered, and the principal visited the Josephine. As he went over the side, he saw Adler, Phillips, and others of the runaways, who belonged to the consort, on deck, and he concluded that his plan had worked as well in her as in the ship.

"Well, Mr. Fluxion," said he, as he grasped the hand of his able assistant, "I see the Josephine has not yet been taken away from you."

"No, sir. We had but a dozen mutineers on board," replied the vice-principal, "and they are about the sickest dogs you ever saw. I kept them in the steerage, and fed them on salt beef and hard bread, as you suggested to me."

"Did you give them any water?"

"Not a drop. After I learned that your ruffians had stove the water tanks, I concluded they were all in the same boat, and that my fellows were as responsible for the deed as yours. I suppose it was all a contrived plan before we left Havre."

"I don't know whether it was or not. I should have treated it in a different manner if the young rascals had not dragged in a large number of the students who seldom give us any trouble."

"The plan worked well, though I did not very strongly approve of it at first. Last night, the rebels sent for me, and begged, with tears in their eyes, to be permitted to return to their duty, promising to be faithful as long as they remained on board. I gave them a pretty severe lecture, but they declared they had nothing to do with staving the water tanks in the ship, and did not know anything about it. I'm not apt to believe what those fellows say."

"It matters little whether they knew it or not; they certainly agreed together to refuse to do duty. Well, they have come to their senses now, and both vessels seem to be in good order. Of course, after what has happened, it is not proper to take these mischief-makers with us into Germany," added Mr. Lowington.

"Certainly not," replied Mr. Fluxion, promptly.

"Then, as you are going to Italy, what shall be done with them while we are absent?" asked the principal, anxiously.

"My sister, who intends to spend the winter in Italy with her husband, desires to see me on a matter of business connected with her private property. As she is an invalid, I think she wishes to consult me in regard to the disposition of her estate, so that her children may enjoy it after her decease; for, as I have told you before, her husband is not a reliable man. If it were a matter of any less consequence, I would not think of leaving."

"Undoubtedly it is your duty to go, and you must do so. But I do not like the idea of leaving thirty such students as Howe, Little, and Phillips in the sole charge of Dr. Carboy. He is a good man; but he has not quite tact and energy enough for such a responsibility."

"Suppose I take them with me," suggested Mr. Fluxion, with a smile.

"That is hardly practicable."

"I mean in the Josephine," added the vice-principal.

"It's a long voyage round through the Strait of Gibraltar."

"I am in no hurry to reach Italy. How long shall you be absent in Germany?"

"About three weeks."

"Say twenty-one days," said Mr. Fluxion, musing. "The Josephine is a fast vessel. Under the most favorable circumstances, she would make the run in eight days. A fair passage would be twelve days. If I remain one day in Genoa, where my sister lives, the cruise would last twenty-five days."

"A few days' time, or a week, is of no consequence," added Mr. Lowington.

"But suppose you take the ship to Lisbon, on your return, and I will meet you there, say about the twenty-seventh or eighth of the month."

"I rather like the plan; but isn't it a little hard on the boys?"

"Not at all. It's giving them plenty of sea-service; but that is what they need for their complaint. We shall feed them well on fresh provisions, and it is a pleasant trip up the Mediterranean at this season of the year. But I only mention the idea to solve the difficulty you suggest."

"I will consider the matter, and give you an answer before night," added Mr. Lowington, thoughtfully.

"If the plan is adopted, I should like to have Peaks and Bitts with me, to act as watch officers with Cleats and Gage."

"You shall have them," replied Mr. Lowington, as he directed the officer of the boat to call his crew, who had been permitted to come on board.

In the first cutter's crew were three of the runaways,

who had taken the opportunity to communicate with Adler, Phillips, and other of the runaways in the consort. After each party had related to the other its experience in rebellion, and commented on its unsatisfactory results, they touched upon the old topic — how to get to Paris, where remittances from their friends were waiting for most of them.

"Old Carboy is to have charge of us while the crowd are gone," said Sheffield, irreverently. "We can easily come it over him."

"If we can only get on shore, we are all right," added Phillips.

"Only we have no money to pay our fare to Paris," interposed Adler.

"I can raise some," suggested Sheffield. "My father sent me a letter of credit on a Paris banker; but any banker will let me have some money on it, if I draw on Paris in his favor."

"That's the idea!" exclaimed Adler. "I have a letter also."

"But we are not to go together this time," added Little.

"Any way, if we are only to go," said Phillips, as the coxswain of the first cutter called away his crew, and ended the conversation.

It was renewed as soon as the ship was reached and the boat hauled up. The runaways had abandoned all thought of joining the excursion to the Rhine; and. "how to get away" was an exciting topic to them. In the tops, out on the bowsprit, and in other secluded places, small knots of them gathered to discuss the subject. Promises made to do better were forgotten, and the bitter experience of the past was wholly ignored. If they could get away from the ship or the consort, — in whichever one they were to be confined, — they would make amends for all their sufferings and all their humiliations. Herman and Little were especially earnest, though they still avoided their late leader, Howe. Perth was regarded as lost to them, for he wore a white ribbon on his breast, and had done his duty as an officer.

"We will all be pious for a day or two, till Carboy closes his eyes," said Little. "You, and Ibbotson, and I will look out for ourselves, and the rest of the fellows must do the same. I have an idea."

"Have you? What is it?" demanded Herman.

"We shall all be sent on board the Josephine as soon as the lambs get ready to start for Germany."

"Yes, I suppose so," added Herman, eagerly.

"Then it will be an easy matter. But I don't want to talk about it yet. Too many cooks spoil the soup," continued Little, with his air of mysterious assurance.

"Tell us what it is. We won't mention it."

"I've got it all arranged; and if the rest of our fellows are smart, they can take advantage of it. We all know this harbor pretty well," added the little villain.

"Why don't you tell us what the idea is?"

Little rose from his seat in the main-top, and looked over to see that no inquisitive person was concealed on the cat-harpings.

"You are not to mention it to any one, you understand, or hint at it. We three, I repeat, are to look out for ourselves only. Ibbotson is to find the money to get to Paris, and I furnish the brains."

"What am I to find?"

"Find your way to Paris, if you can. You are a good fellow, Herman, and I will take you in because you are some punkins."

"But you have'nt told us the plan," said Ibbotson, not particularly pleased with the self-sufficiency of his little companion.

"I will tell you," whispered Little, throwing an arm around the neck of each of his friends, and drawing their heads together near his mouth. "At night, when everything is quiet, one of us will just unbit the cable, and let it run out. Then another shall sing out that the vessel is going adrift. That will make a row. Then we will try to do something. You, Herman, and I, will offer to carry a line to another vessel — the ship, for instance. Carboy — who don't know any more about a vessel than a kitten does of the ten commandments — will tell you to do it. Then we three will jump into a boat, and carry off the line. We can carry it to the ship, or not, just as we think best; but you may bet your life we don't return to the Josephine! How does that strike you?"

"Yes; but where are Cleats and Gage all this time? They know all about a vessel, if Carboy don't," suggested Herman.

"Wherever you please," replied Little, confidently.

"Suppose they happen to be on deck, and are disposed to take the boat and carry out the line themselves?"

"So much the better! Thanks to the prudence and good management of the principal, there are four boats belonging to the Josephine," answered the little villain, who appeared to have provided for every emergency which could possibly occur. "The moment the boatswain and carpenter are clear of the vessel, we will suggest that another line ought to be carried to some other vessel; and Mr. Carboy will see the necessity of the measure."

"Perhaps he won't see it," interposed Ibbotson.

"Then I'll fall overboard."

"Fall overboard?"

"Precisely so," replied Little.

"I don't see what that has to do with it," said Herman.

"Don't you? Well, I hope you and Ibbotson would have the courage and the energy to save me from a watery grave, and all that sort of thing."

"What! jump in after you?" inquired Herman.

"No! How heavy your wits are to-day! You need not dampen your trousers. Just drop the fourth cutter into the water, pick me up, and then we will find our way to the shore."

"Some other fellows might take it into their heads to rescue you from a watery grave, and all that sort of thing," added Herman.

"If they do, so much the better for them. You and Ibbotson must make sure that you get into the boat, whoever else does. There will be no officers to bother, unless Perth happens to be left on board. If he is, all right. He will know what to do. If the other fellows don't want to go to Paris with us, or rather on their own hook, they can return to the vessel, and mildly break it to the professor, that we were all drowned. There will not be a particle of trouble about the business. There are twenty other ways of managing the case. As soon as the lambs are off, and we are put on board of the Josephine, we will arrange everything."

"Perhaps we shall remain in the ship," suggested Herman.

"So much the worse for the ship, for her cable can be unbitted, as well as the schooner's."

"That's so."

"In the dark, with the ship adrift and liable to be thrown on shore, or to run afoul of another vessel, there will be a big excitement, and we can do anything we wish. When the rest of the fellows see what is up, they can take care of themselves," continued Little, who did not believe in the possibility of a failure.

"Very well; we will suppose we get on shore all right — what then? We shall be in Brest, which is a fortified city, with gates through which none can pass without permission," said Ibbotson.

"Never mind the gates. We shall leave by railroad for Paris. As soon as you raise some money to pay for the tickets, I will take care of the rest."

"I have no doubt we can raise the money. My father sent me a letter of credit for five hundred francs. I heard my cousin say he could get money in any large city on his letter of credit, for the bankers know each other," added Ibbotson.

"If he had only sent you a circular letter of credit, you could draw almost anywhere," said Herman.

"Well, if we can't raise any money on the letter, I have a gold watch that cost about a hundred dollars in New York. I can raise two hundred francs on it, and redeem it when we come back," continued Ibbotson.

"That's the talk!" exclaimed Little. "I like to see energy in a fellow. There isn't a ghost of a doubt in my mind but that we shall be in Paris in two or three days from now."

This interesting conversation was interrupted by the boatswain's call, piping all hands to muster. The crew were then drilled for an hour in all the evolutions of getting under way, and making sail. The runaways dared not repeat the experiments which had been tried with so much apparent success at Havre, for they feared the squadron would be sent to sea again if the drill was not perfect. The various movements were admirably performed, and entirely to the satisfaction of Captain Shuffles. The ship's company were then piped to dinner. When they came on deck, the signal, "All hands, attend lecture," was flying on board the ship. This was a hopeful sign for those who were impatient to visit the Rhine, and most of the crew were ready to hear Professor Mapps's description of Germany.

While the ship's company were waiting for the arrival of the Josephine's, a very interesting ceremony was performed in the waist. The Grand Protectress of the Order of the Faithful raised the members of the second degree to the third, adorning them with the white ribbon. They had been faithful in the discharge of all their duties, and Grace insisted that all the members should now stand on an equal footing. Those who wore the yellow ribbon were advanced to the second degree; but Grace promised them that if they listened attentively to the lecture, they should receive the white ribbon before night.

With the crew of the Josephine came Mr. Fluxion, who immediately retired to the main cabin with the principal, where the further details of the cruise to Genoa were discussed. It was finally agreed that the vice-principal's plan should be adopted, and that the Josephine should sail as early the next day as she could be fitted out for the voyage. The two vessels were to meet at Lisbon, near the end of the month, and from that port proceed on the homeward voyage. Peaks and Gage were sent for, and were very willing to be temporarily transferred to the consort; while Leach was to remain as ship-keeper, in charge of the Young America, during the absence of the party in Germany.

While the professor was engaged upon his lecture in the steerage, Mr. Fluxion returned to the consort with the two forward officers, and, taking in the head steward, proceeded to the shore. In half an hour a water boat was alongside the Josephine, filling up the water tanks and casks. Later in the day several shore boats came off to deliver the provisions and supplies which the steward had purchased. Before night the Josephine was ready for the long cruise up the Mediterranean, though none of the students on board of the ship knew that anything unusual was in progress.

CHAPTER XI.

A SHORT LECTURE ON GERMANY.

IN answer to the summons of the boatswain, "All hands, attend lecture, ahoy!" both ships' companies assembled in the steerage of the Young America. The Arbuckles had seats near the foremast, on which the professor displayed his maps, diagrams, and other illustrations of his teachings. These lectures were received with different degrees of favor by various students. While such as Paul Kendall, Shuffles, Gordon, and Tremere regarded them as very valuable privileges, others considered them as intolerable bores. Some were interested in a portion of the descriptions and historical details, others closed their ears to the whole, though all listened to anything that could be considered a story.

The runaways were among those who regarded the present lecture — since they did not expect to visit Germany — as an intolerable nuisance. They were careful to select places where they could listen or not, without attracting the attention of the professor. Herman and Perth had seated themselves near one of the gangways before the boatswain sounded the call. The latter held a very doubtful position on board. Although he wore the white ribbon of the Order of the

Faithful, it was a problem whether he was in sympathy with the objects of the institution. He had declined to serve as a seaman in place of the mutineers; but in spite of his refusal, he took his place at the capstan, and went aloft when the order was given to shake out the topsails. He did not like the idea of being alone, and if he did not formally recant in so many words, he did so by his actions. No fault could be found with him, so far as the faithful discharge of his duty was concerned; still his position was not altogether satisfactory.

Not only the faculty and the officers were in doubt in regard to his standing, but also his former associates. He had done nothing to indicate his regret for the past, on the one hand, and nothing to assure his runaway friends that he was still in sympathy with them. The principal did not know where to put him, and, consequently, was unable to decide whether or not he should be relieved from the penalty of his transgressions in the Josephine, and be permitted to accompany the party to Germany.

"Are you going to the Rhine with the rest of the fellows, Perth?" asked Herman, as they seated themselves at the opening of Gangway B.

"That's more than I know; but I suppose not, for I am considered too wicked," replied the master, lightly.

"I thought you had joined the lambs."

"*Nicht viel!*"

"What do you mean by that?"

"Not much!"

"We all thought so. You have hardly spoken a

word to one of our fellows since you went into the cabin," added Herman.

"Well, I've prayed for you all the same. I declined to take a seaman's place when you fellows in the steerage slopped over, and wouldn't come to time."

"You didn't, though!"

"I did, though; but I couldn't stand alone, and I sort of backed out, just as the rest of you did, and went to work at the braces and buntlines."

"Then you really are not a lamb?"

"Not if I know myself! I didn't do anything to get into the cabin; so it isn't my fault that I'm there. Whether I go to the Rhine or not, I suppose it is certain enough that the rest of our fellows will not."

"No; we have spoiled all our chances."

"There's no doubt of that," laughed Perth.

"But we are going to Paris," added Herman, in a whisper. "We have the wires all laid down."

"Are you, though?" said Perth, deeply interested in the communication. "I should like to go with you."

"But we are not going in a bunch; only two or three in a squad. Don't say anything to any of our fellows about it."

"I never says nothing to nobody," laughed Perth. "But I want to know more about it."

"The arrangements are all made, and I don't think there is any chance to fail."

"Good!"

But the professor commenced his lecture at this point, and the steerage was hushed, so that it was not prudent even to whisper. The students were all required, at these lectures, to be prepared with paper and pencils, so that they could take notes, especially of dates and statistics.

"Our party consists of Little, Ibbotson and myself," Herman wrote on his paper, which he placed so that Perth could read it.

"Have you any stamps?" Perth wrote.

"No; but Ibbotson has a letter of credit on which he can raise some."

"My uncle, in Glasgow, sent me twenty pounds — four five-pound notes — at the request of my father. I got it at Havre," wrote Perth. "I will join you in Paris if I go to Germany; if not, I will start with you. Pop. N. Ger., 28 mill.; S. Ger., 12.5 mill.; total, 40.5 mill.; about equal to pop. of France."

The sudden change in the style of the second master's notes is accounted for by the fact that the principal entered the steerage at the moment indicated by the break in the conversation between the two runaways. They were in the rear of all the other students, and were fully exposed to Mr. Lowington's gaze as he passed out of the main cabin. Perhaps he did not think it was quite natural for such students as Perth and Herman to be engaged so industriously in taking notes; or it may be that his practised eye fully comprehended at a glance the nature of their occupation. The instant the door opened, Herman slyly slipped off the sheet on which he had been writing, and thrust it into his pocket. Perth had written over one of his small pages of note paper, and begun upon a second. He had, when his companion had read what he wrote upon it, slipped the first sheet into the atlas, which served as a desk for him.

Mr. Lowington walked to the vicinity of Gangway B, and paused there. Perth turned down the upper part of the sheet, on which he had written the last part of his message to Herman, so that nothing objectionable appeared on it, even if the principal took it into his head to look over his shoulder. Perth was not at all flurried — he was too old a rogue to commit himself by any weakness; and when he had written down the statement of the professor, he paused and looked at the speaker, as though he was wholly and entirely absorbed in the lecture. The entrance of Mr. Lowington caused many of the students to look behind them, as boys will do in school, on the smallest pretence. Mr. Mapps insisted upon the students' attention, and he paused till his hearers had gratified their curiosity.

Mr. Lowington did not appear to be quite satisfied with the conduct of Perth, and, reaching over the shoulder of the second master, he took the paper from the atlas. Of course this act produced a sensation among the boys; the most insignificant event creates a sensation in the school-room. Mr. Mapps lowered the pointer, and intimated by his actions that he did not intend to proceed till order was restored. Perth was confounded this time, if he never was before.

"What kind of a lecture are you delivering, Mr. Mapps?" asked the principal, with a smile.

"A lecture on Germany, such as I have usually given on these occasions."

" As this young gentleman writes it down, it seems to me rather a singular lecture. I will read it." Perth wanted to drop through into the hold.

"'I will join you in Paris if I go to Germany; if not, I will start with you. Population North Germany, twenty-eight millions; South Germany, twelve and a half millions; total, forty and a half millions; about equal to population of France.' The latter part seems to be a little more germane than the first part. ' I will join you in Paris if I go to Germany,' is rather paradoxical, and I conclude that the young gentleman has not correctly reported this part of your lecture."

" I think not, sir," laughed Mr. Mapps. " I do not remember saying anything about going to Paris."

" Well, Mr. Perth, I recommend that you take a seat nearer to the professor, so that you can understand him better; for certainly you make very bad work of taking notes," added Mr. Lowington, as he pointed to a seat near the foremast.

Perth walked forward, and took the place indicated. Mr. Mapps proceeded with the lecture; but it is doubtful whether the second master understood him any better than before, he was so completely absorbed by the consideration of the little difficulty into which he had so heedlessly plunged himself. After all, the situation was not so bad as it might be. The principal could make nothing of the sentence he had read, and as nothing had been found upon Herman, he could trust to his ingenuity to explain away the meaning of it. So he used his brain in trying to devise a solution of the sentence which would satisfy the principal, instead of attending to the lecture, which he feared would have no practical value to him.

A large majority of the students were deeply interested in the remarks of the professor, and as they were to be in Germany in a few days, even the dry statistics were considerably valued. As it would not be civil to report the professor's lecture from the middle, where it was interrupted by the entrance of the principal, it is necessary to return to the commencement of it.

"What is the German for Germany?" asked the professor, as he picked up his pointer.

"Deutschland."

"The French?"

"Allemagne."

"Germany can hardly be called a nation, though in some respects it is similar to the United States. It is a confederation of nations, though the people speak the same language, and are united by many other common ties of manners and customs, as well as of contiguity of territory. But it is peculiar in some respects, as, Prussia is a nation, under its own king and laws; but only a portion of it belongs to Germany. Austria* is an empire, under its own emperor; but only a part of his dominions are represented in the Germanic Confederation. Its several states are united for some specific purposes, such as the collection of

* Professor Mapps describes Germany as it was before the war of 1866, and the subsequent reconstruction of North Germany. In "NORTHERN LANDS, OR YOUNG AMERICA IN PRUSSIA AND RUSSIA," the present status of Germany will be explained.

certain taxes, and mutual defence. In other respects its empires, kingdoms, duchies, &c., are independent nations, making their own laws, and regulating their own affairs."

" I don't exactly understand the relations of Austria and Prussia to the Germanic Confederation," said Paul Kendall. " How can part of them belong to the confederation without the whole?"

"Very easily," replied the professor; "though, if you ask me why a' part, and not the whole, of Prussia or Austria should be included in the Germanic Confederation, I cannot tell you, unless it be to preserve ' ancient landmarks.' The province of Prussia proper was not German; and that may be a very good reason why it never should be. Germany is a league of the several sovereignties into which the old German empire had fallen. The archduchy of Austria was, and Hungary was not, German, in the reign of the emperors. Holstein-Lauenburg* belongs to Denmark, but belongs, at the same time, to Germany. Of the eight provinces of Prussia, two are not included in the confederation. Of the twenty-one states or provinces which constitute the Austrian empire, eleven are German.

"I can see no good reason why, if the Germanic league is of any service, the provinces of Prussia and Posen should not be admitted, as well as the other six divisions of the kingdom of Prussia. We take the fact as we find it. Germany, then, is simply a union of states for certain purposes. It is not, in any proper

* Annexed to Prussia in 1866.

sense, a nation. It does not send representatives to foreign countries, and it can make laws and regulations only to cover the purposes of the league.

"In 1863 there were thirty-four states represented in the confederation. The empire of Austria cast four votes in the general convention; the kingdoms of Prussia, Bavaria, Saxony, Hanover, and Würtemburg, also four each; other states, grand duchies, duchies, electorates, principalities, landgraviates, and free cities, from one to three, according to their size and importance. These representatives meet at Frankfort, which is the capital of Germany. The population of Northern Germany is about twenty-eight millions; of Southern Germany, twelve and a half millions; making about forty and a half millions, or about equal to that of France.

"Of the early history of Germany there is no authentic record. The ancient Romans had no knowledge of the people north of the Danube and east of the Rhine, except as the barbarous tribes who made incursions into their territory. When Gaul came into the possession of the Romans, they learned more of the barbarians of the north, who were called Germani — a word which is probably derived from *ger*, a spear, indicating their warlike character. Among these tribes were the Teutons, the Saxons, the Franks, the Goths, the Vandals, the Gauls, whose names are common in history. Clovis, the ancient sovereign of the Frankish empire, and his successors, conquered these tribes, and incorporated their territory in the Empire of the West, which reached the height of its glory under the reign of Charlemagne. His son

Louis was too weak to rule so vast a realm, and in 843 the empire was divided into three parts, and given to his three sons. France became the portion of Charles the Bald; Italy, of Lothaire; and Germany, of Louis. At this time the German kingdom extended from the Rhine to the Elbe, and from the German Ocean to the Danube.

"During the succeeding century, Germany was partitioned into three smaller divisions, became a part of France again, and the throne was subverted by the nobles, who elected the kings. Portions of Italy, and other territory beyond the Elbe, were conquered. I will not weary you even by mentioning the line of kings who followed. Their dominions were torn by dissensions, while they struggled to increase their power. In 1273, Count Rudolph of Hapsburg was elected emperor, and, after a fierce struggle with the unruly barons, succeeded in establishing his authority, and in obtaining possession of the dukedom of Austria, and several other provinces. The house of Hapsburg has to the present time retained the throne of Austria.

"Jealous of the growing power of the Hapsburgs, the nobles elected Adolph, Count of Nassau, Emperor of Germany; but Albert, Rudolph's son and successor, wrested the crown from him. The Hapsburgs had possessions in Switzerland, when the house obtained its power in Austria, and they held them as dependencies upon the dukedom. The Swiss revolted in the reign of Albert, and their long and severe struggle for independence was commenced at this time.

"During the reign of Sigismund, one of the successors of Albert, John Huss, the reformer, was burned at the stake at Constance, whither he had gone with the safe-conduct of the emperor. His martyrdom caused the Hussite war, in which several severe battles were fought, including one at Prague. In 1593, Maximilian I. succeeded to the throne; and in his reign the Reformation by Luther began. Charles V., the grandson of Maximilian, — of whom I spoke to you in giving the history of Holland and Belgium, — united the crowns of Spain, Germany, the Netherlands, and Naples, and the empire became the leading power of Europe. The Reformation produced fierce dissensions and savage contests. Charles was obliged, sorely against his will, to grant privileges to his Lutheran subjects. But he was disgusted with power, and resigned his crown. He was succeeded by his brother, Ferdinand I., as Emperor of Germany, and by his son, Philip II., as King of Spain; to whom, also, he gave his possessions in the Netherlands. The dissensions in the empire enabled France on the west and Turkey on the east to wrest valuable possessions from it. The successors of Charles V. were unable to breast the storm of progress successfully, and the imperial authority was completely shattered. The power of the petty rulers of small states increased and overshadowed that of the central authority.

"The emperors Ferdinand and Matthias treated the Protestants with so much severity, committing the most flagrant outrages upon them, that it brought on the Thirty Years' War. When Matthias died, the insurgents declared the throne vacant, and chose the **Elector Frederick emperor.** The Protestant princes fought for him, while the Catholic powers sustained Ferdinand II., Archduke of Austria. Peace was established, by the treaty of Westphalia, in 1648, by which Germany lost a portion of her territory. After these events, the power of the emperors waned still more, until their title was little more than a surname of the rulers of Austria. When Prussia became a great Protestant power, under Frederick the Great, she was a check upon Austria, and prevented the latter from reëstablishing the ancient power of the German empire.

" The French revolution practically destroyed the empire. Francis II. of Austria, overwhelmed by Napoleon, ceded to him the country on the left bank of the Rhine. When the Rhenish Confederation of Napoleon was formed, in 1806, Francis resigned the crown of the German empire, which was thus formally dissolved. Many changes in territorial limits were made, and the free cities lost their independence. The country was either actually or virtually subject to Napoleon, who dictated its policy, and levied heavy contributions upon it.

" As it was not possible for all these small states to maintain their separate independence unaided, when the Allied Powers had driven Napoleon from Europe, and restored the nations to their original condition, it became necessary to regulate the affairs of Germany. Prussia objected to an independent empire, whose power might endanger her safety and progress ; and a confederation of the states was formed in 1815, which exists at the present time." *

* Dissolved in 1866.

The professor continued to describe the country, and to define the powers and duties of the Federal Diet; but as many changes have been made in the government and in the states, it is not necessary to transcribe his remarks to these pages. He promised, as occasion might offer on their travels, to give the students further explanations of the nature of the territory, governments, and local peculiarities of the several states they might visit. The boys were satisfied with this arrangement, and the session was closed. The boatswain immediately piped all hands to muster on deck.

"Whom do you purpose to join in Paris, if you go to Germany?" asked Mr. Lowington, when Perth appeared among the officers.

"My uncle," replied the second master, promptly.

"Your uncle from Glasgow, I suppose you mean."

"Yes, sir. He wrote me that he should be in Paris early this month."

"How happened you to be writing the sentence on your paper?"

"I was writing a letter which I intended to copy with ink, as soon as I had time."

"Have you the rest of the letter?"

"No, sir; I tore it up just now."

"Will you be kind enough to produce your uncle's letter?" said the principal, quietly.

"I don't keep my letters, sir; and I destroyed it as soon as I had read it."

"I suppose you did," replied Mr. Lowington, significantly. "But if you don't go to Germany, what then? I think you wrote the words, 'I will start with you.'"

"Yes, sir."
"Start from where?"
"From here."
"I don't understand it."
"I was going to write to uncle Donald, that, if I went to Germany, I would see him in Paris as we pass through that city. If I did not go, I wanted him to come here, and take me to Paris with him."

"And you think this explains what you wrote upon your note paper?" inquired the principal.

"As I understand it, sir, it does."

"Was Herman expected to join your party?"

"No, sir."

"I observed that he seemed to be much interested in what you were writing, and that you took some pains to let him see your paper. Your explanation is not satisfactory, and I should not dare to take you to Germany, lest you should miss your uncle on the way. Perhaps he had better come to Brest himself. When do you expect him?"

"I don't know when he is coming, sir," replied Perth, rather abashed to find his explanation had obtained so little consideration.

"Have you any money, Perth?" asked Mr. Lowington, suddenly.

"No, sir."

"Not a few francs, even?"

"Perhaps I have a few English pence."

"Haven't you a few English pounds?"

"No, sir."

"Just think a little, before you answer."

"If I had even a pound, I should be likely to remember it, sir."

"I should say you would; and twenty times as likely to remember it, if you had twenty pounds," added the principal.

"O, I haven't anything like that, sir."

"You have an astonishingly bad memory, Perth. You received a letter from your uncle in Glasgow, while you were at Havre. Do you remember that?"

"Certainly I do, sir," replied Perth, wondering what the principal could mean by such pointed questions.

Was it possible that Mr. Lowington had read what he wrote on the first sheet of note paper? He thrust his hand into his pocket, and the sheet was there as he had taken it from the atlas.

"You do remember the letter?"

"To be sure I do, sir."

"And don't you remember that there were four five-pound notes in it, numbering from thirty-three thousand eight hundred forty-five to eight, inclusive? It is very singular, indeed, that you have forgotten this little circumstance."

Perth was confounded by this revelation. He saw that he was caught, and that it was useless for him to say anything more; so he wisely held his peace.

"If your uncle has not changed his mind within three days, he has no more intention of coming to France than I have of going to Glasgow. I received a letter from him to-day, since the ship came to anchor, forwarded from Havre after we left. The writer was confined to the house with a severe attack of rheumatism. In the quiet of his chamber, he had an opportunity to consider whether he had done right to send you twenty pounds, even with the advice of your father, without informing me of the fact. He thought the sum was a large one for a young man to have, and he desires me to see that you make a proper use of it. I will trouble you to hand me the money, which shall be placed to your credit, and receipted for by the pursers."

"I haven't the money now, sir," replied Perth, who was fully resolved to run away at the first convenient opportunity, and wanted the money to pay his expenses.

"Where is it?"

"I sent it to a banker —"

"Silence! Don't blacken your soul with any more falsehoods, Perth," interrupted the principal, sternly.

"You may search me, sir," replied the second master, throwing out his arms, as though he were ready to submit to the operation.

"I may, but I do not choose to do so at present. Keep your eye on him, Peaks," added the principal, as he walked forward to his usual stand on the hatch.

"You are foolish, Master Perth," said the old boatswain, shaking his head; for he had been the only person who had listened to the interview, and appeared to be present for a purpose.

Perth put his hands in his pockets. He felt the paper on which he had written during the lecture. It would be a dangerous document in case he should be searched; for its contents would expose him, and implicate others. As slyly and as quickly as he could, he took it out, tore it into small bits, and threw it out the open port into the water.

"What's that?" demanded Peaks, seizing him by the collar.

"You are too late," answered Perth.

"What was it you tore up?"

"The five-pound notes."

"Tell that to the marines!" exclaimed the old sailor.

"They are gone to Davy Jones's locker now," replied Perth, shaking his head.

Peaks instantly reported the matter to the principal, who, however, did not deem it necessary to take any immediate action. Probably he did not believe the young wretch had destroyed the bills; or, if he had, it was his own loss. Perth stood silent and sullen, while Mr. Lowington spoke to the students, announcing the arrangements for the excursion to the Rhine. The delinquent was certain, by this time, that he was not to be one of the party; but he hoped, if he saved his money, that he should find an opportunity to escape from the squadron soon after his shipmates started on their journey.

CHAPTER XII.

A MYSTERIOUS MOVEMENT.

"YOUNG gentlemen," said Mr. Lowington, as he stepped upon the hatch, after disposing of Perth's case, "we shall commence our tour to the Rhine to-morrow morning."

A hearty demonstration of applause greeted this announcement, and doubtless those who had been faithful from the beginning realized a certain sense of triumph, because they were justified in their hopes.

"We shall leave in the first train for Paris, where we will spend the night, and proceed to Strasburg the next day. From this point we shall enter Germany, and after visiting several places of interest, such as Fribourg, Baden, Schaffhausen, Stuttgart, Carlsruhe, Heidelberg, and Frankfort. We shall take the steamer at Mayence, and go down the Rhine as far as Cologne. This excursion will enable you to see all of the river which is worth seeing. You have already seen the Rhine in Holland, and at Basle. All its picturesque portions are crowded into the space of less than a hundred miles, which you can witness from the deck of a steamer in a single day, if such haste were necessary.

"As we leave at an early hour in the morning, it

will be best to make our arrangements to-night. On our return to Havre, Captain Shuffles requested me to allow all hands to join in this excursion."

A few half-suppressed hisses from some of the runaways were promptly drowned in a sea of applause from the Order of the Faithful.

"I had the subject under consideration, and it would have afforded me very great pleasure to grant the request; but the conduct of those in whose favor it was made has been such, since we left Havre, that I am unable to grant it. I shall, therefore, be obliged again to leave thirty-one of your number on board of the Josephine during the absence of the others."

The runaways, to the astonishment, if not the horror, of the Faithful, warmly applauded this announcement. It was equivalent to saying they did not wish to join the excursion. The principal made no remark, though the applause was certainly impudent; but doubtless he was fully reconciled to the little arrangement he had made with Mr. Fluxion.

"Those who are to go will bring their bags on board of the ship, and sleep here to-night," continued Mr. Lowington. "Those who are not to go will take their bags on board the Josephine. If there is any doubt as to who the thirty-one are, their names will be read."

No one called for the reading of the names, for there was no one who needed to be enlightened. The students were dismissed, and the boats from the consort returned. In a short time, the runaways, who belonged to the ship's company, appeared upon deck with their luggage. They seemed to be rather jubilant than otherwise; and though their manner was very offensive, the principal took no notice of it, as it was not openly insolent, consisting only of a real or assumed expression of pleasure at the sentence pronounced against them. All of them expected to escape from the consort during the administration of Dr. Carboy, and they regarded a couple of weeks in Paris and Switzerland, free from restraint, as ample compensation for the deprivation.

"Let those laugh that win," said Herman, when Horne, one of the Faithful, ventured to sympathize with him in the misfortune of being left behind.

"I don't see what you can win doing duty and learning your lessons on board of the Josephine," added Horne.

"Don't you cry, my hearty. You will hear from us by the time you get half way down the Rhine; and if we don't have a better time than you do, it will be because we don't know how."

"Well, I suppose you do know Howe," answered Horne, with a smile, which indicated that he enjoyed even a sickly pun. "I should think you had known him to your sorrow."

"Howe has played out. I expect Lowington will get boozy on this excursion."

"Why so?"

"Because he's going to take a Horne on the trip."

"Pretty good! I see you know Howe."

"We know how to have a good time, and we can do it without any sheep's wool."

"Are you going to run away in the Josephine again, Herman?"

"No; that's played out."

But the runaway was reminded, by this question, that he had been talking rather imprudently, and he left his companion for more genial associates.

Perth still stood on the quarter-deck, waiting the action of the principal, who had sent the head steward to overhaul the state-room of the delinquent. The money could not be found in the cabin, though several of the officers, who were there, assisted in the search.

"What have you done with the twenty pounds sent you by your uncle, Perth?" asked Mr. Lowington, when the steward had reported to him.

"Thrown it overboard, sir," replied Perth, with a malignant glance at the boatswain.

"He threw some bits of paper he had torn up into the water," added Peaks. "Whether it was the bank bills or not, I don't know, but I don't think it was."

"Very well," added Mr. Lowington, who never permitted a delinquent pupil to see that he was disturbed and annoyed, even if he was so. "You will bring your bag on deck, and go on board of the Josephine."

"I'm ready, sir," replied Perth, with brazen assurance.

"As your conduct is hardly becoming an officer and a gentleman, you will clothe yourself in a seaman's dress," added the principal, taking the shoulder-straps from his coat. "When a young man can stand up and reel off a string of lies without blushing, he is not fit to associate with those who are competent to be officers of this ship."

"I earned my rank, sir," said Perth, who had an

idea that he should sleep in the cabin of the Josephine during his intended short stay on board of her.

"And forfeited it by your gross misconduct. You will obey the orders given you," added the principal, as he turned and walked away.

Peaks did not take his eye off the offender, but attended him to the cabin, where he was supplied with a seaman's suit. Perth objected to changing his clothing with a pertinacity which provoked the boatswain.

"If you say you won't change the clothes, I will report to Mr. Lowington," said Peaks.

"Well, I won't."

"All right, my hearty;" and the old sailor left the state-room.

But he had not reached the deck before Perth hailed him.

"I will put them on, Mr. Peaks. I've thought better of it," said he, throwing off his frock coat, as the boatswain appeared at the door of the room.

"All the better for you, my lad. I thought you wanted to spend a week or two in the brig," replied Peaks.

"I think it is a hard case, after a fellow has earned his rank, to take it from him," muttered Perth, as he proceeded to put on the sailor's suit.

"An officer should be a gentleman," growled the old sailor.

But the boatswain had been overreached, after all. The four five-pound notes had been sewed into the waistband of Perth's trousers; and this was the particular reason why he objected to losing his rank, if he had to lose his pants with it. Peaks would not take his eye off him long enough to allow him to tear out the bills; but when the boatswain went to report to the principal, the opportunity was obtained, and promptly used. The money was saved, and he yielded the point. He was conducted to the deck, and when the boats brought the Josephines, who were to visit Germany, to the ship, the runaways were sent to their new quarters, or rather their old ones, for they had spent three weeks in her before, under the superintendence of Mr. Fluxion. Before supper time the change was effected. Dr. Carboy, at his own request, — for he preferred the trip to the Mediterranean to that into Germany, — was transferred to the consort for the cruise, with Peaks and Bitts.

The "happy family" were now united on board the ship, and all the active discordant elements of the squadron were collected in the consort. With only a very few exceptions, both parties were satisfied with the arrangement. The runaways perhaps experienced a feeling of relief that they were no longer in danger of being watched and overheard by the "lambs." They had only to look out for the adult officers now, and in the steerage they were by themselves.

Yet the appearance of Peaks on board of the consort with his bag was rather ominous. Bitts was not regarded with the same dread. There were now four adult forward officers in the Josephine; but the old boatswain was the only one who inspired any special terror. Little's brilliant scheme to enable his small party to escape seemed to be endangered by Peak's coming, for he was an exceedingly prompt, decided and vigilant man. The four old sailors, on an emergency, could handle the Josephine alone.

"What do you think now?" said Herman, when everything on board the consort had settled down into order and quiet.

"I don't like to see old Peaks on board," replied the little villain. "He is a tough customer, and may bother us."

"That's so."

"But I think we can wax him."

"I hope so. We have Tom Perth now to help us. We must take him into our squad, and then we shall just make up a crew for the third or fourth cutter."

"I don't like too many."

"But Perth has the rocks in his pocket now — twenty pounds, or five hundred francs," suggested Herman.

"That's an inducement."

"Certainly it is. We can cut for Paris the moment we get on shore."

"All right. We will try it on about to-morrow night. But don't say a word to a single other fellow. We must look out for ourselves this time, and not attempt to carry all the rest of the fellows on our backs," added the prudent Little.

"It looks mean to do so."

"No, it don't. I have told them all to look out for themselves."

"But they don't even know how the thing is to be managed."

"No; and they shall not know it. If they don't know enough to go ashore when the vessel is adrift, let them stay on board."

"Well, Perth is the only fellow to whom I mentioned it."

"That's all right; but don't let him say anything about how the thing is to be done."

"He don't know. I only told him we had a plan which could not possibly fail."

"It won't, if Peaks don't make trouble. We must let off the gun when he is not on deck," continued Little.

"We shall be able to see, after to-night, how things are to be done on board, and whether any of the men are to keep watch," added Herman. "We needn't give up if we don't happen to get off to-morrow night, for we have two or three weeks to do the job in."

Little, seated out on the bowsprit, rehearsed his plan again, and went into all the minor details. They were presently joined by Perth, and the whole affair was explained to him. He approved it, and made a number of suggestions in regard to the boats.

"I am bound to go this time," said Perth, earnestly. "I don't stay another week in the Academy. I have had my shoulder-straps stripped off, and am pointed at by the lambs as an example of a naughty boy. I bluffed them all on board the ship, but with me the die is cast. If your plan don't work, I shall jump overboard, and swim ashore. I have been degraded and disgraced, and I can't possibly stand it any longer."

"We are all in the same boat; and if we can't get off any other way, we will set the vessel afire, and swim ashore by the light of it," added Little.

"You are the fellow for me!" exclaimed Perth.

"I don't want any milk and water about this scrape. If we can't make it go in one way, we will try another."

Peaks, who was planking the deck, extended his walk to the forecastle, and the trio discontinued their conversation. They were satisfied that setting the vessel adrift, some time in the night, would accomplish their purpose, and they were willing to wait till the next evening. They had some difficulty in escaping the observation of their companions who were not in the secret; but they assured them something would be done just as soon as Mr. Fluxion started for Italy, which it was understood, would be on the following day.

Berths were assigned to the temporary crew of the Josephine, and at an early hour they turned in. None of them were detailed to keep the anchor watch on deck; but in the night Little crawled out of his berth, and went up the ladder. All was still on deck, and he could not see that any one was on watch. Seven bells struck on board a man-of-war at anchor near the vessel. It was half past eleven. He crept stealthily to the forecastle, where he found Bitts, who was asleep under the lee of the capstan. This discovery satisfied him that the forward officers were to keep the anchor watch. The arrangement was not favorable to the carrying out of Little's scheme; but if the man on deck would only sleep, it would not make so much difference.

Little carefully studied the situation, which suggested to his fertile invention half a dozen expedients, in case he failed at the proper time to unbit the cable. Four of them could jump into one of the cutters, lower the boat from the davit, and might reach the shore before a single man could call assistance, and get another boat into the water. One of them could pretend to be sick, and, sending the watchman to the cabin to procure medicine, escape while he was looking for it. And so the little schemer went on till he had a quiver full of expedients, any one of which promised to be successful. Having satisfied himself that he had not been reckoning too fast, he went below again, and turned in.

At daylight in the morning all hands were called on board of the Young America. An early breakfast was taken, and a steamer came alongside to convey the happy party to the shore. The hands on board the Josephine were turned out at the same hour, and they had the satisfaction of seeing the members of the Order of the Faithful depart on their pleasant tour to the Rhine. Breakfast was served to them at the usual hour, and when Herman and Little went on deck, after the meal, they saw a man in a canoe coming alongside. He looked like a pilot, but neither of the two runaways who saw him suspected that he had a mission on board. He came on deck, and was duly welcomed by Mr. Fluxion.

"What does that covey want here?" said Little.

"I don't know," replied Herman.

"He has made his canoe fast astern, as though he meant to stay here some time."

"O, he's only loafing, and wants to see a Yankee ship and a Yankee crew," laughed Herman.

Little did not exactly like the coming of the pilot; not that he had any suspicion of the actual programme, but he was afraid the vessel might be moored in some less convenient place for the escape than her present berth. As the runaways finished their breakfast, they came on deck, and some of them recognized the pilot as the one who had brought the Josephine into port the day before.

"All hands, on deck, ahoy!" shouted Peaks, blowing a pipe more shrill than had ever before been heard on board of the consort.

All hands were on deck already, but the call produced a decided sensation. Something was to be done, and all hands fell to discussing probabilities with a zeal, which ought to have brought forth correct conclusions. The general opinion seemed to be, that nothing more than a sermon was coming off, though the vice-principal was not much given to preaching. If Mr. Fluxion was going to Italy, it would be necessary for him formally to transfer his authority to Professor Carboy. On the whole, therefore, the prospect was rather pleasing than otherwise. Herman, and some of the others who were deeply concerned in coming events, advised all the fellows to behave well, and take the preaching kindly, so that the officers need not " smell a mice."

"All hands, up anchor, ahoy!" roared old Peaks, piping a blast which seemed to come from the breath of a north-wester, while the leading spirits were counselling meekness and submission.

"What does that mean?" demanded the astonished Perth.

"O, nothing! Only we are going to have another anchorage," replied Herman.

"Lively, my hearties," said the boatswain, as he stepped forward into the waist. "Don't you hear the pipe?"

"I hear it; but we haven't been stationed in this vessel," replied Herman.

"That's very true, my lad; for once you speak the truth."

"You are a little fast, Peaks," said the vice-principal, coming up from the cabin with a paper in his hand. "Here is the bill, and we will station the crew before we do anything."

Every one of the runaways was stationed for each of the various evolutions of getting under way, making and taking in sail, reefing and tacking. They were all good seamen, and it was not necessary to drill them in their duties. The boatswain again piped, "All hands, up anchor, ahoy!"

The hands took their stations promptly enough, and when the anchor was hove up to a short stay, the foresail and mainsail were hoisted.

"Clear away the jib and flying-jib!" shouted Mr. Fluxion, who gave all the orders himself, though they were repeated by Peaks and Cleats, who acted as first and second officers.

"All ready forward, sir," reported Cleats.

"Man the capstan! Stand by the jib-halyards!"

"Anchor a-weigh, sir!" said Cleats, who was doing duty on the forecastle.

"Hoist the jib!"

"Up with the jib!" repeated Peaks.

As the anchor came up to the hawse-hole, the jib filled, and the vessel began to move.

"Cat and fish the anchor!" called the vice-principal; and his order was passed forward.

"Cat and fish the anchor!" exclaimed Perth. That

doesn't look as though we were going to another anchorage."

"It's all right; we can't go far," added Herman.

While those who were stationed on the top-gallant forecastle were engaged in catting and fishing the anchor, those who had been assigned to places on the topsail and top-gallant yards were sent aloft.

"Lay aloft, sail-loosers!" continued Mr. Fluxion, and the top-men and top-gallant-men ran up the rigging as nimbly as though they had perfectly comprehended the purpose of the officers. "Lay out and loose!"

"All ready!" shouted Bitts, who had gone aloft with the top-men.

"Let fall!"

"Let fall," passed from Peaks to Bitts, and from the latter to the top-men.

"Man the topsail and top-gallant sheets and halyards. Sheet home, and hoist away!"

The topsails and top-gallant sails were speedily set, the braces were manned, and the yards trimmed. Gage had the helm, the pilot standing near him to give out the courses. The main gaff-topsail was next set, and the Josephine was then under full sail. With the wind fair, and everything drawing, she flew through the Goulet at the rate of ten knots an hour. Peaks was as busy as a bee, and in person saw that every rope was properly coiled up or flemished, that the cable was in order to run out when needed, and in general, that everything was in ship-shape order.

As good seamen, the young gentlemen understood that these careful preparations did not indicate merely a change in the holding-ground of the vessel. Everything about the Josephine seemed to be shrouded in profound mystery. Peaks kept all hands at work till the strict order of a man-of-war prevailed in every part of the deck and rigging. He did not say anything, or do anything, which afforded the slightest hint in regard to the destination of the consort. Mr. Fluxion planked the quarter-deck, and did not manifest the least sign of an intention to go to Italy. The movement was utterly incomprehensible, and the runaways began to look very anxious.

After passing through the Goulet into the open sea, the fore and main sheets were manned, the yards braced up, and the course changed to the south-west. Off the Chaussée de Sein, the pilot was discharged, and the Josephine sped on her way, with a fresh breeze a little forward of the beam. Still the vice-principal planked the quarter-deck, and no one said anything to solve the mystery. Peaks had caused everything to be done which he could find to do, and all hands were " sogering " about the deck.

" Mr. Peaks, pipe down the port watch," said Mr. Fluxion, at last, as though every word cost him a month's salary, he was so chary of them.

The acting first officer obeyed the order, and the port watch were dismissed from duty. Like old sailors, they went below, partly from the force of habit, and partly to discuss the unaccountable movement of the vessel. Perth and Herman were both in the starboard watch; but Little and Ibbotson put their heads together as soon as they were in the steerage.

" I don't understand it," said Ibbotson, shaking his head.

"Nor I either; but I think it will come out all right," replied Little, who was always disposed to put the best face upon doubtful indications.

"Do you suppose we are homeward bound?"

"Of course not. Look at the tell-tale. We are running about south-west by south."

"Perhaps that's the course on the great circle."

"Nonsense! We shall fetch up on the coast of South America, if we keep this course long enough."

"I don't know about the course, but I have made up my mind that this is about what it means. I'll bet all the bad marks I shall get for the next quarter, that we are homeward bound."

"No such thing."

"I believe it," persisted Ibbotson. "Lowington did not know what to do with us, while he is in Germany, and so he has sent us home."

"South-west by west won't take us home. Fluxion is only giving us an airing for a day or two, just to see how we behave, and to give us a little wholesome discipline. If we are good, he will return to port, and start for Italy. What is Dr. Carboy here for, if we are bound home?"

"What is he here for? Because Mr. Stout is not here. I suppose they have changed places for a few weeks. The ship goes home next month."

"Don't you cry! In a day or two, if not before night, we shall be back again in the harbor of Brest. I'm willing to bet all my bad marks against all yours, that we get ashore in less than forty-eight hours."

"That's heavy betting, but it won't settle anything. There is Peaks; suppose we ask him," suggested Ibbotson, as the old boatswain came down the ladder.

"You can call up spirits from the vasty deep, but they won't come. You can ask him, but you might as well put the question to the anchor-stock."

"Where are we going, Mr. Peaks?" asked Ibbotson, as gently as though he were addressing a lady.

"Going to sea," replied Peaks, gruffly, as he went on his way, deigning no further answer.

"No use," said Little. "If we only wait, we shall know in a day or two. In the mean time we must be as proper as the parson's lambs."

Still the Josephine sped on her way, and no one was the wiser.

CHAPTER XIII.

FROM STRASBURG TO CONSTANCE.

THE party on board of the Young America were in the highest spirits on the morning of their departure. All of them had now been decorated with the white ribbon of the Order of the Faithful. Even Raymond and Lindsley were entirely satisfied with the good faith and fairness of the principal — better satisfied than they were with their own conduct. What had before been regarded as defeat was now triumph, for a failure to achieve success in doing wrong is actually victory, especially if followed, as in this instance, by real regret, genuine penitence.

Grace Arbuckle, perhaps conscious that she had exerted a salutary influence upon the students through the pleasantry of the Order of the Faithful, was as happy as the young gentlemen themselves. She appeared on deck at an early hour, and when the officers and seamen presented themselves, in their best uniforms, wearing the white ribbon, she was so delighted she could not help laughing heartily.

"Commodore Kendall, are you going to wear that ribbon to Paris?" she asked, as Paul touched his cap to her.

"Certainly I am. I should as soon think of going without my coat as without that," replied he.

"But how absurd!"

"Absurd? *Vous ne pouvez pas faire un sifflet de la queue d'un cochon*," added he, very seriously.

"*C'est vrai;* but what has that to do with the ribbon? Do you mean to call that a pig's tail?"

"No; on the contrary, it is the wing of an angel — it was bestowed by you. I only mean to say it would be quite impossible to go to Germany without this ribbon. It is our talisman to keep us faithful to duty; and I am afraid we should get into mischief if we went without it. Every member will wear his decoration. But, Miss Arbuckle, I think you ought to wear the white ribbon also."

"I!"

"Certainly. You are the Grand Protectress of the order. Do wear it, Miss Arbuckle, with a rosette, to indicate your superior rank. It would please all the members very much."

"I will, if you desire it," replied Grace, more seriously.

"We all desire it."

"It shall be done, if you wish it."

"Thanks."

Grace tripped lightly down the stairs to the cabin, but presently returned, wearing the white ribbon, surmounted by a very tasty rosette, composed of white, blue, and yellow ribbons, to denote the several degrees of the order. Paul was in raptures, and when the ship's company saw the decoration she wore, they saluted her with three rousing cheers, which she gracefully acknowledged.

"We must perpetuate this order, Shuffles," said

Paul, as they stood in the presence of the Grand Protectress.

"I think we must," replied the captain.

"We will organize more systematically when we have time."

"And have a suitable emblem to distinguish the members."

"The white ribbon must not be discarded," protested Paul, glancing at Grace.

"Certainly not; but we will have a gold anchor, say, from which the ribbon shall be suspended," added Shuffles. "On the anchor shall be engraved the single word FAITHFUL."

"And 'Vous ne pouvez pas faire,' &c.," laughed Paul. "I think we must ask the Grand Protectress for a suitable emblem."

"You have great confidence in me, and I will give the subject faithful consideration," said Grace.

"Our motto is an excellent one, I think," continued Paul. "To us it will always mean that you cannot redress a wrong by resorting to dishonorable measures."

The conversation was interrupted by the call to breakfast. Before the meal was finished, the steamer that was to convey the party on shore came alongside. By the time she had made fast, and run out her planks, the boatswain piped, "All hands, on deck with bags, to go ashore." The stewards conveyed the baggage of the Arbuckles on board, and the ship's company marched in single file to the deck of the steamer. There were no turbulent spirits among them, and everything was done in order. In due time the party reached the railroad station, and seated themselves in the special cars, which had been provided for their use.

The Arbuckles, Dr. Winstock, Paul, and Shuffles occupied one compartment of a carriage, and, as usual, the pleasant and well-informed surgeon of the ship, who had been a very extensive traveller, was a living encyclopædia for the party. The course of the train was through Brittany, of which Dr. Winstock had much to say. It is a poor country, not unlike Scotland, though it has no high mountains. The lower order of the people wear quaint costumes, and have hardly changed their manners and customs for three hundred years.

"Do you see that building in the churchyard?" said the doctor, as he pointed out the window.

"What is it — the hearse-house?" asked Paul.

"No; I think they don't use hearses much here. It is a bone-house."

"A what!" exclaimed Shuffles.

"A bone-house, or *reliquaire*. The poor people in this part of France are very ignorant and superstitious. *Requiescat in pace*, so far as the mortal remains of their dead are concerned, has no meaning to them, for they do not let them rest quietly in their graves, as we do. After the bodies of the deceased have gone to decay, the skulls and bones are removed from the coffins, and placed in the bone-house. The names, or the initials, of the departed are painted upon the forehead of the skull."

"How horrible!" exclaimed Grace.

"Doubtless it is so to you; but to these people it is

an act of affectionate remembrance," added the doctor; "as sacred and pious as any tribute we render to our loved and lost ones."

Dr. Winstock continued to describe the various places through which the train passed, answering the many questions proposed by his interested auditors. At noon they arrived at Rennes, where the excursionists lunched, and some of them, perhaps at the expense of the inner man, were enterprising enough to see a little of the city, which contains forty thousand inhabitants, and was the ancient capital of the dukedom of Brittany.

"This is Laval," said the doctor, an hour and a half after the train left Rennes.

"See there!" exclaimed Grace, pointing to a man clothed in goatskins, the hair outside. "Is that Robinson Crusoe?"

"No; that is the fashion for the peasants in this part of Brittany. They don't depend upon Paris for the *mode*. I suppose you have all heard of the Vendéan war."

"Yes, sir. The people of La Vendée were royalists, and fought against the republicans as long as there was anything left of them," replied Paul.

"La Vendée lies south of the Loire; but one of their greatest battles was fought near Laval, in 1793. They conducted themselves with fearful desperation, and after the republicans had sent word, as the battle waned, to the Convention at Paris, that La Vendée was no more, the wounded leader of the insurgents was carried through their ranks, and they rallied, gaining the day in a decisive victory, by which the government troops lost twelve thousand men."

Fifty-six miles farther brought the excursionists to Le Mans, where the Vendéan army was finally destroyed by the forces of General Marceau. The carnage was terrible, and extended even to the massacre of many of the wives and children of the royalists. An obelisk to the memory of the republican general, who was born at Le Mans, informs the reader that he was a soldier at sixteen, a general at twenty-three, and died when he was twenty-seven.

At Chartres, forty-seven miles from Paris, the train stopped half an hour, and the party had an opportunity to see the cathedral, the most magnificent in France, and one of the most ancient. It is four hundred and twenty-five feet long. Henry IV. was crowned in it in 1594, for the reason that Rheims, where coronations formerly took place, was in possession of the Leaguers.

At seven o'clock, the train arrived in Paris, and the party hastened to the lodgings which had been engaged for them. In the evening they attended the grand opera, at the invitation of Mr. Arbuckle, and the next morning proceeded to Strasburg. After a short delay, the party continued the journey, crossing the Rhine into Germany, and halting at Offenburg, a small town, where hotel accommodations had been bespoken. After supper, the excursionists were collected in a large room, and Professor Mapps took a position in front of them.

"Young gentlemen, where are we?" he asked.

"In Germany."

"Very true, but rather indefinite," added the professor.

"In Baden," said Paul Kendall, who, as usual, had taken pains to study up the situation.

"In the Grand Duchy of Baden."

"What is a Grand Duchy?" inquired one of the students, who was doubtless bothered, as others have been, by the varying titles of the German states.

"It is a territory having an independent local government. There is no reason why it should be called a Grand Duchy, unless it is because it is larger than a simple Duchy, though this rule does not always hold good, for the Duchy of Brunswick has double the territory and double the population of the Grand Duchy of Mecklenburg-Strelitz. The titles of the states seem to be entirely arbitrary, and, according to the fancy of their rulers, they were called kingdoms, principalities, electorates, palatinates, margraviates, Grand Duchies, or Duchies. The Grand Duchy of Baden is larger than the Kingdom of Saxony. These designations have been occasionally changed, as the states increased in size, or as their rulers desired a grander title. In 1803 Baden was a margraviate of one fourth its present extent. Napoleon gave the title of Elector, and afterwards of Grand Duke, to the Margrave Charles Frederick, as his territory was increased.

"Baden has about six thousand square miles, or is about equal in size to Rhode Island and Connecticut united. It has a population of one million three hundred thousand, which has hardly increased during the last fifty years, for the reason that so many of its people have emigrated to the United States. The country is mountainous, and contains the Schwarzwald. What does that mean?"

"The Black Forest," replied several.

"A mountainous region, which has been the paradise of story-tellers. The highest peak is the Feldberg, forty-six hundred and fifty feet high. Its principal river is the Rhine, which forms its western and southern boundary, and has many branches in this country. The Neckar is the largest, crossing Baden in the north. The river which you observed in this place is the Kinzig. The Danube, which the Germans call the Donau, rises in Baden. In the southeast the country borders on Lake Constance, or, in German, Boden See. The climate is salubrious, but it is cold in the mountains, where they have snow during the greater part of the year.

"Baden is divided into four circles, or provinces, which are again divided into bailiwicks, or counties, and communes, or towns. Two thirds of the people are Roman Catholics; the rest are Protestant, with a sprinkling of Jews, who are found in all parts of Germany. There is a Catholic university at Freiburg, and a Protestant one at Heidelberg, which is so celebrated that it has not a few American students. There are two thousand common schools, and several establishments of higher grade.

"The government is an hereditary constitutional monarchy, the Grand Duke being the sovereign. It has a legislative body, composed of two chambers, the upper of which consists of the nobility and members appointed by the Grand Duke, and the lower of sixty-eight deputies, chosen indirectly by the people. But I do not think it is necessary to describe, at any great length, these small German states, and I give you Baden as a specimen of what most of them are."

The next morning the company took the train for Freiburg, and in a couple of hours reached their destination, where they immediately divided themselves into small parties, in order to see the cathedral, or minster, and other sights, within the allotted time. Those who travelled in the same compartment of the railway carriage usually came together on these occasions for the same reason that united them on the road. Paul Kendall zealously placed himself at the side of Grace, though she was as impartial as a just judge between him and the captain of the ship.

The minster is a Gothic church, and almost the only one in Germany which is actually finished. It was commenced in the twelfth century, and one of the princes of Zähringen, from whom the present Grand Duke is descended, contributed largely to the vast expense; but it would probably have been unfinished, like many similar grand structures, if the people of Freiburg had not taxed themselves to the utmost, and made great sacrifices to insure its completion. The spire is of beautiful fret-work, nearly four hundred feet high. The interior is grand, and something about it gives the beholder a peculiar feeling of solemnity — perhaps the thought that men have worshipped there for six hundred years. It contains some choice paintings, which are carefully cherished as the productions of the old masters. A glance at the university, the Kaufhaus, the statue of Schwarz, the inventor of gunpowder, and a walk around the *Schlossberg*, or Castle Hill, which commands a splendid view of the Black Forest Mountains, exhausted the place, and at the time appointed the party reassembled at the railroad station, where Mr. Arbuckle had gathered together half a dozen diligences, in which the company were to proceed to Schaffhausen, in Switzerland. He knew how much interest the story-readers feel in the Black Forest, and as the party had already visited Basle, he proposed to take his charge across the country, which would enable them to see some of the finest mountain scenery in Germany, and more of the manners and customs of the people than could be observed in the large towns on the railroad. He had already sent forward his courier to make preparations for the accommodation of his party.

Two days were to be occupied in reaching the Rhine. The first part of the journey was over a level plain highly cultivated. The road soon begins to ascend; and this locality is called *Himmelreich*, or Heaven, to distinguish it by contrast from the *Höllenthal*, or Valley of Hell, a deep and romantic gorge which lies beyond. The students enjoyed the scenery, and those who were disposed, walked for miles up the long hills, to the great satisfaction of the driver. The students of the German language had abundant opportunities to practise their gutturals, and none but sufferers know what a pleasure it is to have a genuine native understand their sentences.

The pedestrians made brief halts at the water-mills, houses, and fields on the way, and were invariably treated with the utmost kindness and consideration. "*Bitte, geben sie mir ein Glas Wasser,*" was repeated so many times that all understood it. The fact that they were Americans insured them a warm welcome, and many an inquiry was made for "*meinem Sohn* in Amerika." The "walkists" enjoyed this intercourse with the people so much that they walked till they were unnecessarily fatigued.

"*Bitte, geben sie mir Geld,*" said a German, stepping up to the carriage which contained Dr. Winstock, and those who were so careful to keep near him.

He was a young man, with a big pipe in his mouth, a big stick in his hand, and a big knapsack on his back. He was pretty well dressed, and was in company with three others, who asked for money in like manner of different persons of the party. The doctor asked him a few questions, and then gave him two or three kreutzers, which he accepted with many thanks.

"Those are very respectable beggars," said Paul, as the man left the diligence.

"They are not beggars, but *handwerksburschen.*"

"What are they?"

"Travelling journeymen. No apprentice can obtain his freedom, and be competent to set up in business for himself, till he has spent several years in travelling, and in working at his trade in foreign countries. This is to increase his knowledge and his skill, and you will see hundreds of them on the roads all over Germany. They become, under this system, very skilful workmen, for they learn the various methods of work in different countries. They often understood two or three languages besides their own. They keep a kind of diary of their travels in a book furnished to them by the trade-society to which they belong, in which also their employers write testimonials of their good conduct. It is often the case that they cannot obtain work, and are compelled to ask charity on the roads. It is a hard life to lead, but it produces skilful mechanics."

"What was that man's trade?" asked Grace.

"He is a baker."

At a solitary inn in Steig the party found a dinner ready for them, consisting mainly of trout, which were very nice. From this point the road went up a steep hill, which required an extra horse to each diligence, though most of the boys walked up. At Neustadt, a town of fifteen hundred inhabitants, vast numbers of wooden clocks are manufactured, and the raising of singing birds is a common occupation. Just before sunset the excursionists arrived at Donaueschingen, where they were to spend the night. The place contains about three thousand inhabitants, and is the residence of Prince Fürstenberg, who was one of the mediatized sovereigns — his territory having by treaty been assigned to Baden.

A walk to his palace was immediately taken by the tourists. It is a plain modern edifice, with an extensive garden, which the travellers were permitted to visit. In one corner a circular basin was pointed out to them by their guide. The water, clear as crystal, bubbled up from a spring in the bottom, and was conveyed from the basin, by an underground tunnel, into the Briegach, a stream which flows down from the mountains.

"This spring is said to be the source of the Danube," said Dr. Winstock. "From this point the stream takes the name of Danube, though that into which it flows comes from miles away."

"'Large streams from little fountains flow,'" replied Paul.

"Yes; and from a great many of them," added the surgeon. "The country in this vicinity is like a sponge, it is so full of springs, which feed the great river. The Neckar rises a few miles north of us. We are, therefore, on the summit of the water-shed of Europe; for of two drops of rain which fall side by side near us, one may find its way into the Danube, and be carried down to the Black Sea, while the other, by the Neckar and the Rhine, may reach the North Sea."

The students wandered about the town till it was too dark to see anything, and most of them were tired enough to sleep, even under the feather beds which the Germans insist upon using as a coverlet. In the morning the journey was renewed in the diligences. The scenery was still very fine, and from the top of a high hill called the Rande, the students obtained a splendid view of the mountains of Switzerland, of the broad expanse of Lake Constance, and the towers of the city. Descending the long hill, the tourists entered Switzerland, and at five o'clock were set down at the Schweitzer Hof in Schaffhausen, near the falls.

The students had been riding so long that they were glad to be at liberty again, and hastened into the hotel gardens, which extend down to the river. It was rather late to visit the falls, and the company were piped together around a kind of kiosk, in which Professor Mapps presented himself.

"Do not be alarmed, young gentlemen," said the instructor, good-naturedly. "I will not detain you long, but I am reminded that I have not given you the Rhine in detail. Here on its banks, and in sight of its grandest cataract, I will say a few words to you about it. The river rises in two small lakes in the mountains near St. Gothard, seventy-five hundred feet above the sea. It descends four thousand feet in going twelve miles. Fifty miles from its source, at Reicherau, it is two hundred and fifty feet wide, and becomes navigable for river boats. Its volume of waters is continually increased by the flow from its branches, till it discharges itself into Lake Constance, which may be regarded as a widening of the river.

"The lake is forty-four miles long and nine miles wide. Its greatest depth is nine hundred and sixty-four feet. Its waters are dark-green in color, and very clear. Twenty-five different kinds of fish are mentioned as caught in the lake. It is navigated by steamers, eight or ten of which ply between the various ports, and carry on considerable commerce. It is thirteen hundred and forty-four feet above the level of the sea.

"The Rhine issues from the lake at Constance, and, flowing a few miles westward, again expands into the Unter See, which is thirty feet lower than the upper lake. It gradually contracts till the stream is about three hundred feet wide at this point. Steamers formerly ran from Constance to Schaffhausen; but since the completion of the railroad they have discontinued their trips. The falls which you see, and will visit on Monday morning, are seventy feet high. Below the cataract the river is navigable for boats without obstacles as far as Laufenburg, where its width is reduced to fifty feet, and its waters rush down a series of rapids. Here boats ascend and descend by the aid of ropes, after their cargoes have been discharged. At this place the young Lord Montague, the last male of his line, was drowned while his boat was descending the rapids in this manner. On the same day his family mansion in England was destroyed by fire. From this point to Basle the fall is only fifty feet.

"From Basle to Mayence, a distance of two hundred miles, the Rhine flows in a northerly direction. The current is very swift as far as Strasburg, to which place it is navigable for vessels of one hundred tons, though they are "tracked" by horses on the upward passage. The bed of the river is wide in this part, and contains numerous islands. At Mayence the course of the river changes to west, and again at Bingen to the north-west, where the mountains again force it into a narrow channel; and for fifty miles the stream flows through a beautiful region, where the hills extend to its very banks, and many of their summits are crowned with old castles. Below Cologne, the Rhine runs through a low and flat country. The lower part of the river I have already described in Holland."

The professor finished his brief lecture, and the party spent the rest of the day in wandering about the garden, and in watching the flow of the mighty river, as it tumbled over the precipice. The next day was Sunday, and the excursionists attended church at the town three miles distant. On Monday morning the tourists crossed the bridge, and hastened to the garden of the Castle of Lauffen, where were platforms, stagings and kiosks, for the convenience of visitors, which afford the best views of the cataract. One of these balconies projects out over the fall, and the party gathered on this, and beclouded with mist and spray, gazed at the wild rush of waters. Two rocks on the precipice separate the cataract into three divisions. Below is a semi-circular basin, whose waters are lashed into a heavy sea by the plunging torrent which falls into it. Boats ply between the foot of the rock on which the Castle of Laufen stands and a square tower on the opposite shore. These light craft make heavy weather of it, but with ordinary caution they are safe enough.

There was nothing else to see at Schaffhausen, and the excursionists took the train for Constance. The last portion of the trip was on the banks of the Unter See, separated from the main body of the lake by a peninsula. The ride was less than two hours, and the party reached the " Goldener Adler " in time for dinner. Most of the Swiss hotels serve two or three dinners, *table d'hôte*, every day, the first being at one, and the last at five o'clock, the prices of which are from three to five francs.

" Young gentlemen, in what country is Constance?" asked Professor Mapps, when the party had assembled to visit the objects of interest in the town.

" In Switzerland."

" No."

" We certainly crossed the Rhine on an iron bridge, when we came into the place," replied one of the students.

" That is very true, but Constance belongs to the

Grand Duchy of Baden. It was formerly a free city, but was annexed to Austria in 1549, and ceded to Baden in 1805. It once had forty thousand inhabitants, but now has only eight thousand. It is a very old city, as you may judge from the buildings you have already seen, many of which are just as they were four hundred years ago. "The town is of great historical interest."

"What was the Council of Constance, sir?" asked one of the students.

"I will tell you when we visit the Kaufhaus," replied the professor.

Attended by several guides, the excursionists walked to the minster, a Gothic structure founded in the eleventh century, but rebuilt in the sixteenth. The guides indicated the spot where Huss stood when sentenced to be burned to death. From this church the party went to the Kaufhaus.

CHAPTER XIV.

THE STORM ON LAKE CONSTANCE.

THE Kaufhaus is situated near the border of the lake. It was built for a warehouse in 1388. The party were conducted immediately to a large room with wooden pillars.

"This is the Kaufhaus, and this apartment is the one in which the Council of Constance held its sessions," said Mr. Mapps.

"What's a Kaufhaus?" asked one of the boys who did not study German.

"What does *Kaufen* mean?"

"To buy."

"Then it is a *buy*-house. It is a company's hall, like Goldsmiths' Hall, Fishmongers', and others in London. The Council of Constance assembled in 1414, and continued its sessions for three years and a half. It was called to regulate the affairs of the Catholic Church, especially in regard to the schism caused by some of the popes taking up their abode in Avignon, France. Gregory XI. went from the residence of his immediate predecessors to Rome in 1377, where he died the next year. The Romans wanted a native of their own city to be pope. An Italian — Urban VI. — was elected by the cardinals; but, as he was not a Roman, there was much dissatisfaction. The French cardinals protested against the election, and created Robert of Geneva pope, under the titleof Clement VII., who established himself at Avignon. Urban had three successors, the last of whom was Gregory XII. The Avignon pope was followed by Benedict XIII., who maintained his claim to the papal chair till his death in 1424.

"There were two popes: the church was divided, and in doubt as to which was the rightful successor of St. Peter. Gregory declared, at his accession, that he would resign if Benedict at Avignon would do the same. An attempt was made to get rid of both of them, so that they could agree upon a third. The Council of Pisa deposed both, and elected Alexander V. Benedict refused to vacate his chair; and Gregory retained his position because his rival refused to compromise. Instead of getting rid of one, the church had now three popes who claimed the chair. Alexander died in 1410; and his successor, John XXIII., called the Council of Constance. It was not a meeting of bishops merely, but was attended by cardinals, archbishops, ambassadors of kings, knights, and delegates from universities. John presided at the first session, and was invited to resign the pontifical office. He promised to do so if Gregory and Benedict would do the same; but the next night he fled secretly to Schaffhausen, and from thence to Freiburg. After much trouble, negotiations were opened with him, and he resigned his office. He was afterwards thrown into prison with Huss. Gregory was a good man, and gave the council no trouble, and for the sake of peace yielded up his high office. But Benedict was obdurate to the end, claiming to be pope, even after all his followers had forsaken him. The council attempted to make terms with him; but when he refused to yield, it condemned and deposed him, electing Martin V. to the papal chair.

"The council also gave its attention to the heresy of Wycliffe, whose doctrines it condemned, commanding that his books should be burned, and decreeing that his remains should be disinterred and burned. Huss was condemned to the stake; and his disciple, Jerome of Prague, having retracted his anti-Catholic doctrines, and then relapsed, shared his fate a year afterwards."

In the hall are the chairs occupied, at the sittings of the council, by the Emperor Sigismund and by the pope; a model of the dungeon in which Huss was confined, with the real door and other parts which had been preserved, and the car on which the reformer was drawn to the place of execution. The house in which he lodged is pointed out in one of the streets. The field wherein he suffered, with the spot where the stake stood, is shown to those who are curious enough to visit it.

The students examined the quaint old buildings in the town with much interest. In the middle of the afternoon, they embarked in the steamer for Friedrichshafen. The weather had been warm and oppressive, for the season, for the last two days; and there were strong indications of a change. A barometer at the hotel in Constance indicated an unusual depression. The students dreaded a storm of long continu-

THE ADVENTURE ON LAKE CONSTANCE. — Page 227.

ance, they were so impatient to see the wonders which were yet in store for them ; and the idea of being shut up in a small hotel, for two or three days, was not pleasant in the anticipation, whatever it might prove to be in reality.

By the time the steamer was half way to her destination, the wind began to come in fitful gusts, increasing in force, till the captain of the steamer wore a rather anxious expression on his face. The young salts laughed at the idea of a fresh-water tempest; and if anybody else was alarmed, they were not. The steamer began to tumble about ; but nothing serious occurred, though some of the lady passengers were sea sick. Others, who had never seen a storm at sea, were frightened, and screamed every time the boat gave a heavy lurch.

" Do you think there is any danger, Commodore Kendall," asked Grace, thrilled by the cries of the females.

" I don't see how there can be. If this boat is good for anything, she ought to ride out one of these fresh-water gales," replied Paul.

" It is going to be a fearful storm."

" I should think it would be, from the indications of the barometer."

" Do you see that boat, Paul ? " said Shuffles, pointing to one of the Swiss small craft, which was laboring heavily in the billows.

" She is making bad weather of it," added Paul, as he examined the position of the storm-tossed craft.

" The boatman don't seem to know what he is about," continued Shuffles, who had for some time been studying the movements of the boat. "She lowered her sail a while ago, and she seems to be rolling at the mercy of the waves."

The steamer was headed towards her, and the party on board of her soon discovered that the boatman was trying to put a reef in his sail. Besides himself, the boat contained a lady.

"I suppose that is a Swiss boatman," said Shuffles. "If he is, he knows no more about a boat than a mountaineer who never saw one."

"That's so," added Paul, anxiously.

"He has put her before the wind, and is trying to hoist his mainsail."

A fierce gust struck the canvas, as he began to hoist it, carrying out the boom, and whirling the boat up into the wind. Certainly the person on board of her had pluck enough; for he stuck to the halyards, though he was nearly jerked overboard by the sudden pitching and rolling of the craft. Recovering the sheet which had run out into the water, he took his place at the helm. He flattened down the sail, when the flaw had spent its force, and headed his boat towards Friedrichshafen. The next gust that struck the sail carried her down so that the water poured in over her lee rail by the barrel. The lady screamed lustily; and the tones of her voice indicated that she did not belong to the Swiss peasantry.

"Help! Help!" she shrieked; and her voice thrilled the souls of all on board the steamer.

"Cannot something be done?" cried Grace.

"I don't see what can be done," replied Paul.

"The boatman is a fool!" said Shuffles, impatiently. "Why don't he let out his sheet, or luff her up?"

"Can't you do something?" pleaded Grace, earnestly, as she clung to the railing over the cabin ladder.

"Help! Help!" shouted the boatman, in good English; and it was plain that he was not a Swiss.

Indeed, the lady and gentleman could now be seen plainly enough to ascertain that they were English or American. Both of them were well dressed, and both were quite young.

"We can launch the steamer's boat, if the captain will let us," suggested Paul.

The wind threw the boat round at this moment, and the sail shook violently in the blast. Then it filled again, and drove her directly into the path of the steamer, which was now close aboard of her.

"Stop her! Stop her!" shouted several persons, in French and German.

The captain gave the order to stop the engine; but it was doubtful whether it was given in season to save the unfortunate couple in the boat. Paul and Shuffles rushed to the bow of the steamer, and the latter climbed upon the rail just as the mast of the boat swayed over against the stem. He seized it, and nimbly slid down into the craft. As the steamer was running nearly against the wind, her headway was easily checked by a turn or two of the wheels backward; though the boat bumped pretty hard against the steamer once or twice.

Shuffles evidently believed that skilful management alone could save the sail-boat, and the lives of those who were in her. His mission, as he understood it, was to supply this needed skill. The steamer had only a single boat on deck, which was so dried up by the sun, that none of the salt-water tars believed it would float. She had only a single pair of oars, and it would be impossible to make any headway against the gale in it. The captain declared that he could only save the imperilled voyagers by running alongside their boat, and taking them out of it: he could do nothing by sending his jolly-boat after them.

By excellent good fortune, the steamer was checked at the right moment; though Shuffles supposed the boat would be stove, and he only got into her for the purpose of assisting the young lady. The captain backed his vessel so that she left the craft alone again. But the bold commander of the Young America was not dismayed by the situation. He instantly let go the halyards, and secured the sail as it came down. He glanced at the trembling lady, who crouched in the stern to save her head from the threshing of the boom. Grasping one of the oars, he pulled the boat around till she lay head to the wind. She was almost water-logged, and he saw that it was necessary to relieve her of some of this extra weight before she could be manageable.

"Won't they save us?" gasped the lady, glancing at the steamer, which was drifting rapidly away from them.

"Don't be alarmed, miss," said Shuffles, as he seized a kind of tub which was filled with fish-lines and other angling gear.

"What shall I do?" asked the young man, whose

pluck had by this time become quite exhausted in his vain battle with the elements.

"Can you pull an oar?" demanded Shuffles, rather sharply, of the clumsy boatman.

"I can."

"Take this one, then, and keep her head as it is now."

The young man took the oar, and pulled as he was directed; and Shuffles went to work vigorously with the tub, in throwing out the water. He labored so diligently and effectually, that in a few moments he had relieved the boat of the great burden of water within her. While he did so, he gave the young man such directions as enabled him to keep the craft poised with her head to the fierce gusts that beat upon her. In this position she rose and fell on the great billows, and shipped very little water. The steamer had started her wheels again; but while she did not venture very near the boat, she lay by to render assistance if the latter were swamped. The lady, finding that the frail craft, under her present management, behaved very well, sorely as she was tried by the tempest, was encouraged.

"Can I do anything?" she asked, in soft notes, though they were still shaken by her fears.

"No, miss: if you will only keep perfectly still, I can take care of her."

"Here is a basin," said she, holding up the implement. "Shall I throw the water out of her?"

"If you please," answered Shuffles, willing to encourage her; for even the belief that one is doing some good, in an emergency, assists in quieting one's fears.

She went to work with a zeal which indicated a strong will, and if she did not accomplish as much as she wished to do, it was only because the uneasy tossing of the boat defeated her good intentions.

"Steady!" said Shuffles, to the young man at the oar. "You heave her round so that she will take the wind on the other hand. Now pull away with all your might!" he added, as the boat began to fall off.

"Are we going to stay here all night?" asked the other, who was nearly exhausted by the violence of his efforts to keep her head up to the blast.

"No, no!" replied Shuffles, impatiently, as he put out the other oar, and assisted his companion, when the boat was in danger of catching the wind on her beam. "I will get sail on her in a few moments."

In the lull of the blast, the young commander overhauled the sail, and corrected the non-nautical reefing of his companion.

"Now, mind your eye!" shouted Shuffles, as he grasped the halyards.

"What shall I do?"

"Pull away!"

"I'm losing my wind," gasped the sufferer, who had really struggled with the oar till his exertions and excitement had nearly disabled him.

"Pull away for half a minute more," replied Shuffles, as he ran up the main-sail, which beat and thrashed fearfully in the gale.

Having secured the halyards, the new skipper sprang to the helm, and seized the main sheet. Placing the lady on the weather side, he seated himself on the rail, with the sheet in his right hand, and the tiller in his left.

"Now let her go it!" he shouted to the young man. "Jump up to windward, and keep your weather eye open!"

The weary oarsman was glad to be relieved from his exhausting task, and promptly obeyed the order. Shuffles had put two reefs in the sail; but without the most skilful handling, the boat could not carry even this short canvas in such a fierce tempest. It was not such a sea as rages in a storm upon the ocean, but it was altogether too rough for any ordinary boat. It was not a long, bounding, rolling billow, but a short, angry wave, that tried the timbers of the Swiss boat. As soon as the rower ceased his occupation, the head of the craft fell off, the sail filled, and she careened down to the gunwale.

"We shall certainly tip over!" gasped the lady, clinging to the rail.

"Don't be afraid, miss. This boat behaves very handsomely, and is stiff enough to weather a gale," added Shuffles, confidently, as the little vessel leaped upon one of the snappy, snarling billows, and then plunged down into the trough of the sea.

"I never was terrified in a boat before," said she, shaking with alarm.

"It is a heavy storm, and not just the weather for a lady to be out in. Don't be frightened, miss. The boat is doing very well under her double reefs, and she will weather it, if you only believe in her."

There came another tremendous gust, which seemed to strike the boat like a blow from an immense sledgehammer; and she bent down under it till her rail was buried in the foaming waters. Shuffles " touched her up" a little, and let out the sheet till the sail shook in the blast. The boat righted, and for a moment had a partial respite from the savage pounding of the tempest. The young man, who clung to the weather rail with a tenacity which indicated that he had not yet recovered his self-possession, glanced ahead, and then at the steamer, whose course now diverged from that of the sail-boat, and the two craft were increasing their distance from each other.

"We wish to go to Friedrichshafen," said he, apparently troubled by the discovery he had made.

"So do I," replied Shuffles, quietly, without taking his eye from the sail.

"This will not bring us there," added the ex-skipper.

"Any port in a storm," said the gallant helmsman. "If I let the boat fall off enough to lay a course for Friedrichshafen, she will fill in the twinkling of an eye."

"I don't see why she should," added the young man, evidently not satisfied with the action of the new skipper.

"I think you ought to see it, after you have half filled the boat yourself on that tack. Don't you understand that it would throw the boat into the trough of the sea, and make her roll? Look at that steamer. I am not sure that she will not be obliged to throw her head up into it, and lay too for a while."

"Pray do just as you think best, sir," interposed the lady.

"That is what I intend to do, miss. Really there is only one thing you can do when it blows like this — keep her head up to it."

Again it was necessary for Shuffles to use all his skill and strength, as the heavy gusts were repeated, to prevent the boat from filling. Easing off the sheet, and crowding her up into the wind, the boat weathered another shock, and then had another brief respite. The spray dashed in the fierce blast like hailstones into the face and eyes of the intrepid captain, and he was nearly blinded by the charge. His hands were full, holding the tiller and the sheet. Securing the latter with his knee, he tried to take his handkerchief from his pocket, to wipe the water from his eyes. But a jerk of the boat compelled him to grasp the helm suddenly, and the wind carried away the handkerchief like a feather.

"My eyes are full of spray," said he, without even glancing at the flight of the lost article.

"You have lost your handkerchief," replied the young lady, tenderly. "Pray take mine."

"I am obliged to use both hands. May I trouble you to wipe the water from my eyes? I can hardly see, I am so blinded."

The young lady promptly complied with the request, and holding on to the rail with her left hand, she wiped the water from the captain's eyes.

"Thank you," said he, greatly relieved by the act.

"Let me change seats with you, Feodora," interposed the young man. "Perhaps I may be able to assist in working the boat."

"Sit still! Don't move!" shouted Shuffles, sternly.

"I only wish to help you," replied the other.

"You will help me most by keeping entirely still," answered Shuffles, as another fierce blast struck the sail, and required the skipper's whole attention. Again the cutting spray blinded him, though, as any other skilful boatman can, he was able to comprehend by the feeling the motion of the boat.

"Shall I wipe your eyes again?" asked the young lady.

"If you please."

Gently, her eyes beaming with interest and sympathy, the lady wiped the drops of water from his eyes. Though her companion said nothing, he did not seem to regard the operation with much favor. Very likely he thought it was quite unnecessary to wipe the skipper's eyes at every fresh gust. Again he proposed to change places with her; but Shuffles peremptorily forbade the movement, either because he thought the young lady could wipe his eyes better than the young man, or because he was afraid some accident would happen in making the change.

The storm rather increased than diminished in violence, and for an hour Shuffles held on his course. The steamer had gone into Friedrichshafen, though she had been obliged, in some of the fiercest blasts, to throw her head up into the wind, and hold on till its fierceness subsided a little. After every gust, the young lady wiped the eyes of her gallant preserver, for as such she regarded him; and such he doubtless was, for the boat would have gone to the bottom long before without his skilful assistance. She soon learned to perform the kindly office without a word, though the captain did not fail to thank her every time.

The boat did not make rapid progress; by keeping her close-hauled, continually easing off the sheet, and touching her up, she made considerable lee way. At the end of two hours, and when it was beginning to grow dark, Shuffles found himself nearing the shore on the north side of the lake. He must either make a harbor or go about on the other tack. It was impossible to land on the exposed shore, against which the waves were beating in the madness of their fury. He was at least ten miles above the port to which he and his passenger wished to go. Directly ahead of him was a point of land, which projected out into the lake. Beyond it there was an indentation in the shore, within which he might possibly find a partial shelter from the fury of the storm. It was doubtful whether he could weather the point; but he did not wish to tack, and stand farther out into the lake. The night was coming on, and all his skill and courage could not insure the safety of the boat in the darkness and on unknown waters.

Hauling in the sheet a little, he braced the craft sharp up, and struggled with the elements to clear the headland. He looked anxiously into the green waters for any shoals on the lee bow. Fortunately there was no obstruction in his path, and the boat weathered the headland, though without the fraction of a point to spare. Easing off the sheet, he ran the boat into the bay, and in a few moments she was slightly sheltered by the shore to the eastward. This friendly relief enabled him to keep her away a little, and run for the head of the bay, where he perceived an opening, which looked like the mouth of a river.

No longer cramped by the helm and the sheet, the boat flew on her course, and Shuffles presently satisfied himself that the opening he saw was really the mouth of a stream. He realized that the battle had been fought and won, but he said nothing to his fellow voyagers, who were silent and anxious. On sped the boat, and as the waves became less furious, he gave her more sheet, and she darted into the still waters of the river, which was not more than a hundred feet wide, and with banks high enough to afford perfect protection to the storm-shaken craft. As she rushed into the quiet stream, Shuffles let go the sheet, and the boat gradually lost her headway. Putting the helm down, he ran her gently upon the shore, and the grating of her keel upon the gravelly bank was sweet music to the ears of the voyagers.

"You are all right now," said Shuffles, as he rose from his seat in the stern sheets.

Almost for the first time since he boarded the sail-boat, he looked into the face of the young lady. Her clothing was thoroughly drenched by the spray, and her face was moist as though she were a mermaid just emerged from the depths of the ocean. But even in her present plight Shuffles saw that she was a very pretty girl. She was shivering with cold, and it was necessary to do something for her comfort.

"We are really safe," replied the lady, with a grateful smile. "We owe our lives to you, sir."

"We are exceedingly grateful to you for your service," added the young man.

"I am very glad to have had an opportunity to serve you," replied Shuffles, addressing his words to the young lady.

"I shall remember you, and be grateful to you as

long as I live," continued the lady, warmly, as she bestowed upon him an earnest look, which a skilful observer would have interpreted as one of admiration.

"But where are we?" asked the young man.

"I don't know, except that we must be ten or a dozen miles to the eastward of Friedrichshafen," answered Shuffles.

"What shall we do?" asked his male companion.

"There are probably houses not far distant. You had better go on shore, and when you see one, let us know it."

"Perhaps you would prefer to go," suggested the young man, glancing at the lady.

"Having worked hard in the boat, I prefer to rest a little while," replied Shuffles.

"Go, Sir William," added the lady, reproachfully.

Sir William! Captain Shuffles was rather taken aback to find he had been sending a young baronet to look for a house; but then he regarded himself as the peer of any baronet, and he did not apologize.

Sir William leaped over the bow of the boat to the shore, and climbed up the bank. He cast a glance back at the companions of his voyage, and then disappeared.

"I think you must be a sailor, sir," said the young lady, when her friend had gone.

"I am, miss. I am; at least I ought to be, since I am the captain of a ship."

"A captain — and so young! O, I know what you are!" exclaimed she. "You belong to the American Academy Ship."

"I do."

"But I did not see you at the emperor's ball in Paris."

"No. I was absent on duty."

"I had the pleasure of dancing with a captain on that occasion."

"I was appointed on the first of this month," explained Shuffles.

"I know your uniform very well; and I am glad to see you. I am sure you are worthy of your high position."

"Thank you, miss. You are very kind."

"I should have been at the bottom of Lake Constance at this moment, if you had been less gallant and skilful."

"Perhaps not," replied Shuffles, wondering all the time who the young lady was.

The hail of Sir William from the bank above interrupted the conversation. The boat had grounded a rod from the bank of the stream, and Shuffles gallantly bore the fair passenger to the shore in his arms. Assisting her up the bank, the party soon reached a cottage a short distance from the mouth of the river. The young nobleman imperiously ordered great fires and refreshments. He spoke German fluently, and his commands were promptly obeyed. The rain now poured down in floods, and the party congratulated themselves upon escaping this added discomfort.

CHAPTER XV.

LADY FEODORA AND SIR WILLIAM.

HOUR after hour the storm-beaten party sat before a blazing fire in the cottage of the German peasant. Their clothing was dry, and they were quite comfortable. The only thing that disturbed them was the anxiety of their friends at Friedrichshafen. Possibly something else disturbed the young baronet, for the lady, ingenuous enough to talk and act as she felt, seemed to be delighted with her gallant preserver. After they entered the house, Shuffles heard Sir William call her Lady Feodora. She also belonged to the nobility, and he soon learned that she was the youngest daughter of the Earl of Blankville. Sir William's father was dead, and though only eighteen, he was a baronet. They were travelling with their friends.

Lady Feodora declared that she adored sailors, and Sir William was afraid she spoke only the truth. They had been affianced by their parents; but the young lady did not seem to feel a very deep interest in the baronet; and on the other hand, she did seem to feel a deep interest in the commander of the Young America. His courage, skill, and energy had made a deep impression upon her; and the signal service he had rendered called forth all her gratitude. She was only

16

sixteen, and perhaps had not judgment enough to see that it was perilous to cast pleasant glances at a young American tar, and might disturb the calculations of her prudent parents.

The wind howled, and the rain poured all night long; but the party were in comfortable circumstances. They were too thankful to have escaped the perils of the storm to complain of the rudeness of their quarters. It was not possible to go to their friends either by water or by land, till the tempest had abated, and they were disposed to make the best of their situation.

"I was not aware that they had such heavy storms on these fresh-water lakes," said Shuffles, after they had partaken of the simple fare set before them by their host.

"Nor I," replied Lady Feodora. "If I had, I should not have gone so far in an open boat. We went across the lake to Romanshorn, but Sir William said he knew all about a boat."

"So I do, under ordinary circumstances," replied the baronet, rather nettled at the implied censure.

"It was a very savage storm," added Shuffles.

"I never saw anything like it, even in the Channel," said Feodora. "But you seemed to handle the boat just as easily as though the wind came only in zephyrs."

She bestowed another glance of admiration upon the modest tar, who explained that he had always been used to boats from his childhood, and he felt more at home on the deck of a ship than he did in the parlor of his father's house. They talked of the perils of the day till midnight. A bed had been provided for the lady, but the two young gentlemen lay on the floor before the fire. In the morning the clouds broke away, and the sun rose bright and clear. The calm that follows the storm prevailed upon the lake. The party ate their simple breakfast, and Sir William paid liberally for their accommodations at the cottage.

The manner of reaching Friedrichshafen was thoroughly discussed. They could go to Lindau, and take the steamer, or proceed in the sail-boat. Sir William proposed to take Feodora with him, while Shuffles sailed the boat back alone. The lady protested. She was not afraid-to sail back in the boat, if the captain would manage it; and this arrangement was finally agreed upon, though the baronet was not at all pleased with it. They embarked, and a little breeze came to their aid; but it was eleven o'clock when they reached their destination.

"I do not know at what hotel our ship's company is stopping," said Shuffles, as they landed.

"My friends are at the Deutschen Haus; and you must come there with us," replied Lady Feodora. "My father and mother are there, and they will be delighted to see you."

"Perhaps our people are there," added Shuffles.

They walked to the hotel named, and found that the American party was there. As they approached the house, an elderly lady and gentleman rushed down from the veranda, and grasped Feodora in their arms at the same moment. They were her parents, and wept tears of joy over her safe return.

"We thought you were lost," said the fond mother.

"I have sent boats in every direction to look for you," added the father. "Mr. Lowington, the principal of the Marine Academy, who is here with his students, assured me you were safe."

"I am safe, father, thanks to Captain Shuffles," replied Feodora, turning to the young commander.

"His Lordship, the Earl of Blankville," interposed Sir William, introducing the hero of the day.

The gentleman grasped the hand of Shuffles, and expressed his gratitude in the warmest terms.

"We have heard part of the story, and we watched the boat till it disappeared in the distance," added his lordship. "It was a terrible hour for us all."

"Worse than death," sighed the countess, as she pressed her daughter to her heart again.

"Mr. Lowington assured us that the young man who had so daringly thrown himself into the boat would certainly take her to the shore. But we could only hope, rather than believe."

"It was a heavy blow," said Shuffles.

"It was fearful!" exclaimed the earl, with a shudder, as he thought of the anxiety and terror they had endured. "I owe you an everlasting debt of gratitude."

"I only did what the occasion seemed to require of me, and I am as thankful as any one can be, that I succeeded in getting the boat to the shore," answered Shuffles.

"It was remarkably fortunate that you were at hand, for I don't believe there is another person on the continent of Europe who could have managed the matter so cleverly."

"Really, I think your lordship over-estimates my services."

By this time Mr. Lowington and the young America's party came out to welcome Shuffles. They astonished him by giving three rousing cheers, and the captain was again on the top of the wave of popularity. Mr. Lowington said he was satisfied, at the time of it, that he would take the boat to the shore, and save both of his passengers, so great was his confidence in Shuffles. The earl acknowledged that his prediction had been fully verified.

"You had a rough time, Shuffles," said the principal.

"Rather, sir;" and the affair was discussed at length.

"We have seen the town; but we cannot leave by train for Ulm till two this afternoon. If there is anything here you wish to see, you must improve your time," added Mr. Lowington.

"What is there to be seen?"

"Nothing but the Château of the King of Würtemberg, and some old buildings. But Mr. Mapps is about to give a lecture, from which you shall be excused if you desire it."

"No, sir; I think I will hear the lecture," replied the captain, as he followed the principal into the coffee-room, where all the students had collected.

Lord Blankville's party had been informed of the lecture, and desired to attend. Shuffles had hardly seated himself when they entered the room. Lady Feodora had hastily made her toilet; but she looked like a queen, and the captain could hardly believe she was the same person. Those who had attended the emperor's ball in Paris recognized her, and paid their respects. Ben Duncan declared she was as " stunning " as when she wore her white ball-dress. Shuffles gave her a seat, and had the courage to take one by her side, before Sir William could secure the enviable position.

"Würtemberg is a kingdom belonging to the Germanic Confederation," the professor began. "It has an area of about seventy-eight hundred square miles, varying but a few miles from that of the State of Massachusetts. It has a population of one million seven hundred thousand, which during the last ten years has diminished on account of the large emigration to the United States. The government is an hereditary monarchy, and, like so many English stock companies, 'limited.' Freedom of person and property, liberty of speech, and liberty of conscience, are guaranteed by the constitution; but liberty of the press, like the monarchy and the stock companies, is also 'limited.' The legislature is composed of two houses, the higher one being made up of princes and nobles. The present king is Charles I., whose wife is the daughter of Czar Nicholas I. of Russia. The royal family is quite numerous in its various branches, and is connected by marriage with many of the royal houses of Europe. The former Duchy of Würtemberg was made a kingdom in 1806, by Napoleon, after having been enlarged by the annexation of several smaller states. Stuttgart, the capital, is also the largest town, containing a population of fifty thousand. I close this lecture, which I think has not been a very tedious one, with this remarkable fact: In 1840 there was not to be found an individual in the kingdom, above the age of ten years, who could not read and write."

"Is that all?" asked Lady Feodora.

"That's all this time; but sometimes we have to take it for a couple of hours," laughed Shuffles.

"I'm sure I wish he had said more. What do you do now?"

"We go to Ulm at two this afternoon. After that we go to Stuttgart, Carlsruhe, Baden, and then down the Rhine."

"We must go with them, pa," added she, turning to the earl.

"We shall be ready to go to Ulm this afternoon in the same train," replied her father.

"I am delighted!" exclaimed Feodora. "I hope we shall go with you down the Rhine."

Sir William, for some reason or other, did not hope so. In fact, he was rather dumpy and morose.

"Possibly you will," suggested Shuffles.

"What a happy life you must lead, captain!"

"Perhaps you would not think so, if you were at sea with us, when we have to stand watch in the night and the storm, whether it blows high or blows low."

"But you are the captain."

"I was a seaman. It is nearly an hour till dinner time; and I think I shall take a run down to the Château of the king. Of course you have been there," said the captain, suggestively.

"I have, but I should be delighted to go again."

A carriage was called by the earl. It had seats

for only four, and Feodora's father and mother had decided to go. So had Sir William; but his lordship hinted that, as the baronet had already visited the Château, he might stay at the hotel and play with her ladyship's poodle dog. It would require too much space to narrate all that was said and done on this little excursion; but the two young people were very much pleased with the Château, after and very pleased with each other, probably more pleased with each other than with the Château, though the latter was a very beautiful place, as it ought to be for the summer residence of a king. Captain Shuffles handed the noble young lady out and in the carriage, handed her up various steps, into various grottos; indeed, he handed her up and down everything that would afford him any excuse for offering his assistance. Lady Feodora certainly appreciated his kindness, and rewarded him with many a smile.

They returned to the hotel; and though the noble party were in the habit of dining at the aristocratic hour of six, they took places at the *table d'hôte* with the republicans. The party hastened to the railroad station after dinner, and at the appointed hour, were on their way to Ulm. The compartment in which Dr. Winstock, Paul, and the Arbuckles rode, contained one less than usual, for Captain Shuffles — not entirely to the satisfaction of Sir William — occupied a place with the party of the earl. The railway carriages in Germany are generally built with a first-class compartment at one end, while the rest of the space is devoted to the second-class passengers. The former is very luxuriously furnished, the seats having stuffed arms and backs, with a table between the two rows of seats, while the latter has about the same arrangement as is found in the ordinary cars in the United States.

"We have lost our good friend Captain Shuffles," said Grace, with a pleasant smile.

"Perhaps our loss is his gain," added Paul.

"Lady Feodora is very pretty."

"Very; and interesting, too."

"I really pity her every time I look at Sir William."

"Why?" asked Paul, curiously.

"Because she is doomed by her parents to be his wife; and he is a selfish, supercilious fellow, if he is a baronet."

"Her parents seem to be very fond of her; and I am sure they will not sacrifice her, if she don't like him."

"There are a great many considerations of policy which influence these great families," replied Grace. "She seems to like the captain much better than she likes Sir William."

"And I know that he likes her."

"Let us hope for the best," said Grace, gayly, as she glanced out the window at the fine mountain scenery.

"How far is it to Ulm, Dr. Winstock?" asked Paul.

"Fourteen miles," replied the surgeon, with a twinkle of the eye which seemed to mean something.

"Fourteen miles!" exclaimed Paul, glancing at his

watch. "Why, we ought to be nearly there by this time, then."

"The German trains rarely go more than four miles an hour."

"Why, that's no faster than a smart boy can walk."

"Rather, I think."

"You are joking, doctor."

"I never was more serious in my life. This train is not going more than four miles an hour."

"I should say it was going at the rate of twenty."

"I am afraid you have not read your guide-book since you came into Germany," laughed the doctor. "Perhaps it has not occurred to you that a German mile is equal to about four and two thirds English miles."

"I didn't think of that."

"It is sixty-four and a half English miles from the point where we started to Ulm; and the time is over three hours. We shall arrive there at half past five," continued Dr. Winstock.

"I thank you for setting me right," replied Paul. "I have been bothered with the German money."

"I have a copy of the last issue of Harper's Hand Book for Travellers, which I obtained in Paris. It is a capital work for the tourist, for it does not compel him to carry a whole library of guide-books, and is complete enough for ordinary purposes," said Dr. Winstock, taking the neat little volume from his bag. "In connection with each country, you will find the value of its money in United States currency, and the names and value of the several coins in use. In the Prussian states, values are reckoned in *thalers* and *silver groschen.* A *thaler* is about seventy-three cents. A *silver groschen*, of which thirty make a *thaler*, is worth two and two fifths cents."

"What's a *florin* ?"

"A *florin* of Baden, Würtemberg, &c., is forty cents; but a *florin* in Austria is forty-nine cents. The former has sixty *kreutzers*, of two thirds of a cent each, the latter one hundred, of about half a cent each. In Prussian Germany, twelve *pfennings* make a *silver groschen*. Five pfennings, therefore, are about equal to a cent. Of course these values vary with the rates of exchange, and even in the different countries where the currency is used."

It was dark when the train arrived at Ulm, though the tourists obtained an obscure view of the Danube, on which the city is located. After supper, Professor Mapps gave a brief account of the place to the students. It is a fortress and frontier city of Würtemberg, on the right bank of the Danube, and has twenty-five thousand inhabitants. It is largely engaged in linen manufactures, and snails are fattened in the surrounding region, and sent into Austria and other countries, where they are highly esteemed as an article of food. For three centuries the town was an imperial free city, and one of the most thriving in Germany. It is noted in modern times for the disgraceful capitulation of General Mack, in 1805, who surrendered thirty thousand men and sixty guns to the French.

The party slept at the Kronprinz Hotel, and the next day, after a glance at the minster, — which is ranked among the six finest Gothic cathedrals in Germany, and is now a Protestant church, — the excursionists resumed their journey, arriving at Stuttgart in two hours and a half. This city is on the Neckar, and is situated in the midst of a beautiful country, the slopes of whose hills are studded with vineyards. The party, having no time to spare, immediately devoted themselves to the business of sight-seeing, hastening first to the palace of the king, said to contain as many rooms as there are days in the year, though our arithmeticians did not count them. It is a grand edifice, with a tremendous gilt crown over the chief entrance, so that strangers in the city cannot possibly mistake the royal character of the building.

Only a few of the numerous apartments were visited, which contained some fine pictures by German artists, and sculpture by Thorwaldsen. The palace may be said to be in both town and country; for while the front opens upon the grand square of the city, the rear faces an extensive park, which reaches far out into the rural region. The king's stables, containing the finest Arabian horses in Germany, were visited by a portion of the party. The public library next claimed attention. Its catalogue of three hundred thousand volumes includes over three thousand manuscripts, half of which are very rare and valuable. The collection of Bibles, amounting to eighty-five hundred in number, and in sixty different languages, is doubtless the most extensive in the world. The museums of the fine arts and of natural history used up the rest of the day.

The next place to be visited was Carlsruhe, the capital of the Grand Duchy of Baden. It was only a three hours' ride from Stuttgart, and, as the trains connected, the principal decided to proceed at six o'clock in the evening, for he could not otherwise reach his destination till noon the next day. The earl's party had taken apartments at the Hôtel Marquardt for the night, and Shuffles sent word to them that he was about to leave. He was invited to the elegant parlor occupied by his lordship, where he proceeded at once to take leave of Lady Feodora.

"Probably we shall never meet again," said he. "If we —"

"Pray, don't say that, Captain Shuffles," interrupted she, with an expression even more sad than that which the young captain wore. "I hope we may meet many times yet."

"We may, but it is not probable that we shall," added Shuffles. "After remaining a week or ten days longer in Germany, we shall go to Brest, and from there sail for the United States."

"But your ship crosses the ocean again next spring, I think I heard the principal say," interposed the earl.

"Very true; but I may not come in her — I don't know."

"I will not believe we are not to meet again. You must come to England and visit us at Blankville. We shall all be delighted to see you."

All except Sir William.

"I hope I shall have the pleasure of meeting you again. If I do not, I shall remember the hours I have spent with you as the pleasantest of my life," continued Shuffles.

"But I am not going to think of such a thing as

not seeing you again," persisted Lady Feodora. "I shudder every time I recall the circumstances under which we met. But for your daring courage and your wonderful skill, both Sir William and myself would have been drowned."

The young baronet looked as though the actual situation was not much improvement upon the possible one suggested by his affianced, if he was to be " cut out " in this extraordinary manner.

"You over-estimate the value of my services; but however you regard them, I shall always rejoice that I was able to serve you. I must leave now."

" But we shall meet again, and very soon, too," said Lady Feodora, as she extended her hand to the young officer.

The other members of the party each in turn took him by the hand. The earl and his lady manifested a warm interest in the young hero, and seconded the wish of their daughter that they might meet again.

"I am really sorry you are going," said Sir William; but it is doubtful whether he was as sincere as his friends. " Couldn't you contrive it some way so as to drop in upon us at Blankville? It would really be a very great pleasure — it would, upon my honor."

" I am afraid it will be impossible," replied Shuffles, as he bowed himself out of the apartment.

Perhaps Sir William was the only happy person in that group, for there was no doubt that he was glad to get rid of the troublesome hero.

The ship's company took the train at the appointed time, and by ten o'clock were in their rooms at the Hôtel Erbprinz, in the capital of the Grand Duchy of

Baden. As soon as it was light in the morning, the students were scattered through the streets of the town, which, like those of Washington, radiate from a common centre, where the king's palace is located. The meals of the party at the hotels were usually served separate from those of other guests, and at breakfast Professor Mapps had an opportunity to say a word about the city. He told them, what many of them had already ascertained, that it was a very pretty, but very quiet place. It is of modern growth, being unable to boast of much more than a century's duration. Charles, the Margrave of Baden, built a hunting-seat on the spot in 1715, which, on account of the seclusion of the place, he called " Charles's Rest." In the course of time, his retreat was invaded by others, and a city grew up around him, which was called Karlsruhe — the German for the name the Margrave had given his hunting-seat.

The Schloss, or palace, did not essentially differ from a dozen other similar structures the party had seen. In fact, palaces and cathedrals were getting rather stale with them, and they coveted a new sensation, which they were likely to realize at their next stopping-place. Before noon the tourists reached Baden-Baden, and were pleasantly installed at the Hôtel de l'Europe. As the season was somewhat advanced, there was plenty of room, though the glories of the German watering-place were not seen at their height.

The place is called Baden-Baden to distinguish it from Baden in Austria and Baden in Switzerland. It is beautifully located in a lovely valley surrounded by the hills of the Black Forest. Although it has but seven thousand permanent inhabitants, not less than forty thousand visitors have made their abode within its precincts in a single season. It is the most fashionable, and at the same time the most attractive, of the German watering-places. The nobility and gentry, as well as the blacklegs and swindlers of all the nations of Europe, gather there. The country around the town is romantic and pleasing, and with good roads through the forests and up the hills, there is a great variety of delightful walks and drives. Everything which nature and art could do to make the place and its surroundings an attractive abode, has been done.

On the rocky hills above the town are the old and the new castles of the Grand Duke of Baden. The former is of Roman origin, and was occupied by the reigning dukes in the middle ages. The latter is the summer residence of the present sovereign. At the foot of the rocks on which the modern structure is located are the hot springs, thirteen in number, to which the town owes its origin as a health-giving abode. This part of the place is called "Hell" on account of the heat of the springs, which does not permit the snow, even in the coldest weather, to remain upon it. The hottest of these springs has a temperature of $54°$ Réaumur, equal to $153\frac{1}{2}°$ Fahrenheit. Their water is led by pipes to the "Trinkhalle" and baths in the village, the passage having but little effect upon its temperature. A kind of temple is built over the principal spring, which furnishes the hottest and most copious supply of water. There is sufficient evidence that the Romans used these fountains for vapor baths, and other medicinal purposes. The water is perfectly clear, has a saltish taste, and at the spring is not unlike weak broth, though it has a disagreeable odor. It is beneficial for dyspepsia, gout, rheumatism, and scrofulous diseases.

After dinner the tourists commenced their explorations by a visit to *das neue Trinkhalle*, or the New Pump Room, opposite the hotel. The spring waters are conveyed to it in pipes, and in the season the place is crowded with visitors, who drink them in the morning.

The *Conversationshaus* is the grand centre of attraction. It is a magnificent building, surrounded by splendid gardens. In front of it is a Chinese pagoda, intended as a music stand for the band, which plays there twice a day. It contains a large assembly-room, where the company dance at times, a restaurant, a theatre, and other apartments. There are also rooms for gambling, which is the staple amusement, not only for the blacklegs and swindlers, who resort to the establishment, but for the noblility and gentry. The *Conversationshaus* is rented by the government to a company, who pay fifty-five thousand dollars a year for the monopoly of the gaming tables, and pledge themselves to spend one hundred thousand dollars annually upon the walks and buildings. Of course players must lose vast sums of money to enable the keepers of the establishment to pay these large prices. All classes of people gamble, and about one fourth of those who engage in the seductive play are ladies — or rather women, though they include not a few of the nobility.

Balls, concerts, promenades, and the theatre, as well as the exciting amusement of the gaming tables, keep the visitors well employed during the season; and when they weary of the din of gayety, a walk of five minutes will lead them to the solitudes of the forests and the mountains. There is a library and reading-room in operation in the midst of the scene of the revelry. The students spent the afternoon in wandering through these brilliant halls; and some of them observed, with a feeling akin to terror, the operations of rouge-et-noir and roulette. No one spoke at the tables, and no one but players were allowed to be seated. If any of the boys, after the exciting sport had become familiar to them, were tempted to try their hand, they had not money enough to make it an object, which proved the wisdom of the principal's policy in managing their finances for them.

The next forenoon was devoted to a visit to the two castles above the town. Only the ancient one has any special interest, and this is noted for the curious dungeons in the rock beneath it. The castellan, or keeper, conducted the party down a winding staircase, to an ancient Roman bath, by a passage made in modern times; for originally the only access to the dungeons was by a perpendicular shaft in the centre of the castle, which is still in existence. Tradition declares that the prisoners, blindfolded, and lashed to an armchair, were lowered through this shaft to the gloomy vaults hewn out of the solid rock. The dark and mysterious dungeons were closed by a stone slab, revolving on a pivot, and weighing from half a ton to a ton. One room, larger than the others, was the rack-chamber, which contained the instrument of torture; and in the wall several iron rings still remain.

In a passage-way there is a deep aperture, now boarded over, but formerly covered by a trap-door. The victim doomed to the rack was led to the passage, at the end of which was an image of the Virgin, which he was required to kiss. In approaching it, he stepped upon the trap, and was precipitated into the depths below upon a wheel armed with knives, upon which he was torn in pieces. The story is, that this horrible pit was discovered in searching for a little dog which had fallen through the planking, when the wheel was found, with its knives rusty, the fragments of bones and garments still clinging to them. But people who go to see sights ought not to be disappointed — and some allowance should be made before accepting all the stories of guides and keepers of mysterious dungeons. Doubtless these subterranean apartments were the meeting-places of some secret tribunals, such as the Vehmic courts, which existed in the middle ages in Westphalia. Scott and Göthe have made use of these dungeons in their works, and our students regarded them as a splendid field for the later writers of sensational fiction.

The party walked through the upper portion of the castle, and obtained a fine view of the surrounding country from its openings. The rest of the day was spent in the gardens, assembly-rooms, and other places of interest. In the first train, the next morning, the excursionists went to Heidelberg, fifty-eight miles distant.

CHAPTER XVI.

UP THE MEDITERRANEAN.

THE Josephine still sped on her course, southwest by west; and still the mystery of her destination remained unsolved. Little was hopeful, while Ibbotson was despondent. Mr. Fluxion planked the quarter-deck as industriously as though he were walking on a wager, or had the dyspepsia, which could only be cured by plenty of exercise.

"What do you suppose this means?" said Perth, when the port watch had gone below.

"I don't know: it's a poser to me," replied Herman, as he seated himself under the shelter of the top-gallant forecastle. "But I can't think it is anything more than a short cruise for the sake of the discipline."

"It can't be a long cruise, for no provisions and water were taken in," added Perth. "I think, if we behave first rate, we shall return to Brest in a day or two."

"We will be as proper as the lambs themselves."

"How is it about Fluxion's going to Italy?" asked Perth.

"I know only what the fellows say. Everybody believes that he has to go there to see some friend who is sick."

"Where are we going, Mr. Briskett?" inquired Perth, as the head steward came forward to take a look ahead.

"Going to sea," replied he.

"Where are we bound?"

"Bound to sea."

"But how long are we to be out?" persisted Perth.

"Well, I don't know; but I am fully of the opinion that we shall be out till we go into port again."

"Won't you tell us, Mr. Briskett?" interposed Herman.

"Tell you what?"

"Where the vessel is going."

"Going to sea," answered the head steward, good-naturedly; for he rather enjoyed the perplexity of the crew.

"Is there any secret about the ship's destination?"

"You must ask Mr. Fluxion. He is on the quarter-deck, and I dare say he will be very happy to give you any information he thinks it is proper for you to have."

Mr. Briskett, having taken his long look ahead, turned on his heel, and went aft again.

"Where are we going, Mr. Bitts?" said Herman, to the carpenter, who had been within hearing during the dialogue with the head steward.

"Going to sea."

"Yes; but where are we bound?"

"Bound to sea."

"But how long are we to be out?"

"Well, I've boxed the compass, taken an observation, worked up an altitude, swung six and cast out nine, — and I've made up my mind that we shall be out till we return to port again. I may be wrong, but you can figure it up for yourself."

"O, come! Is there any secret about the vessel's destination?" added Herman.

"There's Mr. Fluxion, wearing out the planks of the quarter-deck. He's a good sailor, and a gentleman from his top-lights down to his keelson; and if you ask him, he'll tell you all he has a mind to."

"If he's a gentleman, I hope the forward officers will take lessons of him," added Herman, disgusted with the conduct of the carpenter.

"I shall, for one; for we have so many unlicked cubs on board now, that I am afraid my manners have suffered by being among them," laughed Bitts. "But do you really want to know where we are going, young gentlemen?"

"I do, for one," replied Perth, promptly.

"You won't say a word if I tell you — eh?" added Bitts, very seriously.

"Not a word."

"Well, we are bound down to the coast of Africa to get a cargo of gorillas. Mr. Fluxion is going into the show business."

"You get out!" exclaimed Perth, vexed to find himself "sold."

"I don't know but the plan was changed," continued the carpenter. "Some of them were afraid we might get things mixed on board; and after we got the cargo in, we couldn't tell the gorillas from the runaways."

Bitts thought he had said a clever thing; and, chuckling at his own wit, he turned on his heel, and walked aft to the waist.

"It's no use to ask them anything," said Herman.

"I suppose we may as well keep still, and wait till something turns up," added Perth.

"I don't see that we can do anything else."

"Unless we start the water in the tanks," suggested Perth.

"And have our own supply cut off. I had enough of that sort of thing in the ship. If we don't behave well, the first thing Fluxion will do will be to put us on salt horse and hard bread."

"We won't do anything yet. In my opinion, we shall go into port in a day or two."

At eight bells the starboard watch were piped to dinner, being relieved by the port watch. The wind continued fresh and fair; and the Josephine flew on her course, logging from ten to twelve knots all day. The portion of the crew off duty were not required to recite any lessons, or do anything else. The severe course of study to which Mr. Fluxion had subjected them, during the absence of the rest of the company in France and Switzerland, had enabled them to make up all deficient lessons. The principal had requested Mr. Fluxion not to assign any studies to his charge, unless it became necessary to do so in order to keep them out of mischief. The crew were to serve in quarter watches, from eight at night till eight in the forenoon, though the acting watch officers were to serve full time.

Night came on with the breeze freshening, and the top-gallant-sail was furled. The Josephine then had all she could carry, for Mr. Fluxion was not a fair-weather sailor, and always crowded on all the vessel would stagger under. The wind was more to the eastward than when the schooner left Brest, which still kept it fair. At eight bells in the evening, the first part of the starboard watch took the deck; and the night wore away without any exciting incident to break the monotony. Peaks and Cleats were thorough seamen, and being in authority, they compelled every seaman to do his duty.

The sea was rough in the Bay of Biscay, and the Josephine, though she made good weather of it, was rather wet on deck. But she was making a splendid voyage so far. On the forenoon of the second day out, Perth and Herman, having the watch below, had another discussion in regard to the probable length of the cruise. The vessel was still headed away from Brest; and even if she put about then, it might take her two or three days to work back to the port where they had left the ship. The prospect was decidedly sickening. The Josephine was far out of sight of land, and still headed south-west by west. The officers were as taciturn as on the previous day, so far as the destination of the vessel was concerned, though they were very considerate in every other respect. There was nothing to do after the decks had been washed down in the morning. The wind was a little lighter, and, in addition to the top-gallant-sail, the fore square-sail was set, so that her speed was at no time less than ten knots, and most of the time it was twelve.

"What do you make of it now, Little?" said Ibbotson, just before noon on the second day out. "Do you think we shall get back to Brest in a day or two?"

"Of course we shall."

"Bah! What's the use of talking?" We couldn't beat back to Brest now in three days."

"Perhaps we shall make some other port in France," suggested Little, with a sickly smile.

"What! steering south-west by west? Not much! I tell you we are homeward bound."

"Nonsense! Not unless we are going by the way of Cape Horn, Behring's Straits, and the North-west Passage! Keep cool, Ibbotson; we shall come out right yet."

"But we are sold. Lowington has the weather-gage of us, and we are beaten at our own game."

"Not yet."

"Yes, we are. We shall not see the coast of France again this year. I'll bet you Fluxion's starboard whisker, our cruise for this season is up."

"Don't croak."

They all croaked when the vessel had been out thirty hours, and was still persistently headed to the south-west. The day wore wearily away, crowded with doubt, anxiety, and perplexity to the runaways. At three in the afternoon, when the starboard watch were on deck, Peaks, by order of Mr. Fluxion, stationed a lookout in the fore-top. Perth and Herman were the first to do this duty.

"I suppose our game is all up," said the latter, as they seated themselves in the top.

"It don't look very hopeful; but I suppose we are going somewhere," replied Perth. "When we make a port, I'm off, if I have to swim ashore."

"I'm with you; but those five-pound notes will suffer in the water."

"I will look out for them," answered Perth, grating his teeth with anger. "I think we are reduced to common sailors, and I can't stand it."

"One thing is certain; we can't help ourselves. If Fluxion chooses to go round the world with us, we can't do anything but submit."

"I'm not so sure of that. When we find out where he is going, we can figure up what it is best to do. We are not babies, and thirty-one of us can do something. But we will keep still till we ascertain where we are going."

"Look ahead!" said Herman, pointing a little over the port bow. "Isn't that land?"

"It looks like it; but don't say anything yet."

"What can it be?" asked Herman.

"It is Cape Ortegal, if it is anything, on the north-west corner of Spain. We can tell, in a few hours after we come up with the cape, how they head her."

They watched the dark, hazy line for half an hour longer, and then shouted, "Land, ho!" The announcement made a sensation among the runaways, but it afforded no revelation of the purposes of the vice-principal. Still the Josephine sped on her way, and in a few hours was up with Cape Ortegal. She kept on the same course, with the coast of Spain in sight, till dark. Mr. Fluxion remained on deck; for he attended to the navigation himself. At twelve o'clock at night, the first part of the port watch came on deck, and Little and Ibbotson tried to ascertain where they were. The tell-tale still indicated south-west by west as the course. A bright light on the shore bore south-east by south. Mr Fluxion watched the light and the compass.

"Keep her south-west by south," said he to the hands at the wheel.

"South-west by south," repeated one of the seamen.

"Trim the sails, Mr. Peaks," added the vice-principal.

"Ay, ay!'sir. Man the fore-sheet! Now walk away with it! Avast! Belay!" said the acting first officer; and the manœuvre was repeated upon the mainsail.

The yards were trimmed for the new course, and there was nothing more to be done. The seamen not occupied at the helm, or on the lookout, stowed themselves away in comfortable places.

"We are going nearly south now," said Ibbotson, as he and Little seated themselves under the weather rail.

"South-west by south," added Little, gloomily; for even he had almost lost hope.

"I heard Perth say there were over two points and a half variation; and that makes the course about south by west. Where do you suppose we are bound?"

"I can't guess. I suppose we shall fetch up somewhere. When we do, I'm off as soon as the mud-hook finds bottom. I'm not sure that I shall wait till we go into port," added Little, desperately.

"Why, what can you do?"

"We are not more than ten or fifteen miles from the coast of Spain. If we could only drop a boat into the water, I would risk getting ashore."

"You can't do that."

"Fluxion has turned in now. Cleats and Bitts have the next watch," continued Little, suggestively.

"They won't let you off."

"Bitts goes to sleep; and Cleats may go below for something," said Little, dropping his voice to a whisper. "We will talk it over to-morrow with Perth and Herman."

"But you can't do anything."

"Perhaps we can," answered the little villain; but there was not much of his usual elasticity of spirits in his tones.

Ibbotson had no faith, and did not even care to talk about what seemed to him such an impracticable scheme. At four bells they were relieved, and the night wore away without any incident. All the following day the Josephine kept in about the same position with regard to the shore, running rapidly to the southward. Mr. Fluxion "made no sign," and the acting officers were as reticent as ever.

"Perth, I have an idea," said Little, as they met on deck.

"So have I," replied the disgusted leader of the runaways. "I have an idea that we are going round the world. This is our third day out, and no signs of turning back."

"I mean that I have a plan."

"You always have a plan," added Perth, with a sickly grin.

"If you don't want to hear it, all right; but I mean to get out of this scrape, if I can."

"So do I. If we don't do something we shall be the laughing-stock of the whole ship's company, if we ever join them again, of which I have some doubts. Lowington has hauled us up to the bull-ring this time, if he never did before. He has the weather-gage of us."

"That's so."

"If you have a plan, let's hear it."

"O, I won't trouble you with it. You don't think much of my plans."

"Yes, I do. I regard you as a genius in that line. You gave us the plan by which we got off in the Josephine."

"This little thing is for our four fellows only," continued Little, mollified by the credit awarded to him.

"All right; propel."

"We are only ten or fifteen miles from land. This is Portugal off here, I suppose."

"Yes; we shall be off Cape Roca to-night, if the wind keeps up, and I think we go within five or six miles of the shore."

"So much the better."

"Well, what's up?" asked Perth, with a yawn which indicated that he had not much hope of any scheme.

"Cleats and Bitts will be on the mid watch to-night. I notice that Cleats goes into the cabin once or twice in our quarter watch, and I suppose he does in yours."

"Yes, after his coffee, I suppose. He always comes back eating a biscuit."

"Just so; and Bitts goes to sleep."

"Not often."

"I've seen him asleep."

"The officers on duty have to keep on their feet all the time," said Perth.

"No matter if they do. Bitts leans against the foremast, and goes to sleep. He isn't used to being on watch lately."

"Well, go ahead."

"When Peaks goes below, we will draw the slide on him, and lock him into the cabin," added Little.

"Good! Go on," replied Perth, beginning to be interested. "Bitts is still on deck."

"Pass a line around him, and make him fast to the foremast while he is asleep."

"It will be apt to wake him."

"No matter; he is fast."

"He will make a noise."

"But the other officers are locked into the cabin."

"It might work. What then?"

"Lower the second cutter, and go ashore."

"They would pick us up as soon as they broke out of the cabin. The other fellows would work against us if we don't take them with us."

"Well, make a big thing of it, and take all the fellows and all the boats," said the accommodating little villain.

"That would do better; and there isn't a fellow on board who isn't up to such a move."

"That's so."

"It will take some time to work up the idea, though we have the steerage all to ourselves," added Perth, musing.

The conspirators discussed the scheme at every opportunity during the day, and imparted it to the rest of the crew. Some of them suggested objections, but all of them were willing to take part in the enterprise.

for they were so utterly disgusted with the course of Mr. Fluxion, that anything was preferable to submission.

"Suppose we get ashore," said Sheffield. "We shall be in Portugal, perhaps fifty miles from any large place."

"Cape Roca isn't twenty miles from Lisbon," replied Perth. "We can walk that distance in a day."

"What are you going to do in Lisbon? Not one of us can speak a word of Portuguese."

"We can do just the same as we should have done in Brest, and raise money on our letters of credit, and get to Paris. We can take a steamer back to Brest. The fare will not be more than ten dollars apiece in the fore cabin."

"Why not wait till we see where we are going?" suggested Sheffield.

"It may be too late then," answered Perth. "If Fluxion should suddenly head the vessel to the westward, that would mean home. The cook says we have fresh provisions enough for thirty days, which they took in while we were attending lecture."

"Does he know where we are bound?"

"No; or if he does, he won't say anything."

"I don't believe in landing at any such place as Lisbon, or anywhere in Portugal; though, of course, I will do what the rest of the fellows wish."

Perth and Little were too impatient to postpone the enterprise, though they acknowledged the difficulty of landing in Portugal. They worked up the details of the plan, and a part was assigned to each of the runaways. Phillips was to secure Bitts, with the assistance of half a dozen others. Perth was to close the companion way, lock it, and also drive a nail into the slide to make it sure. Greenway was to cover and secure the sky-lights. Herman was to fasten the door leading from the cabin to the steerage with a handspike. Ibbotson was to bar the door of the forecastle, where the cooks and under stewards slept. Others were to back the head sails, so as to lay to the vessel; and when all these things had been done, the boats were to be lowered,— the places of all the party having been assigned to them,— and they were to pull for the shore.

The night came on, and the light on Cape Roca was identified by Perth, at four bells; but a fog set in from seaward, and he decided that it was not prudent to take to the boats under such circumstances, for the reason that the boat compasses were in the cabin, and could not be obtained. At seven bells on Saturday morning the Josephine was off Cape St. Vincent.

"Keep her south-east," said Mr. Fluxion to the quarter-master at the wheel, when the headland bore north-east from the vessel.

"South-east!" exclaimed Perth, when the order had been repeated. "That means the Straits of Gibraltar. Fellows, we are bound up the Mediterranean."

"What does it mean?" inquired Herman.

"Fluxion is going to Italy," replied the leader, bitterly. "He is taking us with him!"

Perth's conclusion was passed along till every seaman on board understood it. The mystery was solved at last. There could be no doubt of the correctness of the solution, and great were the wrath and indignation of the runaways. It was abominable to compel them, the sons of gentlemen, to work the vessel as foremast hands, while she was employed on Mr. Fluxion's private business. It was an insult to them, an insult to their parents, and an outrage upon humanity in general. It was not to be endured, and rebellion was a duty. Little's plan was in higher favor than ever.

The wind was light, and the vessel, close-hauled, made but five and six knots during the day. At night she was out of sight of land. All day Sunday she made but little progress, and lay in a calm for several hours. Towards night, however, a fresh westerly wind came to her aid, and on Monday morning the crew saw the mountains of Europe and Africa vying with each other in sublimity, though they were too sour to appreciate the grandeur of the scene. The vessel hugged the Spanish shore, and Perth was on the lookout for an opportunity to spring the trap; but the sea was so rough and choppy, and the current so swift, that he was not willing to embark in the boats. It looked altogether too perilous. Besides, Bitts did not lean against the mast and go to sleep, and Cleats sent a hand down to bring up his luncheon, and the vice-principal staid on deck nearly all night.

"I think Fluxion smells a mice," said Perth, the next day.

"Why so?" asked Little.

"Because he stays on deck more than half the night."

"He is anxious about the navigation, perhaps."

"It is plain sailing here," added Perth. "I think he has seen our fellows talking together a great deal."

That was really the case. The vice-principal understood boys thoroughly. He had observed the earnest talks among little squads, and cautioned the acting officers to be very vigilant. It is enough to say that no opportunity was presented for carrying out the scheme of Little, and the Josephine came to anchor in the harbor of Genoa, ten days after she sailed from Brest. If the runaways had been in a proper frame of mind to enjoy it, there was a great deal to be seen; but they were too much taken up with their grievances to appreciate strange sights or beautiful scenery.

As soon as the schooner came to anchor, three of the four boats were hauled in, and lowered to the deck, where they were turned over to be painted. Bitts and Gage rowed the vice-principal ashore, while Peaks and Cleats, laying aside the dignity of their temporary positions, went to work scraping and painting the bottoms of the boats, which seemed to have been removed from the davits solely for the purpose of preventing any of the crew from escaping. Mr. Fluxion was absent only an hour, and during his absence Dr. Carboy watched the students every moment of the time.

The next morning a shore boat brought off a pale lady, who was understood to be the vice-principal's sister. They spent the whole forenoon in the cabin; but in the afternoon they went on shore together, to draw up and execute certain papers. Perth, in behalf of the crew, asked permission of Mr. Fluxion, just as he was departing, to go on shore.

"Quite impossible, young gentlemen," replied the **vice-principal**. "They are painting the boats, which are not in condition to be used. Besides, there is hardly time, for I hope we shall be able to sail before night."

Perth was very angry, and so were all the others, though they hardly expected the desired permission. Mr. Fluxion went on shore with the pale lady, and Dr. Carboy, Peaks, and Cleats watched the crew with Argus eyes. It was of no use for Little to fall overboard, for there was no boat to send after him. Perth was not quite willing to attempt a swim to the shore, for a fresh south-west wind kept up an ugly swell in that part of the port where the Josephine was anchored. Shore boats were driven from alongside by Peaks. In a word, Mr. Fluxion understood his crew, and knew what he was about. With a ship's company who had been desperate enough to capture the vessel on a former occasion, he was wise enough to keep everything taut. So the runaways could only grumble and growl, and watch the steamers which were constantly arriving and departing.

Before sundown Mr. Fluxion returned alone. He had finished his business with his sister, and the order was given to get under way, after the boats had all been restored to the davits. There was no chance to execute any of the desperate schemes which had been adopted. Discipline was triumphant, and the Josephine sped on her way to the Straits of Gibraltar. Four days out, Cape Antonio, on the coast of Spain, was sighted, and for the next two days the vessel sailed along the coast, with the lofty mountains of Spain in full view.

Mr. Fluxion was communicative enough to say that

the Josephine would put into Lisbon, and await the arrival of the Young America. The intelligence was not pleasant to the runaways. Perth declared that something must be done at once, or at least before the vessel had passed Cape de Gata. Alicante and Carthagena were near, and from either of them steamers frequently departed for Marseilles. They had actually made the trip in the Josephine which they had contemplated before their runaway excursion in her, but under different circumstances from those they desired. If they could get to Marseilles, the rest of the plan might be realized.

They had kept everything in readiness for the enterprise which Little had planned, and for a fortnight had been on the lookout for an opportunity to strike the blow. After the vessel had come up with Cape Antonio, Perth told the fellows he should make the attempt that night, though it would be bright moonlight. The signal for those below to perform the part assigned to them was three raps on the deck, over the steerage, with the heel of the leader. But Perth was not in Cleats's watch; so he and Herman hid themselves under the top-gallant forecastle, when their watch was relieved. About three bells in the mid watch, Little informed the leader that Cleats had gone below.

"Where's Bitts?" whispered Perth.

"In the waist, planking the deck."

"Call Phillips, quick!" added the leader, as he came out of his hiding-place.

Phillips promptly appeared. He was a great, stout fellow, as ugly as he was big. He immediately prepared to do his part. Herman was sent below to see that every seaman in the steerage was awake and ready to act, and he succeeded in eluding the sleepy vigilance of Bitts.

Perth gave the signal for those in the steerage, and at the same time whistled for the information of those on deck. Bitts was not so obliging as to lean against a mast, or anything else, and the conspirators were compelled to take him flying. Phillips had prepared, with a piece of whale line, a kind of lasso, and, stepping up behind him, threw it over his head, drawing it tight around his neck, before the astonished carpenter suspected any mischief. The end of the whale line was then hooked to the clewline of the fore-square-sail, which had been detached for the purpose. The hands at the clewline walked away with it, until the rope bore hard on the throat of the carpenter. All this was done in an instant, for Phillips had carefully adjusted all the details of his share of the work. Bitts tried to cry out; but when he did so, Phillips ordered the hands at the buntline to haul taut.

"Keep still, old fellow, or you shall be hung!" said the ruffian in charge of the deed.

Bitts was obliged to keep still, for when he struggled to release his neck with his hands the rope was tightened. In the mean time, Perth had secured the slide, and those below had barred the doors.

"Clear away the boats!" and all but Phillips, who was obliged to watch Bitts, sprang to their stations for lowering the boats, and in a couple of minutes all four of them were in the water, with the oars tossed, ready to pull for the shore. In the cabin there was a tremendous din, made by Cleats and the other officers, who had been aroused by the noise. They were trying to batter down the door leading into the steerage, but as yet with no success.

"All ready!" shouted Perth.

Phillips, who was the only one of the crew remaining on board, hastily belayed the clewline at the fife-rail, hauling it just taut enough to hold Bitts, without choking him to death. As the ruffian leaped into the boat, to which he had been assigned, Perth gave the order to shove off, and the runaways pulled with all their might for the shore.

CHAPTER XVII.

HEIDELBERG AND HOMBURG.

ON the arrival of the excursion party at Heidelberg, they were conducted, by Mr. Arbuckle's *avant-courrier*, to the Hôtel Prinz Karl, in the market-place, and near the castle, which is the principal object of interest in the town. One of the first persons that Shuffles saw, as he walked up to the hotel, was Lady Feodora, promenading the veranda with Sir William. She looked a shade paler than when the captain had met her last; but her color deepened when she discovered her gallant friend.

"I am delighted to see you, Captain Shuffles!" exclaimed she, deserting her titled companion, and rushing towards him, her cheeks suffused with blushes.

"This is a very unexpected pleasure," replied the commander, his brown face flushing, "but none the less welcome because unexpected."

"How glad I am to see you again!" said she, taking his offered hand, as they met.

"Thank you; but not so glad as I am," added he, in a lower tone.

"I hope you are very well, Captain Shuffles," interposed Sir William, stiffly.

"Quite well, I thank you."

"Lady Feodora has been quite ill," added the baronet, "or we should have been in Brussels by this time."

"I have not been very ill; but father thought we had better remain here a few days. Now I am almost glad I was ill, since it gives me the pleasure of seeing you again," continued the young lady, with a childish candor which brought a frown to the brow of the little baronet.

"You are very kind, Lady Feodora."

Sir William thought so too.

"We have been all over the castle, Captain Shuffles; and I am going to be your guide," continued she, playfully.

"I am afraid your health will not permit you to do so much," suggested Sir William.

"O, I feel quite strong now."

The conversation was interrupted by the appearance of Feodora's father and mother, who extended to Shuffles a cordial and hearty greeting. Mr. Lowington and the party were warmly welcomed by the earl's family. The business of sight-seeing required immediate attention, and Shuffles was taken into a carriage with his English friends; for the daughter insisted upon redeeming her promise. Sir William evidently did not enjoy the excursion; but he was apparently unwilling to be left at the hotel.

Heidelberg is beautifully located on a narrow strip of land between the River Neckar and the vast, high rock on which the castle stands. It has one principal street, nearly three miles long, and contains a population of about seventeen thousand. It is situated in the midst of some of the finest scenery in Germany; and all tourists agree in calling it one of the most delightful residences in Europe. The students walked through the principal street and along the banks of the Neckar until dinner time, when Professor Mapps found an opportunity to say something about the place.

"Heidelberg was once the capital of the Palatinate established here by the Emperor Otto of Germany in the tenth century. The Palatines were sub-rulers, whose duty it was to look after the interests of the emperor. This palatinate, including the northern portion of Baden and a part of Bavaria, became the most powerful in the empire, and was divided into the Upper and Lower Palatinates."

"What does *palatinate* mean, sir?" asked a student.

"It means merely the territory of a sub-ruler, who was called a *palatine*, from the Latin word *palatium*, a palace. When the throne of Germany became elective, these palatines chose the emperor, and for this reason were called electors-palatine, or simply electors. The castle here was the residence of the elector of this division. The town has suffered more from the ravages of war than almost any other in Europe. It has been bombarded five times, burned twice, and captured and pillaged three times.

"The university is one of the most noted in the world, as well as one of the oldest in Germany, having been founded in 1386. It has had at one time nearly nine hundred students, and generally has seven or eight hundred. It employs the most celebrated professors in Europe, especially in the departments of law and medicine. Its library contains some very rare and valuable works, printed and in manuscript."

"What about the duels, sir?" inquired Haven.

"The students here are noted for the duels which take place among them. Four or five have occurred in a single day, and perhaps they average a dozen a week. But I wish to say, in the beginning, that duelling and other vicious practices charged upon the University of Heidelberg are confined to about one fifth of the whole number of students. They are not all duellists, nor all inordinate beer-drinkers. Probably they are no worse than the residents at other universities, though the duels are certainly exceptional. Four fifths of the students here are devoted to their studies, improve their time to the utmost, and never engage in, or even see, a duel.

"These combats — which they are, rather than duels — take place at the Hirschgasse, a lonely hotel on the other side of the Neckar. The fighting and dissipated students form themselves into clubs, called 'chores,' among which a great deal of jealousy and ill feeling prevails. The fights are to avenge insults, to 'see who is the best fellow,' or between representatives of different chores, who battle for the honor of their clubs. The champions fight with blunt swords ground sharp on the two edges. They slash each other, but do not thrust, so that the combats seldom result in mortal wounds.

"In a fight for the honor of the clubs, the parties tie up their necks and right arms in bandages and cushions. When they fight for the satisfaction of an injury or insult, they have no protection. The combat, in all cases, is decided in fifteen minutes; and at the end of this time, the one who has the fewest cuts is declared to be the best fellow. If one of the champions is severely injured in less than fifteen minutes, so that he cannot continue the fight, it is finished up on another occasion. A surgeon is always in attendance to decide whether a wounded contestant is able to go on. The police are on the watch for these fights; but the students station sentinels for some distance from the arena of contest, and the approach of an officer is communicated to them in season to enable the combatants to escape. I need not add, that these duels are brutal and disgraceful. It looks as though the police winked at them.

"In some of these clubs, the ability to drink from a dozen to thirty glasses of beer at a sitting is a necessary qualification for admission. But these beastly and brutal tendencies belong, I repeat, to a minority of the students."

After the lecture, the party started for the castle, Shuffles riding with the earl's family, and Paul with the Arbuckles, while the rest walked. Heidelberg Castle has the reputation of being one of the most imposing and interesting ruins in Europe. The grounds are quite extensive, and full of curious objects. The students wandered through the halls and subterranean vaults till they came to the famous *tun*, which is thirty-six feet long, and twenty-four feet high, having a capacity of eight hundred hogsheads. It was employed to contain the wine of the vineyards; but it has not been used during the last hundred years. A run to the Königstuhl, or King's Seat, — a high hill behind the castle, which commands a magnificent view of the valleys of the Neckar and the Rhine, and of the mountains in the vicinity, — finished the work of the week.

As the next day was Sunday, the party remained* at Heidelberg, and attended church at the English chapel in the forenoon. In the afternoon they visited the Church of the Holy Ghost, which has a partition through the entire length of it, dividing it into two equal parts, one of which is used by the Catholics, and the other by the Protestants. Services in both take place at the same time.

On Monday morning the excursionists, including the earl's party, proceeded to Darmstadt. When Lady Feodora had taken a back seat next to the window, in a compartment of the railway carriage, she insisted that Shuffles should have the seat opposite, much to the disgust of Sir William, who usually occupied that position. In fact, he was angry, and did not take much pains to conceal his ill-will. It is doubtful whether Shuffles understood the matter, but the young lady was very strongly interested in him. She did not like the baronet, and she did like the young commander. As the latter had rendered her a signal service on Lake Constance, she felt justified in extending unusual attentions to him. Sir William was jealous, as well he may have been; for his lady-love hardly condescended to notice him, while all her smiles were bestowed upon the gallant young seaman.

There was nothing especial to be seen in Darmstadt, and after the party had walked through the principal street, and glanced at the Grand Ducal Palace, they were ready to continue their journey to Frankfurt, where they arrived in less than an hour, and repaired to the *Hôtel de Russie* for dinner. Mr. Drexel, one of the landlords, was especially devoted to the party, and afforded them every facility for seeing the city in the shortest possible time. The dinner was capital, and when it had been disposed of by the hungry students, they were in condition to hear Professor Mapps.

"Darmstadt, where we spent an hour this forenoon," said the professor, "is the capital of Hesse Darmstadt, which consists of two divisions of territory, separated by a strip of land belonging to Hesse Cassel and Frankfurt. It has an area of thirty-two hundred square miles, — being about two thirds of the size of Connecticut — and a population of about eight hundred and fifty thousand. It is a constitutional monarchy in its government, the Grand Duke Ludwig III. being the sovereign. The word *Hesse*, applied to several of the German states, indicates that they are parts of the original territory which bore that name. One of its rulers divided his country into four unequal parts, and gave them to his sons. Two of the descendants of these sons dying without children, there remained only Hesse Cassel and Hesse Darmstadt. Hesse Homburg formerly belonged to Darmstadt, but was ceded to another branch of the reigning family in 1622. It is composed of two parts; the smaller, containing forty-three square miles, and eleven thousand five hundred inhabitants, is about ten miles north of Frankfurt; the other portion, having eighty-five square miles, and fourteen thousand five hundred inhabitants, is on the other side of the Rhine.*

"Frankfurt-on-the-Maine, so called to distinguish it from Frankfurt-on-the-Oder, is a free city, and the capital of the Germanic Confederation. It is a little nationality by itself, having the right to make its own local laws, levy duties, and other powers belonging to a state. It is represented in the Federal Diet. This territory includes nine villages, besides the city proper, with a population of about seventy-five thousand. It is a very old city, and is mentioned in history in the time of Charlemagne, who had a palace here. This city is the original home of the Rothschilds, the great bankers, upon whom even princes wait — when they are short of money. The family are Jews, who form a considerable part of the population of Frankfurt. The house in which several, if not all, the prominent sons were born, is shown in the Judengasse, or Jews Street. The laws were formerly very severe upon the Israelites. They were compelled to reside in their own quarter, where the gates were closed upon them at an early hour. A regulation forbade the celebration of more than thirteen marriages among the race in the city within a year. All these stringent laws have been rescinded.

"Göthe, the German poet, was born in Frankfurt; and you will see his house, which contains some relics of him. Luther, the Reformer, also resided here for

---

* Hanover, Hesse Cassel, Hesse Homburg, Nassau, the part of Hesse Darmstadt north of the Maine, Hohenzollern, and Frankfurt were annexed to Prussia in 1866.

a time. The city is noted for the wealth of its merchants, and there are many magnificent private residences within its limits."

The professor finished his lecture, and the party started to see the sights to which he had alluded. The old cathedral, with its unfinished tower, was very much like many others they had seen. Within its chapel all the elected emperors were crowned in front of the high altar. The Town Hall was the scene of the festivities which followed the election of an emperor. He was feasted in the banquet hall, where the kings and princes of his empire waited upon him at table, in token of their subservience. A whole ox was roasted in the market-place, — into which the students looked from the windows, — and the emperor ate a slice, while from a fountain flowing with wine the cup-bearer filled his flagon. The room is hung with portraits of the emperors, under most of which are placed the mottoes adopted at their coronation.

Passing across to the Hirschgraben, the tourists visited the house where Göthe was born. Over the front door is the coat of arms of the poet's father, which consists of three lyres, as if to prefigure the destiny of the genius who first saw the light within its walls. Göthe's room is a garret, wherein his portrait, his autograph, and his washstand are exhibited. His statue stands near the theatre, and one of Schiller in front of the guard-house. From the house of the poet, the party went to the Städel Museum, filled with fine pictures, mostly by Dutch and German artists, **which is named for its founder, a liberal banker, who** gave four hundred thousand dollars to the institution, besides a collection of artistic works. From the museum, the students, after a walk of over a mile, reached the Jewish quarter, glanced at the Rothschild House, the synagogue, and other buildings, returning to the *Hôtel de Russie* at dark.

On the following morning the party went to Homburg, nine miles distant, where they spent the rest of the day. The town is another watering-place, and has increased in popularity till it outrivals Baden-Baden, Wiesbaden, or any other fashionable resort in Germany. It has its medicinal springs, which are beneficial in a variety of diseases. The *Kurhaus* is the most magnificent in Europe, containing lofty halls, elegantly frescoed, for dancing, gambling, for restaurants and reading-rooms. As in Baden-Baden, the gambling monopoly is in the hands of French speculators, and the lavish expenditure upon the gardens, buildings, and other appointments is an instructive commentary on the chances which favor the visitor disposed to try his fortune.

"Commodore," said Ben Duncan, who was now the second master of the Josephine, as they met at the Hotel *Quatre Saisons* in the evening, "I have lost two hundred florins."

"What!" exclaimed Paul.

"Certainly, Mr. Duncan, you have not been gambling," added Grace Arbuckle, looking as sad as though she had lost a dear friend.

"I lost two hundred florins out in that dog-house," replied Ben, who was the wag of the party, and a general favorite.

"What dog-house?" inquired Paul.

"Why, the big one — *auf dem Platz.*"

"Do you mean the Kursaal?" asked Paul.

"Mr. Fetridge calls it a dog-house, in Harper's Hand Book."

"No."

"The cur-house — what's the difference?"

"U in German is pronounced like double o. But you don't mean to say you have been gambling, Ben?" added Paul.

"I said I had lost two hundred florins," replied Ben, with a most lugubrious expression.

"Impossible!"

"I was standing near the table, in the grand gambling *hell*, — I beg pardon, hall, — watching the play, when I saw a Russian czar, king, grand dook, polywog, or something of that sort, win two hundred florins at one fell swoop. Now, thinks I to myself, if I should put down two hundred florins, and win, I should make two hundred florins by the operation. I didn't do it — so I'm two hundred florins out."

Ben dropped his chin, and looked very sad, while Grace and Paul laughed heartily, perhaps more at the "face" the wag made, than at the joke he had perpetrated.

"I hope your losses will always be of this description, Ben," added Paul.

"Probably they will be while each student is allowed only a florin a day for pocket-money," replied Ben. "There is to be a grand concert in the dog-house this evening. Of course we shall go!"

"Certainly."

"Suppose we walk down now."

"If you please; but don't call it a dog-house."

"Well, it is a gambling-hole, and I don't know but it is a libel on the dog to call it so," answered Ben, as they walked towards the Kursaal.

Most of the excursionists were headed in that direction. Shuffles was with the earl's party, though, strangely enough, Sir William was not at the side of Lady Feodora. They seated themselves in the grand apartment, and gazed with interest at the brilliant scene before them.

"Where can Sir William be?" said Lady Blankville.

"I do not know, mother," replied Feodora, languidly, as though she did not care where he was.

"I haven't seen him these two hours."

"Nor I," added Feodora, in a tone which indicated that she did not wish to see him for two hours more.

"I will look for him, if you desire," suggested Shuffles.

"O, no! Do not trouble yourself," replied Feodora. "Perhaps he is looking at the play."

"Pray, do, if you please, Captain Shuffles," interposed the countess.

Lady Feodora was too dutiful a girl to object, and the commander went to the gambling-rooms. At the roulette table he found the baronet, playing with a zeal which indicated that this was not the first time he had indulged in the baneful game. He was not staking large sums, but he was losing about three out of four times that he put down his money.

"I beg your pardon, Sir William, but Lady Blankville is anxious to see you," whispered Shuffles in his ear.

"Lady Blankville!" exclaimed the baronet, turning from the table as he lost his last stake, and walking towards the concert-room.

"Lady Blankville," repeated the captain.

"Lady Feodora is not anxious to see me — is she?" said Sir William, bitterly.

"She did not say that she was," replied Shuffles.

"No; she did not!" added the baronet, stopping suddenly, and looking his companion in the face. "Will you do me the favor to walk in the garden with me?"

"While the ladies are waiting for us, it is hardly proper to be absent from them," replied Shuffles, troubled by the manner of the young gentleman.

"Perhaps you are right," mused Sir William. "Will you meet me alone at the hotel, after the ladies have retired?"

"For what purpose?" inquired Shuffles, nervously.

"I have not time to explain now. Will you meet me?" continued the baronet, earnestly.

"If possible, I will."

They joined the party in the concert-room. Sir William was cool, and inclined to be morose. Shuffles was rather disturbed by his manner, and could not help wondering for what purpose the baronet wished to meet him alone. He had not failed to see that Lady Feodora regarded her travelling companion, whose relations to her he could only infer, with a feeling bordering upon aversion, and that her demeanor towards him was in marked contrast with her bearing towards himself. He was afraid the proposed meeting related to this subject. While the party were listening to the enchanting music of the band, he tried to ascertain whether he had said or done anything to give offence to the baronet. It was not his fault that the lady did not like Sir William, and rebelled against the relation which appeared to exist in form between them. But the captain was willing to give the baronet any explanation he might demand, and hoped that all unpleasant feelings would be removed by the interview.

After the tourists had returned to the hotel, and the ladies had gone to their rooms, Shuffles walked up and down the hall till the baronet joined him. Taking his arm, Sir William led him to an unfrequented part of the garden, and there halted.

"Captain Shuffles, I believe you are a gentleman, and have the instincts of a gentleman," the young Englishman began.

"I trust I have," replied Shuffles, not a little agitated, for the manner of his companion was very earnest and serious.

"You have placed me under very great obligations to you. I cheerfully acknowledge them. I am willing to believe that both Lady Feodora and myself would have been drowned but for your plucky conduct and generous efforts in our behalf on Lake Constance."

"I am very glad to have served you, and I assure you I hold you to no obligations of any kind," replied Shuffles. "I simply did what I regarded as my duty, which my sea life fitted me to perform."

"Having acknowledged my obligations, you will

permit me to add, that I think you are making a very unfair and ungenerous use of your position. After your noble conduct on the lake, I expected something like magnanimity from you. I am sorry to say I have been disappointed," continued Sir William, bitterly.

"Really, I do not understand you," replied the captain, amazed at the sudden turn in the style of his companion.

"Is it possible that you do not comprehend my relations with Lady Feodora?" demanded the baronet. "Let me explain, then, that we have been affianced from our childhood."

"Indeed!"

"You could not help seeing that our relations were of this kind."

"I did suppose there was something of this description."

"Then allow me to say again that you have made a very ungenerous use of your position."

"In what respect?"

"You have extended to Lady Feodora many attentions," said the baronet, becoming more and more excited.

"Only ordinary courtesies."

"But such courtesies as belong to me rather than to you. I am devotedly attached to her."

"If any of my attentions were not agreeable to the lady, she had only to decline them."

"There you presume upon the position which circumstances have given you."

"If Lady Feodora is attached to you —"

"She is not attached to me."

"Then you make a very ungenerous use of your position," retorted Shuffles, rather warmly.

"What do you mean, sir?" demanded Sir William.

"If your parents and hers made a bargain for her which she repudiates, I say it is ungenerous in you to use such an advantage as that bargain gives you."

"Do you mean to insult me?"

"Certainly not; only to speak as plainly as you have spoken. If my presence is disagreeable to the lady, I will avoid her."

"Your presence is not disagreeable to her," added Sir William, unable to conceal his vexation.

"Then you will excuse me if I decline to treat her with the rudeness you suggest."

"I find I am mistaken in you, and I regret that you compel me to ignore the obligations under which you have placed me."

"I cheerfully absolve you from any obligations which may weigh heavily upon you. But I assure you, I have no ill-will towards you, and I shall continue to treat you with courtesy and kindness. In about a week, our ship's company will return to Brest, and sail for the United States. It is not probable that I shall ever see Lady Feodora or you again."

"Will you pledge yourself never to see her again after this week?" demanded Sir William.

"I will not — certainly not," replied Shuffles. "I do not purpose to interfere in any way with your relations to her. If she desires to see me, and it is possible for me to see her, I shall not deny myself that pleasure."

The baronet suddenly turned upon his heel, and

walked rapidly towards the hotel. Shuffles was amazed. He could not conceal from himself the truth that he was deeply interested in Lady Feodora, though no thought of anything beyond friendship occurred to either of them. They might or might not continue in company for another week, and then part, in all human probability, forever in this world. Still, the situation was novel enough to be exciting, and he lay awake, thinking of it, for several hours that night. But in the morning Sir William appeared as usual, and probably, on reflection, had decided not to do any desperate deed.

At seven o'clock the excursionists returned by train to Frankfurt. It was decided then that, as Wiesbaden, one of the celebrated German watering-places, was only a repetition of Baden-Baden and Homburg, the company should proceed direct to Mayence, where they arrived by nine o'clock.

CHAPTER XVIII.

CASTLES, VINEYARDS, AND MOUNTAINS.

AS the students were crossing the bridge to Mayence, they obtained a full view of one of the great rafts of timber which float down the Rhine, and of which Professor Mapps had spoken to them at Dort, in Holland. However, it was much smaller than those of which they had heard, and they hoped to see another. The students were not disposed to "do" Mayence, being too impatient to witness the glories of the Rhine. But most of them, from a sense of duty rather than from an interest in the place, visited the principal attractions of the city.

"Mayence is the French name of the town," said the professor of geography and history, as the students collected in the railroad station, previous to the tramp. "The German name is Mainz, which is pronounced Mynts — y like long i. If you pronounce it in any other way, a German will not know what you mean. It was an old Roman town. A fortress was established here to keep back the barbarians. It was formerly a larger and more important city than at present, having now a population of only forty thousand.

"This place has done two grand things for civilization and for Europe. It was the cradle of the art of printing, and furnished the man who suppressed the robber knights. As you go down the Rhine, you will see the ruins of many old castles on the hills by the banks of the river. The nobles, who occupied them as strongholds, carried on a system of robbery, levying duties upon all who travelled on its waters or passed through their territory. Arnold von Walpoden suggested the plan which led to a confederation of the cities for the driving out of the knightly highwaymen, and the destruction of their strongholds. They were feudal lords, and the breaking of their power opened the way for the progress of civilization.

"Mayence was the birthplace of Gutemberg, who invented movable types for printing, and reduced the art to practice. You will see the site of the house where he was born, and the building which contained his first printing-office."

After this brief explanation the party walked to the cathedral, a very ancient structure, possessing much historical interest. Opposite the theatre they saw the statue of Gutemberg, and the guide pointed out the place where his house stood, and the old building in which he and Faust took their first proofs from types.

At twelve o'clock the tourists went on board of the steamer Königin von Preussen, and realized that they had actually embarked for the trip down the Rhine. They had seen the river at Basle, Constance, and Schaffhausen, had crossed it at Strasburg, and obtained views of it from different points on their route. The steamer was unworthy of the noble river, and if the palatial boats of the Hudson could be run upon its waters, they would lend a new charm to the scenery.

The Rhine steamers are small, compared with the Hudson river boats, and far from being elegant. They have no saloon on deck, though a couple of small apartments, abaft the paddle-boxes, are pretentiously called "pavilions." They are appropriated to first class passengers, and are seldom used except by travellers who wish to be very exclusive. The second class passengers occupy the main cabin and the deck abaft the wheels. Meals are served below, or, for an extra price, upon little tables on deck. The third class travellers have the forward deck, with piles of luggage to lounge upon. The relative fares are as the ratios four, six, and nine. From Mayence to Bingen the time is about two hours, and the fares are eight, twelve, and eighteen silver groschen. The steamers stop at all the principal landings, and passengers are occasionally brought off in small boats from other places.

The company dined in the cabin before the Königin started, so as not to lose a single view. The dinner was an excellent one, and cheap, the ordinary price being seventeen silver groschen, or about forty-one cents. When served to private parties on deck, the price is one thaler, or seventy-two cents.

"Are those steamboats?" asked Paul, pointing to a number of boats with houses on deck, and having immense wheels.

"No," replied Dr. Winstock. "They are mills for grinding grain."

"But what turns the wheels?"

"They are moored as you see them in the river, and the current turns the wheels, which are very large, so as to gain power."

"That's a new idea to me," added Paul.

"I have seen just such in the Alabama River, in our own country," replied the surgeon.

"It is certainly a very good way to obtain the power."

The boat started, and soon made a landing at Biebrich, on the other side of the river, where passengers from Frankfurt, Homburg, and Wiesbaden usually take the steamers. As the Königin proceeded on her way, a feeling of general disappointment pervaded the minds of the party, who had not seen the river before.

"It does not compare with the Hudson," protested Paul.

"Wait, Paul!" said the doctor, with a smile.

"How long shall I wait?"

"Two hours. You must not be hasty in your judgment."

"What is this town on the right?" asked Grace.

"Eltville. Do you see the white building in the midst of the vineyards, some distance down the river?" said the doctor, pointing to the shore.

"I see it."

"That is the château of Johannisberg, belonging to Prince Metternich, formerly a celebrated prime minister of Austria. Those vineyards are the most noted in the world. The famous Johannisberger wine is made from these grapes. It sells here for five or six dollars a bottle, where ordinary kinds can be bought for twenty cents, and even less. The grapes are very precious, and are kept upon the vines till they are nearly rotten. Those that fall off are picked up with a kind of fork, so valuable are they deemed. Of the seventy acres contained in the vineyard, only a small portion produces the best wine, which is not found except in the cellars of kings and princes. This is Rüdesheim, where the boat will make a landing," added Dr. Winstock, as the steamer stopped her wheels. "A famous wine is also made here. It is said that Charlemagne, seeing from his castle windows, near Mayence, how early the snow disappeared from the heights below us, ordered vines from France to be set out here; and from these vines is produced the noted Rüdesheimer wine.

"What place is this?" inquired Paul, at a point where the course of the river seemed to be obstructed by rocks and hills.

"Bingen on the Rhine," said the surgeon. "Here the waters of the river are crowded in a narrow space. Look upon the hills around you, and see how every foot of ground is economized for the vineyards. Where the hill-sides are too steep for cultivation, they are formed into terraces, as you see them."

The steamer stopped a few moments at Bingen, which contains about seventy-five hundred inhabitants.

"On our left, now, are the dominions of the King of Prussia — the Rhenish provinces. On our right, as before, is the Duchy of Nassau. What do you think of the Rhine now?" asked Dr. Winstock.

"It is improving, certainly," laughed Paul. "The scenery is really very grand and very fine. I will give it up now. It is finer than the Hudson. But where are the old castles?"

"There is one of them," answered the doctor, pointing to a ruin which crowned a hill on the right. "That is the Castle of Ehrenfels. There is a legend connected with about every one of them. There is the Mouse Tower."

The doctor pointed to a stone structure rising from the river a short distance from the shore. It was certainly a very romantic building, and in a very romantic situation.

"What is the story about this tower?" asked Paul.

"If you take Southey's works when you return to the ship, you will find in them, 'The Tradition of Bishop Hatto.' He was the Archbishop of Mayence, and during a famine kept his granaries, well filled with food, locked, and, by his own profusion and high living, excited his starving subjects to revolt. The prelate ordered the rebels to be arrested, confined them in a building, and set it on fire. Not content with this outrage, he added insult to injury by mocking the wail of the sufferers, and comparing their cries with the squeaking of mice. In the night which followed the diabolical deed, a swarm of mice penetrated to the apartments of the archbishop's palace, attacked him, and tried to tear the flesh from his bones. Appalled by this poetic justice, the cruel prelate fled, and, taking to the river, reached this insulated tower. Suspending his bed in the upper part of the structure, he struggled to escape from the mice, as merciless as he had himself been. But the mice followed him, and he could not avoid the doom that was in store for him. Vainly he resisted. The rats attacked him, and he suffered a lingering and horrible death. It is but fair to add that history gives the archbishop a different character. Do you happen to know the meaning of the German word *mauth?*"

"A duty, or a toll," replied Grace.

"The German for mouse is *maus,* and probably it is in this instance corrupted from *mauth;* for nothing could have made the tower and its owners more odious than the collection of duties from voyagers on the river. There is a sad story connected with the Brömserberg Castle, which we saw above. Brömser of Rühesheim went to Palestine with the crusaders, and, while there, distinguished himself by slaying a dragon which made itself very annoying to the Christian army. He was immediately after captured by the Saracen forces, and reduced to slavery. While in this condition, he made a solemn vow, that if he were ever permitted to return to his castle again, he would give his only daughter to the church. Improving an opportunity to kill his guard, he succeeded in reaching his home, where he was met by his daughter, a lovely young woman, who was betrothed to a young knight. Her father told her of the vow he had taken. Tearfully she entreated him to change his purpose; but his pledge to the church could not be set aside. Brömser threatened her with his curse if she refused to obey. Life had no charms apart from the young knight, and she determined to die. In the midst of a violent storm, she threw herself from the castle battlements into the river, and her corpse was found the next day, by a fisherman, near the Mouse Tower. The boatmen and peasants say, to this day, that they sometimes see the pale form of Gisela hovering above the castle, mingling her wails with the moanings of the storm."

"That's a very pretty story, and I suppose young ladies in that age were like those of the present," added Paul. "Perhaps more so, for now they don't throw themselves from walls into a damp river for such a cause."

"There's another castle!" exclaimed Grace, pointing to the left.

"That is Rheinstein, a castle which has been restored, and is the summer residence of a Prussian prince. Below the castle, where the road runs between the rock and the river, tolls were levied upon Jews who passed that way. And it is even said that the collectors had little dogs trained to know a Jew from a Christian, and to seize him with their teeth."

Castle-crowned heights succeeded each other in rapid succession; and in this part of the river they are so thick, that our students had to keep their eyes wide open in order to see them all. Rocky steeps rose from the verge of the water; and wherever there was any soil, or any earth could find a resting-place, the spot was made into a vineyard. Sometimes the vines have to be planted in baskets, while all the steep hillsides are terraced to the height of a thousand feet above the river. To reach these plats of ground, the peasants, male and female, must climb the steeps, and everything used there must be carried up on the shoulders. The vine-dressers are a very industrious people, and nothing but the most determined perseverance could induce them to cultivate these lofty artificial beds.

The towns on the banks of the Rhine are picturesque, and one never tires of looking at them. Indeed, half a dozen voyages down the Rhine no more than enable the tourist to see all its wonders and all its beauties.

"Stahlech Castle," said Dr. Winstock, pointing to a ruin on the left. "It was the palace of the Elector Palatine. Between the castle and the hill are the remains of St. Werner's Chapel. In the middle ages, it is said that the Jews at Oberwesel, farther down the river, crucified a Christian named Werner, and threw the body into the stream. Instead of descending with the current, it was carried by a supernatural agency up the river, from which it was taken at Bacharach, the town we are approaching, interred, and afterwards canonized. The chapel was built over the grave. Doubtless the story was invented to afford a pretext to rob and persecute the Hebrews, though in former ages such excuses seem to have been hardly needed."

"There is another castle in the river," said Grace, as the boat left Bacharach. "It is an odd-looking building."

"That is the *Pfalz*, and the town on the right is Caub. A toll was paid here by all vessels navigating the river. The Duke of Nassau inherited the right to levy this tax, and exercised the right to collect it, until three or four years ago. The *Pfalz* was his toll-house. In the middle ages, thirty-two tolls were levied at the different stations on the river. Schönberg Castle is on the left. What does the word mean?"

"Beautiful hill," replied Grace.

"It is called so because the occupant had seven

beautiful daughters, who were sad flirts. All the young knights in the vicinity were bewitched by their beauty, but they were so hard-hearted that they would accept none of them; and, as the penalty of their obduracy, they were changed into seven rocks, and planted in the middle of the river, where you will presently see them."

Passing Oberwesel and the Seven Sisters, the water was considerably agitated where the current had formerly produced a whirlpool, in its course among the rocks, which have now been removed by blasting. There was also a rapid just above it, and the place was very perilous for the long rafts, which were sometimes dashed to pieces upon the sunken rocks. The bank of the river on the right rises abruptly to a great height, and the precipice is called the Lurlei. It has an echo which gives back fifteen repetitions of the original sound. It sometimes makes intelligent replies; and wicked students put to it the question, "Who is the burgomaster of Oberwesel?" To which it responds, "Esel," which, in English, means an ass. The burgomaster intends to have it indicted for slander.

This echo, which repeats the sounds from below, and the wild character of the region, have produced a legend that the place is haunted by a beautiful but wicked water nymph, who lured the voyager, by her witching voice, to the rocks and the whirlpool, where his boat was dashed to pieces.

St. Goar and St. Goarhausen are opposite each other, on little shelves under the brow of the continuous range of hills which wall in the Rhine for miles. The railroad extends along the left bank of the river, in the rear of which is Rheinfels Castle, — the most extensive ruin on the river, — nearly four hundred feet above the water. The Mouse, on the other side, is supposed to have some unpleasant relations with the Cat, farther up the stream. On the right, opposite the small town of Salzig, are two twin castles, which go by the name of the Brothers. Their owners, bearing this relation to each other, unfortunately fell in love with the same beautiful lady, fought for her, and both were killed.

"This is Boppart, a very old place, occupied by the Romans," said Dr. Winstock, as the steamer made a landing. "You have noticed that the shelf of land on each side of the river, grows wider and the hills are farther from the stream. Between this point and Bingen, the Rhine makes its passage through the mountains. Some suppose the river, at a remote period, forced its way through the range, and formed the narrow gorge which we have passed, and that the country as far back as Basle was a vast lake, for various sea shells and fossils are found there. Marksburg Castle, on your right, is very much like the one you saw at Baden-Baden; and a walk through its deep dungeons hewn out of the rock, its torture-rooms, and its subterranean galleries, is enough to inspire a sensation novel."

"Dear me!" yawned Grace, "I am almost tired of castles."

"I think Captain Shuffles is also," added Paul.

"I notice that he hardly looks at them. Well, he has something better to look at."

"What?"

"Lady Feodora," laughed Paul.

"The best way to go down the Rhine, if one has the time, is to go from town to town by railway, and then pass through the region in a steamer, to put the effects together. I am sorry you are tired of it," said the surgeon.

"I enjoy the scenery, but I have had about castles enough for one day."

"There are not so many below Coblenz. You have now 'done' the most beautiful portion of the river, and the trip to-morrow will be hardly more interesting than the same distance on the Hudson."

The young people devoted some time to conversation with each other; but the doctor pointed out the Königstuhl, where the seven electors used to sit, and where emperors were elected, and sometimes dethroned.

"Lahnech Castle has a peculiar interest," he continued, as he called the attention of the group to a château on the right. It belonged to the order of Knights Templars, which was founded, in 1118, for the protection of pilgrims, and the defence of the Holy Sepulchre at Jerusalem. The institution became renowned, and extended all over the world. It was very rich and powerful, and therefore disliked by the clergy, who finally overthrew it. Those residing here were attacked in their castle, which was captured only after the last of its brave defenders had been slain. On the other side is Stotzenfels, or Proud Rock — a title which it deserves. Upon it is the beautiful château of the King of Prussia."

A short time after, the steamer reached Coblenz, where the excursionists were to spend the night.

CHAPTER XIX.

COBLENZ AND COLOGNE.

APARTMENTS had been engaged at the *Riese*, or Giant Hotel, near the landing. It was too dark to see anything of the town, but the students wandered about the streets, looking into the beer shops, which they dared not enter, and observing the evening life of the Germans. To many of them this occupation was more interesting than visiting old castles, or even modern palaces, especially after they had become old stories. Paul, Shuffles, and some others found themselves more pleasantly entertained at the hotel.

After breakfast the next morning, the tourists made a business of seeing the place. The town occupies a tongue of land at the junction of the Moselle with the Rhine. It is strongly fortified, on the land side, with works which it required twenty years to build, and there are forts all around the city, which is intended to be a stronghold for the defence of Prussia against an invading army from France.

The Church of St. Castor, at the confluence of the rivers, is a very ancient structure, in which the grandchildren of Charlemagne met to make a division of the empire. Napoleon, on his march to invade

Russia, caused a fountain to be erected in front of this church, bearing an inscription commemorating the event. The French army was overwhelmed, and a Russian force, pursuing the remnant of it, arrived at Coblenz. The general saw the obnoxious record, but instead of erasing it, he added the sarcastic sentence, " Seen and approved by us, the Russian commandant of the city of Coblenz," which remains to this day.

The party visited some of the principal edifices in the city, including the palace, in which the King of Prussia sometimes resides, and then crossed the Rhine on the bridge of boats to the immense fortress called Ehrenbreitstein, the meaning of which is " honor's bright stone." It was a fortress in the middle ages, and was unsuccessfully besieged by the French in 1688, though it was less fortunate in 1799, when the garrison was starved into a surrender, and it was blown up. In 1814 the Prussians commenced the work of restoring it, and since that time they have been continually strengthening and enlarging it. The series of military works, of which this fortress is the principal, are capable of holding one hundred thousand men, but five thousand are sufficient to garrison them. The magazine will hold provisions enough to supply eight thousand men ten years. It mounts four hundred pieces of cannon. The rocks have been hewn out into bomb-proofs and battlements, and art has done its utmost to strengthen the place.

The parade is on the top of the rock, beneath which vast cisterns have been constructed, which will contain a three years' supply of water. In addition to these, a well, four hundred feet deep, cut in the rock, communicates with the Rhine, which is to be used only on an emergency, as the river water is unwholesome. The river seen from the parade is very beautiful, but the company were obliged to hasten back to Coblenz, in order to dine in season for the afternoon steamer to Cologne.

At one o'clock the voyage down the Rhine was renewed, and the students, after their long ramble in the forenoon, were glad to use the camp stools on the deck of the steamer. Village after village was passed, but the scenery was less grand than that seen the day before. There were fewer castles to be seen on the heights, though Dr. Winstock could hardly tell the story of one before another required attention. The railroads which extend along each side of the river, in several instances, passed under castles, towers, and ruins, whose foundations have been tunnelled for the purpose. At Andernach, the mountains on both sides come close to the river again, and the water flows through a kind of gorge between them.

"At Brohl, which you see on the left, a peculiar kind of stone is found, which has the property of hardening under water, and is, therefore, in great demand for the manufacture of cement," said Dr. Winstock. "The ancients used it for coffins, because the stone absorbed the moisture from the bodies. These quarries were worked by the Romans, who had a road to Cologne on the left bank of the river."

"There are mountains on the right," said Grace, some time afterwards.

"Those are the Siebengebirge, as they are called. Though the name indicates seven mountains, there are thirty summits. They are very picturesque, but they are only ten or fifteen hundred feet high," continued the doctor.

"There is a beautiful island in the middle of the river," added Paul. "It has an old building on it, and is covered with trees."

"That is Nonnenwerth, and the building is a convent. Do you see the castle on the left bank, opposite the island?"

"I see it."

"You must read Herr Bernard's Legends of the Rhine. You will find the book in Cologne, both in German and in English, though the English of the latter is execrable. You will find in it the story of Rolandseck, the castle on the left, and Nonnenwerth. Roland was the nephew of Charlemagne. He was engaged to a daughter of the Lord of Drachenfels, whose castle you see on the opposite side of the river. He went away to the wars, and during his absence, a false report came back that he was killed at Roncesvalles. His betrothed, in despair, entered the convent on the island, and took the black veil. Roland returned, but could not reclaim the bride. He built the castle on the left, where he could overlook her retreat, and lived the lonely life of a hermit. One evening, while he was gazing down upon the convent, he heard the bell toll, and saw a procession of nuns escorting a coffin to the chapel. His page soon brought him the intelligence that his lady was dead. He ordered his horse to be saddled immediately, and hastened to Spain, where, in a battle with the Moors, he was killed."

"Then these are the Drachenfels, on our right," said Grace.

"They are 'The Castled Crags of Drachenfels,' as Byron sings. From the top of this precipice, Cologne, twenty miles distant, can be seen."

"And that large town is Bonn," said Paul.

"Yes; the electors of Cologne — not the city, but the electorate — formerly resided here. The vast palace built for them in 1730, which is nearly a quarter of a mile long, is now used by the University of Bonn, where Prince Albert, Queen Consort, of England, was a student. The city has about twenty thousand inhabitants, and is a very beautiful place. When I was here, six years ago, I went out about a mile and a half to a church, on the top of the Kreuzberg. It formerly belonged to a convent; and in a chapel behind the high altar are exhibited what are called the Sacred Stairs, which led up to Pilate's judgment hall. No one is allowed to ascend them except upon his knees, and the stains of blood falling from the wounds caused by the Saviour's crown of thorns are pointed out. Those believe who can and will. There is a vault under the church, reached by a trap-door in the floor, which, by some remarkable property, has preserved undecayed the bodies of twenty-five monks. They lie in open coffins, clothed in cassocks and cowls. They are dried up, and look like mummies. Some of them were buried there four hundred years ago."

"What a horrible sight!" exclaimed the sensitive Grace.

"I did not see anything very horrible about it," replied the doctor, with a smile; "but I am a surgeon by profession. In Italy and Sicily there are many such exhibitions of the dead."

Below Bonn the banks of the river are level, or gently undulating, reminding the traveller of the Delaware above Philadelphia. The scenery is pleasant, but rather tame after the experience of the Drachenfels. At five o'clock the steamer reached Cologne, and passing under the great iron bridge, and through the bridge of boats, made her landing at the quay. The Grand Hotel Royal, in which accommodations had been engaged for the tourists, is situated on the bank of the river, and many of the party had rooms which overlooked the noble stream. There is no pleasanter occupation for a tired person than that of sitting at one of these windows, watching the flow of the river, and the variety of scenes which its surface presents.

It was a lively scene at the hotel in the evening. A few of the students took a walk through the narrow streets; but Cologne is not a pleasant place to walk in the evening. There are no sidewalks, and some of the streets are not wide enough to allow two vehicles to pass abreast, though in the more modern parts of the place this defect has been remedied. The Hotel Royal has broad halls, though there is no such thing as a public parlor, where the guests may meet together, as in American hotels. Captain Shuffles and Lady Feodora were promenading, while Paul and Grace had seated themselves in the coffee-room.

"I suppose, when we leave Cologne, we shall depart in different directions," said Shuffles.

"Papa says we shall go direct to Calais," replied

Feodora, looking very sad, as, indeed, she felt when she thought of the separation.

"I believe our company are going by Charleroi to Paris, and from there to Brest. Probably we shall never meet again."

"O, I hope we shall!" exclaimed Feodora, looking up into his face.

"It is not very probable."

"You may come to England within a few years, perhaps a few months."

"It is possible. If I come out in the ship next spring, we shall sail up the Baltic, and make our first port at Christiansand, in Norway."

"I am afraid you don't wish to meet me again."

"I would cross the ocean for that alone," protested the gallant young captain.

"If you wished to meet me, I think you would find a way."

"Perhaps I ought not to meet you again," added Shuffles.

"Not meet me again! Pray why not?"

"Sir William very much prefers that I should not do so."

"Sir William!" repeated she, with an inquiring glance.

"I think he does not like my company very well."

"I do, if he does not."

Shuffles did not mention to her that he had conversed with the baronet about the matter, and that the latter had used some rather strong language to him. He was not disposed to make trouble.

"I have some idea of your relations with Sir

William," added Shuffles, with considerable embarrassment.

"I haven't any relations with him, Captain Shuffles," replied she, fixing her gaze upon the floor, while her face crimsoned with blushes.

"I have been told that you were engaged."

"By our parents — yes. By myself — no. I dislike Sir William very much indeed; and I know my father will never do anything that will make me unhappy."

"Pardon me for alluding to the subject," said Shuffles.

"I am very glad you spoke of it."

"I should not have done so, if I had not had some doubts about seeing you again, even were an opportunity presented."

"Doubts about seeing me?"

"I mean because Sir William dislikes me," stammered the captain.

"He ought not to dislike you, after what you have done for him and me."

"He thinks I am too strong a friend of yours."

"I don't think you are. Why, you saved my life, and I should be very ungrateful if I did not value your friendship," replied Feodora, apparently investigating the texture of the wood of which the floor was composed.

"Then you value it because I rendered you a little service on the lake," added Shuffles.

"That assured me you were very brave and noble; and I am sure you have not done anything since which makes me think less of you."

"You are very kind; and it makes me have the

blues to think of parting with you, perhaps never to see or hear from you again."

"Won't you write to me, as Miss Arbuckle does to the commodore, and tell me about your travels, and about your own country, when you return?"

"It would be a great satisfaction to me to have the privilege of doing so," said Shuffles, eagerly.

"I should prize your letters above all others," she replied.

"Will your father allow you to receive them from me?"

"Why should he not?"

"On account of Sir William."

"My father is one of the best and kindest men in the world, and he loves me with all his great soul. He has even told me that I might dismiss Sir William, when we return to England, if I found it impossible to like him," answered Feodora, artlessly; and English girls speak on such subjects with less reserve than American damsels.

"Here comes Sir William. I shall write to you at the first opportunity after we separate."

The baronet had been out to smoke; for young as he was, he had already formed this habit, which was one of Lady Feodora's strong objections to him, — he gave forth such an odor of tobacco. He frowned and looked savage when he saw the young couple together; but they continued their promenade in the hall, though they changed the subject of the conversation.

"Good evening, Sir William," said Ben Duncan, the inveterate joker, who saw the effect produced by the coming of the baronet, and wished to relieve the young couple of his company.

"Good evening, sir," replied the baronet, stiffly; for he was not disposed to be on very familiar terms with the young republicans.

"A friend of mine at the Gas-house—"

"At the what?" demanded Sir William, with a look of contempt.

"I beg your pardon. I mean the *Gasthaus*. But there were two or three English nobs there who were so gassy in their style, that I forgot my Deutch for the moment. A friend of mine at the Gasthaus, *am Holländischer Hof*, expressed a strong desire to see you."

"Indeed! What friend of yours could desire to see me?"

"Well, I call him Elfinstone. If I were more polite than I am, I should say Lord Elfinstone; but he's just as good a fellow as though he were not a lord."

"Is it possible that Lord Elfinstone is in Cologne?" added the baronet.

"Do you know him?"

"I have not that honor."

"I have. I used to sail him in my father's yacht, when he was in New York," replied Ben; who, however, under any other circumstances, would not have troubled himself to make the young nobles better acquainted. "I will introduce you, if you like."

"Thank you," answered the baronet, with a promptness which indicated that he appreciated the honor in store for him. "I shall be under great obligations to you."

Taking the arm of Ben Duncan, who had suddenly risen in the estimation of Sir William, because he was on familiar terms with so distinguished a young gentleman as Lord Elfinstone, they left the hotel, very much to the satisfaction of Shuffles and Feodora.

"Perhaps there is another objection to our meeting again, or at least to permitting a friendship to grow up between us," said Shuffles, continuing the subject.

"What can there be?" asked Feodora.

"You belong to the nobility of England, while I am only the son of a Republican American."

"A fig for the nobility!" exclaimed she. "They are just like other people."

"I think so myself," replied Shuffles; "but there is some difference of opinion on that subject."

Sir William was duly presented to Lord Elfinstone, at the Holländischer Hof, and they did not part till after nine o'clock; so the young couple had the evening all to themselves. After the ice was broken, they probably made some progress in establishing a friendship; but as it is not fair to listen to such conversations, it cannot be reported. The earl and his lady did not interfere, whatever they thought of the confidential relations which appeared to be gaining strength between the captain and their daughter, and they separated only when it was time to retire.

After breakfast the next morning, Professor Mapps had something to say about Cologne, and with the consent of Herr Deitzman, the landlord, it was said in the coffee-room.

"As many of you do not study German, you would **not know what was meant by the name of the city if** you saw it printed in that language," the professor began. "It is written Köln, with the *umlaut*, or diæresis, over the vowel, which gives it a sound similar to, but not the same as, the *e* in the word *met*. It is the third city of Prussia, Berlin and Breslau alone being larger, and has a population of one hundred and twenty thousand. On the opposite bank of the Rhine is Deutz, with which Cologne is connected by an iron bridge and by a bridge of boats. The former is a grand structure, and worthy of your attention.

"Cologne was originally a colony of Rome, from which comes its name. Portions of walls built by the Romans will be pointed out to you, and in the Museum are many relics of the same ancient origin. Agrippina, the mother of Nero, was born here, her father, the Emperor Germanicus, being a resident of Cologne at the time. Trajan was here when he was called to the throne. Clovis was declared king of the Franks at Cologne. In the fourteenth century it was the most flourishing city of Northern Europe, and one of the principal depots of the Hanseatic League, of which I spoke to you on a former occasion. It was called the Rome of the North, and many Italian customs, such as the carnival, are still retained in Cologne, though in no other city of this part of Europe. Several causes — the principal of which was the closing of the Rhine by the Dutch in the sixteenth century — nearly destroyed the commercial importance of the place; but the river was opened in 1837, and the city is now growing rapidly.

"One of the principal objects of interest in Cologne is the great cathedral, called in German the *Domkirche*.

It is one of the largest churches in the world, and if completed on the original plan, it will rival St. Peter's at Rome. It is five hundred and eleven feet long by two hundred and thirty-one feet wide. The choir is one hundred and sixty-one feet high. It has two towers in process of erection, which will be five hundred feet high, if they are ever completed. It was commenced in the year 1248, and the work went on, with occasional interruptions, till about a hundred years ago, when it was suspended by war. Frederick William, King of Prussia, on his accession to the throne, caused the work to be resumed; and it required years of labor and vast sums of money to make the needed repairs, for the structure was a ruin even while it was unfinished. An association has been formed to insure its completion, and the present king, as well as his predecessor, has contributed large sums of money.

"As you came down the river, you saw the huge crane on the summit of one of the towers, used to hoist up stone and other materials. It has been there for hundreds of years. When it became insecure by years of decay, it was taken down; but a tremendous thunder-storm, which occurred soon after, was interpreted by the superstitious citizens as a wrathful protest of the Deity at its removal, indicating that the people did not intend to complete the work, and it was repaired and restored to its original position. Not less than twenty years, with the utmost diligence, will be required to finish the building, and five millions of dollars is the estimated expense."

When the professor finished his lecture, the excursionists organized themselves into little parties to see
21

the sights. As the unruly elements of the squadron were all in the Josephine, the students were permitted to go when and where they pleased. The Blankvilles and the Arbuckles, with Shuffles and Paul, hastened to the cathedral, as it was but a short distance from the hotel. Sir William was not in attendance, being engaged with Lord Elfinstone. Dr. Winstock, as usual, did much of the talking, being entirely familiar with all the localities and traditions of the city.

The Domhof, or square in which the cathedral stands, is partly filled with rude sheds, in which the stone for the building is hewn, and much of the space around the grand structure is covered with stone. Entering the church, the party walked to the middle of the choir. Its vast height, its lofty columns, its arches, chapels, and richly-colored windows filled them with awe and amazement. It was the most magnificent sight they had ever beheld, and with one consent they were silent as they gazed upon the architectural glories of the structure. They were interrupted very soon, however, by the appearance of an official in the livery of the church, who presented a salver for contributions for the completion of the building. The earl and Mr. Arbuckle each gave a napoleon, and other members of the party gave small sums. The gold won the heart of the official, and he was very polite.

Having observed the effect as a whole, the tourists proceeded to examine the church in detail. Behind the high altar is the shrine of the Three Kings of Cologne. They are represented as the Magi, who came from the east with presents for the infant Saviour. Their bodies are said to have been brought by the Empress Helena, mother of Constantine the Great, from the Holy Land to Constantinople, and then sent to Milan; and when this city was captured by the Emperor Frederick, he presented them to the Archbishop of Cologne, who placed them in the principal church. They have always been cherished with the greatest veneration; were enclosed in costly caskets, and adorned with gold and silver of immense value, though these have been mostly purloined, or otherwise appropriated. The skulls of the three kings are inscribed with their names, in rubies: *Gaspar*, *Melchior*, and *Balthazar*. Those who show the tomb of the Magi say its treasures are still worth a million of dollars; but people who go to see sights must see them.

Near the shrine is a slab in the pavement, beneath which is buried the heart of Marie de Medicis, wife of Henry IV., of France, her body having been sent to France. In various parts of the church are ancient and valuable paintings, in several of which the Magi are introduced. The story of the Three Kings is a cherished tradition in several of the cities of this part of Europe, and hotels and other public edifices have been named for them.

Passing out of the church, the party walked around it, in order to obtain a complete view of the exterior, whose grandeur can hardly be overrated, even by the enthusiast in architectural beauty. At a bookstore in the Domhof the party purchased some views of the cathedral.

"I suppose the ladies will want some cologne, if the gentlemen do not," said Dr. Winstock, with a smile.

"I want some," added Paul. "My mother will be delighted with a bottle of cologne from Cologne itself."

"The reputation of the article is world-wide, and I suppose many fortunes have been made in the trade. Farina was the original inventor, and there are not less than twenty-four establishments in this city which claim to be the rightful owners of the receipt for the pure article. I see that Murray and Fetridge both award to Jean Marie Farina the glory of being the right one."

"The original Jacobs," laughed Paul.

"Yes. His place is opposite the Jülich's Platz; and after we have been to the Churches of St. Cunibert and St. Ursula, we will call upon him. There is a cologne shop," added the surgeon, as he pointed to the opposite side of the Domhof. "I bought some there once, and I found it very good."

There are half a dozen churches in Cologne from six to eight hundred years old, and our party looked at them with interest. The church of St. Ursula and the Eleven Thousand Virgins presented to them a very remarkable display. The saint went from Brittany to Rome with her virgin band. On their return by way of the Rhine, they were all massacred at Cologne by the savage Huns. The remains of the saint and her companions have been gathered together, and enshrined in this church. The bones are buried under the pavement, displayed in the walls, or exhibited in glass cases. St. Ursula herself lies in a coffin, and near her are the skulls of some of her preferred companions. The chains of St. Peter, and one of the clay vessels which held the wine of Cana, are also exhibited.

Before dinner time, the party reached the Jülich's Platz, where the original cologne shop is located. A blast of the vapor of the fragrant water was blown in each of their faces by the aid of a machine made for the purpose, and each one bought a supply of the genuine article.

In the afternoon the same party visited the house in the Sternengasse, in which Rubens was born and Marie de Medicis died. There were objects of interest enough in the city to occupy the attention of the excursionists till night.

"Do you find Cologne a very dirty city?" said the doctor, as they were returning to the hotel.

"Rather so in the old market-place," replied Mr. Arbuckle. "As a whole, I don't think it is any dirtier than most of the cities of Europe."

"That is just my view. I find that all the guide-books and all the works of travel insist upon inserting and indorsing Coleridge's lines on the subject."

"What are the lines?" asked Paul.

Dr. Winstock took his guide-book and read,—

> "Ye nymphs who reign o'er sewers and sinks,
> The River Rhine, it is well-known,
> Doth wash your city of Cologne;
> But tell me, nymphs, what power divine
> Shall henceforth wash the River Rhine."

"I protest that it is a slander, whatever it may have been in former times."

The next morning the tourists took the train for Dusseldorf, where they spent the forenoon in examining the pictures of the School of Art, which has its headquarters in this place, and in a walk through the beautiful Hofgarten. From this place a ride of two hours brought the party to Aix-la-Chapelle, where they dined at the Hôtel Grand Monarque.

"Aix-la-Chapelle was the birth-place of Charlemagne, who also died here," said Professor Mapps, after dinner. "The German name of the city is Aachen, which is derived from *Aachs*, meaning a spring. There are several warm medicinal springs here, which have a considerable reputation for their curative properties. The city is called Aix-la-Chapelle from the chapel which Charlemagne built. From him the place derived its chief importance. He raised it to the rank of the second city in his empire, made it the capital of all his dominions north of the Alps, and decreed that the sovereigns of Germany and of the Romans should be crowned here. Between 814 and 1531, the coronations of thirty-seven kings and emperors took place here.

"It has been the scene of many Diets and church councils, and in modern times several treaties have been signed here."

The excursionists left the hotel and walked to the cathedral, which is probably the oldest church in Germany. This is the chapel for which the city is named, and was intended by Charlemagne as his burial-place. It was consecrated by Pope Leo III., assisted by three hundred and sixty-five archbishops and bishops. It was partially destroyed by barbarians, but was rebuilt by the Emperor Otho III., and much of the primitive structure still remains. Under the centre of the dome is a marble slab in the floor on which are the words CAROLO MAGNO, indicating the spot where the tomb of Charlemagne was located. It was probably a little chapel above ground. It was opened in 1165, and the body was found sitting on a throne, clothed in imperial robes, a sceptre in the hand, and a copy of the Gospels on the knee. The crown was on the bony brow, and his sword and other articles near him. All these relics were subsequently used at the coronation of the emperors, but are now kept at Vienna, except the throne, which is still here.

The church has an abundance of relics, including the skull and arm-bone of Charlemagne, though the latter has, unfortunately, turned out to be a leg-bone! It is said that the rest of the bones of his body were found here in a chest in a dark closet; but we are not told by what means they were identified. If some of the apostles, martyrs, and worthies of the past had had a dozen skulls each, sight-seers might be more credulous. There are also in this church a lock of the Virgin's hair, the leathern girdle of Christ with the seal of Constantine upon it, a nail of the cross, the sponge which was filled with vinegar for the Saviour, blood and bones of St. Stephen, and bits of Aaron's rod.

In addition to these precious articles, the cathedral has what are called the Grand Relics, which are shown only once in seven years, and then for but two weeks. At the exhibition in 1860, half a million people resorted to Aix to see them. Charlemagne received them direct from the Patriarch of Jerusalem, and from Haroun-al-Raschid. They are enclosed in a shrine of silver-gilt, of the workmanship of the ninth century. There are four principal articles: The cotton robe, five feet long, worn by the Virgin at the Nativity; the swaddling clothes, of a coarse yellow cloth like sacking, in which the infant Saviour was wrapped; the cloth on which the head of John the Baptist was laid; and the scarf worn by the Saviour, at the crucifixion, which bears the stains of blood. Other articles, such as religious emblems, are doubtless of great antiquity.

The party visited the Hôtel de Ville, on the spot where stood the palace of the Frankish kings, in which Charlemagne was born. This was the last sight to be seen in regular course, and the last city in Germany which the tourists were to visit that season. It had been put to vote whether the company would remain in Aix over Sunday, or make a night trip to Paris, and the latter had been almost unanimously adopted. Captain Shuffles voted against it, because the earl's party were to remain till Monday; but he gracefully yielded, and the tourists left at eight o'clock. Lady Feodora was very sad, and so was Shuffles — Sir William was very glad. His lordship was kind enough to hope that the acquaintance thus begun would be continued by letter, if not possible in any other way.

The excursionists were in Paris at eight o'clock the next morning, and most of them had slept very well in the cars. They were allowed to attend such churches as they pleased, and while some heard the fine singing in St. Roch, others listened to Mass in Notre Dame, while not a few attended at the American Chapel.

On Monday forenoon, after breakfast had been disposed of in the Hôtel du Louvre, Mr. Arbuckle requested all the students to assemble in the grand dining-room. When they were all in the apartment, their kind and liberal friend rose, and was received with hearty applause.

"Young gentlemen, I thank you for this kindly greeting," said he. "I shall never forget the debt of gratitude I owe you, and I hope, when your squadron goes up the Baltic, you will put into Belfast on your way. It has afforded me very great pleasure to contribute something to your instruction and amusement, and I most sincerely regret that we must part to-day. For myself and my family I thank you for all you have done for us."

Mr. Arbuckle paused, and Mr. Lowington, for the ship's company, thanked him for his liberal hospitality, and assured him that "all hands" would remember him and his family as long as they lived.

"I thank you, Mr. Lowington; you are very kind," continued Mr. Arbuckle. "Allow me to speak a word now for my daughter, the Grand Protectress of the Order of the Faithful. Some of the young gentlemen were saying something about perpetuating the association formed on our voyage from Havre to Brest, and Grace desired me to provide a suitable emblem for that purpose. I took the liberty, when we reached Paris, nearly three weeks since, to order a sufficient number of badges for all the members; and this morning I obtained them. They are very neat, and I hope they will please you."

He held up one of the emblems.

"It is a gold anchor, with a star upon it," continued Mr. Arbuckle. "The word FAITHFUL is inscribed upon it. Grace will be happy now to present it to each member of the order."

The students applauded lustily, and one by one they passed before her, and she attached the badge, which was made like a breastpin, to the coats of the members, over the white ribbons. They were admonished always to wear them, and always to be faithful. The Grand Protectress was warmly cheered by the boys, when the ceremony was concluded. The hour of parting had come, for the ship's company was to return to Brest, while the Arbuckles proceeded to London. There was a general shaking of hands, and a general exchanging of kind words. Paul and Grace found the occasion a very trying one. What promises they made to each other need not be repeated.

The Arbuckles attended the party to the station, and when the last words of farewell had been spoken, the train moved off. The excitement of the excursion was ended, and the ride to Brest was rather dull. The buoyant spirit of youth, however, soon furnished a new hope, and they now looked eagerly forward to the meeting of dear friends at home. The train arrived at Brest in the evening, and the students slept that night in their berths on board the ship.

The next morning the Young America sailed for Lisbon. She did not make so quick a passage as the Josephine had made, and after a three days' run, dropped anchor in the Tagus; but the consort had not yet arrived.

CHAPTER XX.

HOMEWARD BOUND.

THE moon shone brightly on the deserted deck of the Josephine after the runaways had departed in the four boats,— deserted by all save Bitts, who was endeavoring to free himself from the rope by which he had been secured. Before the conspirators had gone a cable's length, he succeeded. Reaching the rope over his head, he went up, hand over hand, till he had slack enough to make a bight for one of his feet. Then, holding on with one hand, he loosed the rope from his neck with the other, and descended to the deck.

Rogues always overreach themselves. Phillips had intended to secure the arms of his prisoner by winding a line around his body, but, considering him safe without it, he had neglected to do so. If he had done this, the runaways might have reached the shore before any one could come to the aid of the sufferer. He was free in three minutes after Phillips left him. The boats were pulling for the shore, and those below were laboring to release themselves from their imprisonment. He went to the companion way, and tried to open it; but the nail held it fast. Descending to the steerage, he removed the handspike with which the cabin door was fastened.

"What does all this mean?" demanded Mr. Fluxion, as he hastened on deck.

"The boys have taken all the boats, and left the vessel," replied Bitts.

"Left the vessel!" exclaimed Mr. Fluxion. "Were you asleep on deck?"

"No, sir. Half a dozen of them hung me by the neck till I was nearly choked to death," pleaded the carpenter.

"Where was Cleats?"

"I stepped below for half a minute, and they clapped the slide on over me," answered Cleats, very sheepishly.

"You stepped below! I ordered you not to leave the deck," added the vice-principal, angrily. "You are responsible for this."

"I did not think the young rascals would do such a thing as this," pleaded the culprit.

"I did; and I told you they would do anything. You have disobeyed my orders. Take the helm, Gage."

Mr. Fluxion glanced at the boats, and gave a few hasty orders, by which the Josephine was headed towards the shore. The cooks and stewards in the forecastle were released, and the chase commenced.

"I did not think they were quite so bold as this," said Dr. Carboy.

"They will do anything. Cleats thinks more of his stomach than of his duty, or it would not have happened," replied Mr. Fluxion. "I have seen the boys talking together a great deal on this cruise, and I was sure something was brewing. I charged all the officers not to leave the deck for a single instant. Probably the young rascals have been watching for this opportunity during the whole cruise."

"It is a very foolish movement on their part," added Dr. Carboy.

"Yet if they had kept us in the cabin half an hour longer, it might have succeeded, for the boats would have been out of sight. If they had tied Bitts's arms behind him, it might have been half an hour before we could have broken out of the cabin."

Mr. Fluxion questioned the watch officers very closely in regard to the conduct of the crew on deck, and he soon understood the whole matter. He was very severe upon Cleats for leaving the deck, declared that he could not be trusted, and that he should be discharged. The latter was very humble, acknowledged his error, and made no attempt to palliate it. He had always been faithful, so far as was known, and probably had never been guilty of any graver offence than that of leaving the deck for a few minutes during his watch. But he had been expressly cautioned not to do this, and had sent a hand below for his lunch, until the present time.

In the boats the runaways were pulling with all their might to get out of sight of the Josephine before the officers should set themselves at liberty. Perth urged the oarsmen in the captain's gig to the most tremendous exertion. But in less than ten minutes, and before they had made a single mile, they saw the Josephine fill away, and stand towards them.

"Did you fasten Bitts?" said Perth, to Phillips, who was in the gig with him.

"I did. He couldn't get away, I know," replied Phillips.

"They are after us, and I'm afraid the game is up," added Perth. "The Josephine can make two knots to our one in this breeze."

The leader was very anxious for the result. The plan had really failed because the officers had released themselves so much sooner than was expected. But Perth hoped to make it partially successful. Standing up in the gig, he ordered the other boats to separate, so that the Josephine could not capture them all at once. He directed the first cutter to pull to the northwest, while the gig went to the south-west, and the second and third cutters were to take intermediate points. The Josephine was headed to the north-west, with the evident intention of getting between the boats and the shore. The second cutter would therefore be her first victim; and Perth hoped that, by the time she had picked up the other three boats, his own would be in shoal water, where a schooner of her tonnage could not come.

Little was in command of the first cutter. He obeyed the order of Perth, though he saw it would be a losing game for his boat. In less than half an hour the Josephine came up with him. The wind was due east, which gave the vessel every advantage, and she came about under the lee of the cutter.

"Hold water! Back her!" shouted Little, who had prepared his plan of operations, and intended to pull dead to windward of her, so that she would have to go in stays before she could come up with the boat again.

Peaks spoiled his plan by throwing a boat grapnel into the fore-sheets of the cutter, and hauling her alongside of the Josephine as her sails shook in the wind. Cleats dropped into the boat, and, leaping aft, seized Little by the collar. Gage followed him, and ten of the runaways' were captured. Mr. Fluxion ordered them on board the vessel, and the two men in the boat expedited their movements by some rather rough usage.

The vice-principal said nothing to the discomfited crew of the first cutter, but gave his orders to chase the second cutter. As the Josephine approached her, Peaks and Gage, with two of the stewards, were sent off in the first cutter as the vessel lay to. They grappled the boat, and as no one thought of resisting Peaks, they were readily captured, and driven upon the deck of the schooner. The third cutter was taken with no more difficulty. A few moments later, the Josephine luffed up under the lee of the gig, having towed the first cutter, in which the four men were seated, to this position. The boat pulled towards the runaways. Perth was desperate when he saw how easily he was to be captured.

"Bat them over the head with your oars, fellows!" shouted he. "Don't let them take you!"

The oarsmen attempted to obey this order, and to beat off their pursuers. A brief struggle ensued, in which Perth and Phillips fought with desperation; but Peaks succeeded in getting into the gig, and the strife was ended. With a blow of his fist the stalwart boatswain justified the traditions of himself, and Perth was knocked senseless in the bottom of the boat, while Phillips, with a bleeding face, yielded the day. The runaways in the gig were driven to the deck, as their companions had been, while Perth was handed up by the grim Peaks, put in his berth, and attended by Dr. Carboy.

The long-cherished scheme of Little had ended in disaster, and all hands had been captured. The runaways looked at each other with a sort of astonishment when they found themselves on board again. Doubtless they were satisfied that they had not bettered their condition by what they had done. They obeyed whatever orders were given them, for the terrible Peaks had verified all the stories told of him. He had knocked Perth insensible, and badly damaged Phillips. It was not safe to refuse to do duty, as some of them, in their chagrin, wished to do.

As soon as the boats were hoisted up, and the Josephine headed on her course again, all hands were piped to muster. By this time Perth was able to appear, for he had only been stunned by the boatswain's fist. A savage lecture from the vice-principal was expected; but instead of that, every one of the crew was searched. Perth's twenty pounds was discovered and confiscated, as well as numerous bills on Paris, letters of credit, and similar valuable papers. The conspirators had put them in their pockets to use on shore. Without any further notice of the affair of the night, the vice-principal stationed the watch, and dismissed the rest of the crew.

Mr. Fluxion probably acted on the principle of the celebrated schoolmaster who charged all the faults of his pupils upon himself. If Cleats had not left the deck, the conspiracy could not have been even partially successful, and he charged all the blame upon him. After the affair he increased his own vigilance, adding Dr. Carboy to one watch, and the head steward to the other, so that another attempt to escape must certainly fail.

"I never believed much in that plan," said Herman, the next day, as he and Perth met on deck.

"I did. I won't go back on it now. If we had had half an hour more, we should have been safe. Phillips didn't do as he agreed with Bitts," answered the leader. "He ought to have put a line a dozen times around his body, so that he couldn't move his hands."

"He said he was afraid of actually choking him to death."

"Tying his hands would not have choked him."

"Well, whatever the reason was, the plan failed. We are played out for this cruise."

"Yes, and haven't seen Paris, Switzerland, Germany, or the Rhine," growled Perth.

"I suppose it is our own fault."

"Humph!" snuffed the conquered leader.

"I am satisfied, now, that if we had done our duty, we should have had a better time."

"Repent, then," said Perth, as he turned on his heel.

Possibly there was no other runaway in the crew who confessed as much as this, but it is doubtful whether there was one who did not realize the truth of the statement. All of them were satisfied that it was useless to contend against the discipline of the Academy while it was administered by such men as the principal and the vice-principal.

The Josephine had a fair passage, and reached Lisbon on the day after the Young America had anchored in the river. She was loudly cheered when she luffed up under the quarter of the ship, but not a sound came from the disappointed and disheartened runaways in response, and more fully than the sufferers themselves did the members of the Order of the Faithful believe that the way of the transgressor is hard.

Mr. Fluxion immediately went on board of the ship, and reported to the principal. For an hour they discussed the events of the cruise of the Josephine up the Mediterranean; but both were satisfied that the discipline of the squadron had been triumphant. Mr. Lowington was more indulgent towards Cleats than the vice-principal was disposed to be, and he was put on probation.

Before night the original order on board both vessels was restored, and again the runaways mingled with the faithful ones. Each party had a story to tell, and the glories of the beautiful Rhine lost nothing in the description given by the tourists. The narrative of the adventures of the excursionists was galling to the others, for the latter had nothing but sea life to speak of, unless it was the harbor of Genoa. It was painful to be obliged to say that they had been up the Mediterranean without putting a foot on shore during their absence. Certainly those who had done their duty could appreciate the pleasures of their trip, after contrasting it with that of the runaways; and perhaps they needed this contrast to enable them fully to realize the satisfaction which follows right doing.

Fresh provisions and water were taken in by both

vessels. Only a few of the students went on shore, and those on duty; and at noon on the day after the arrival of the Josephine, the squadron got under way, homeward bound. The usual routine on board was restored, and the studies of the school-room were mingled with the duties of the ship. Only one gale disturbed the serenity of the passage, and both vessels came to anchor in Brockway harbor, after a voyage of thirty days. The runaways had behaved tolerably well during the trip, for they had learned that there was no safety or satisfaction in rebellion and disobedience. They were not reformed, and perhaps never will be; but they were controlled, and saved from a vicious life on shore during the period of the cruise.

Others had been reformed, and converted from evil-disposed boys into well-meaning ones. Shuffles and Pelham were not the only ones who had been turned aside from the error of their ways, though their individual experience has not been detailed. The moral results of the voyage were very good. If the discipline of the ship and her consort had not reformed all the vicious characters, it had restrained their evil tendencies, and kept them away from the haunts of vice, though its most pernicious haunt is within the soul of the evil-doer.

On the other hand, the intellectual results of the cruise were abundantly satisfactory. The students had made excellent progress in their studies, and not a few of them were already competent navigators. There had been hardly a case of sickness on board, and the boys were all in rugged health. Mr. Lowington, therefore, had every reason to be satisfied with the success of his great experiment. He intended to make some changes in the vessels, and return to Europe the following spring, after spending the winter in various ports of the United States.

The Academy had a vacation during the Christmas holidays, and all the students went home. Perth and some others declared they should not return, but their parents thought otherwise, and with hardly an exception, they did return, and the institution continued to prosper.

Shuffles, it need not be said, kept his promise to Lady Feodora, and hardly a week passed in which a letter did not cross the ocean from him to her, and from her to him. One of the latter informed him that Lady Feodora had not seen Sir William for a month; for, with her father's consent, she had dismissed him. Paul Kendall spent much of his spare time in writing letters which went to Belfast. No doubt Lady Feodora will, in due time, become Mrs. Shuffles, and Grace Arbuckle Mrs. Kendall. It may even be said that promises to this effect have already passed between the respective parties. Our readers will wish them joy, and we heartily join in the hope that life will be as happy to them as duty faithfully done can make it.

For the present we take our leave of the Academy Squadron, though we hope in the future to be the chronicler of more of the travel and adventure in foreign lands of YOUNG AMERICA ABROAD.

www.ingramcontent.com/pod-product-compliance
Lightning Source LLC
Chambersburg PA
CBHW030317240426
43673CB00040B/1200